The Addis Ababa House
A Typological Analysis of
Urban Heritage in Ethiopia

The Addis Ababa House
A Typological Analysis of Urban Heritage in Ethiopia 1886–1936

Edited by Piet Nieder

The many faces of Addis today: Pedestrians and giant infrastructure at Meskal Square

With contributions from:
Rami Anis, Henock Ashagre,
Maroua Ben Kiran, Bachir Benkirane,
Yoseph Bereded, Federico Castracane,
Klajd Cullhaj, Christos Dalakouras,
Onur Degirmenci, Arita Dreshaj,
Lía Duarte Rodríguez, Christine Feistl,
Eden Fikrmariam, Feed Furaiji,
Fasil Giorghis, Tadesse Girmay,
Fabian Gutheil, Nagham Hatem,
Sophia Jemaneh, Adèle Lebaudy,
Sara Leoni, Martina Lustina,
Kamal Maharjan, Piet Nieder,
Rumi Okazaki, Livio Sacchi,
Ebrar Sayan, Fkereselase Sifir,
Selen Sönmez, Robert Stahlschmidt,
Ruben Amorim Vasques, and
Addisu Yisma

The many faces of Addis today: Low cost dwellings in central areas here in Lideta

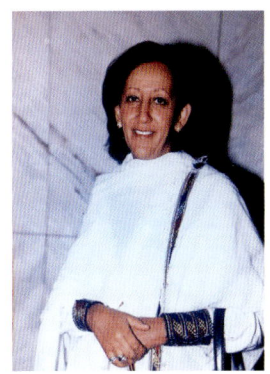

Dear reader,

Now that you hold this book in your hands, another important step has been taken to recognise and value the endangered urban heritage of Addis Ababa.

The protection of heritage is an intergenerational task and I am very glad that international researchers are encouraging students to study the treasures of our urban past. The old architecture from the imperial times of Menelik II and my grandfather Haile Selassie I are living witnesses to the rich history of our capital. Some buildings have withstood the ever-changing winds of history, others have been lost – with or without leaving a trace.

At the age of 22 I had to go into exile; I returned to my home country only 23 years later. When Nahu Senay Girma and I founded 'Addis Woubet' in 2005 and started to collect and document the heritage buildings of Addis Ababa together with Michael Maiwald (GIZ), it was a terra incognita – and to many, even most Addis Ababeans, it still is today.

It is with great pleasure that I have seen the project of this publication evolve. I wish you an inspiring and revealing read!

Yours,

ማርያም፡ ሰና አስፋ ወሰን

Princess Mariam Senna Asfa Wossen

The many faces of Addis today: Livable fragments of the old city in Piassa

Contents

1
Introduction 10

2
Phenotype: The Case Studies 74

3
Genotype: Influence Analysis 166

4
Genes: Architectural Alphabet 204

5
Appendix: Heritage at Risk 218

6
Acknowledgements 264

Model by Sophia Jemaneh

1
Introduction

The many faces of Addis today: Tramline dividing the city in Megenagna

The Addis Ababa House
by Piet Nieder

In its early decades after its foundation in 1886, the young city of Addis Ababa witnessed a very specific form of local architecture. At the beginning of Ethiopia's first urbanisation process, a mixture of vernacular knowledge and a new cosmopolitan mindset led to an architectural type that local professionals call the 'Addis Ababa Style'. With the Italian invasion in 1936, this culturally outstanding period abruptly ended, exactly 50 years after Addis Ababa was founded.

This book aims to shed light on the architectural qualities of the Addis Ababa Style. Yet the term 'style' has a connotation of just being added to a building, as something quite superfluous and exchangeable. The aim of this book is the contrary: It wants to show the underlying architectural logic of the Addis Ababa Style buildings, in its embeddedness in local resources, local climate, and craftsmanship – a result of a refined, cosmopolitan approach to architecture that was open to foreign influences while also valuing the indigenous, vernacular construction know-how of Ethiopia. As most of the buildings shown in this book are residences, we will speak of the 'Addis Ababa House'.

Next to residences, there were also administrative, commercial, and educational buildings constructed during that time.[1] Most of these edifices were owned by the Ethiopian feudal cast from different regions of the country, others by rich merchants, engineers, or political figures of the time – among those many foreigners. The Addis Ababa Style is characterised by the diverse international influences that were not completely new to Ethiopia, but that had found a context in which they could flourish in the new capital. Indians, Armenians, and Europeans worked in the construction sector and contributed significantly with their expertise, be it as architects, designers, or craftsmen. Their expertise was highly appreciated by the Emperor and the feudal cast. This unique integration of different building cultures as well as the variety of functions and professional or ethnic background of the owners led to highly diversified architectural forms, some of which are documented in this volume.

A Hinge Between Indigenous Past and Urban Future

The historical setting in which the Addis Ababa House came into being marked an interesting turning point in Ethiopia's political and cultural history when Ethiopia started to open up to the world. Addis Ababa was initially planned as a temporary camp for Emperor Menelik II and his entourage – as it was common practice at the time that the Emperor was forced to resettle his siege regularly when the local wood that was needed for construction, cooking, and heating was depleted. These were Ankober, Entoto, and then Addis Ababa. Even its name, Addis Ababa, which means 'new flower' in Amharic, indicates not only beauty but also a certain temporality.

---

[1] Important churches were also built during this period of time, but as their architectural forms are quite directed from religious rules, this volume focuses on the profane architecture of the young capital.

Different historical circumstances eventually led to the transformation of Addis Ababa into the permanent capital of Ethiopia – a fact that led to a flourishing construction sector because otherwise, new architectural endeavours would not have been possible. Firstly, the military victory of Ethiopians over the colonial power of Italy in 1896 led to international recognition of Ethiopia as a sovereign state. In the following years, many foreign powers such as France, Russia, Italy, and Great Britain built quite elaborate embassies in Addis Ababa. Foreign diplomats objected to moving the capital. Secondly, as a crucial asset of Addis Ababa, the Ethio-Francais Railway was opened and connected Addis Ababa with the port of Djibouti in 1917. Thirdly, and this might be the most important reason: The eucalyptus tree was introduced to Ethiopia. It grew so fast that the need for wood for building construction and fire-making could once again be met.

These first decades of Addis Ababa from 1886–1936 marked the start of a 'new' époque for Ethiopian architecture. On the other hand, they mark the end of an 'old' époque – an époque that was characterised by a certain 'Africaness' – cultural and political independence from the metropolitan Western powers. This in-between status makes the Addis Ababa House so compelling and unique on the African continent. The Addis Ababa House is a hinge between the indigenous past and urban future.

Emperor Menelik II (about 1900)

With the 1936 invasion of the Italian fascists under Benito Mussolini, who aimed to take revenge for the 'catastrophe' of 1896, this African independence was lost. And even though the occupation of Ethiopia only lasted for five years, this marks a clear rupture in Ethiopian cultural history, which sooner or later also showed in architectural forms. When Haile Selassie returned in 1941 from Great Britain, where he had stayed in exile during the occupation, his architectural preferences significantly changed in favour of European modernism. Thus, the Addis Ababa Style as a local building culture came to an end and its remaining examples were increasingly perceived as outdated.

Feudal Ethiopia came to an abrupt end in 1974 due to a socialist coup d'état. Some members of the imperial family were killed or had to flee the country.[2] Some of the houses owned by feudal families were turned into social housing, so-called 'kebele houses', that were state-owned and rented out for very low prices. This process was legally managed by a new law, by which families were not allowed to own more than one single house. However, there are some examples where the original family remained living until today, such as the Residence of *Sheik* Ojele, a rich merchant from the west of Ethiopia.

Heritage Today

In a country that longs for development – from 2010–2019 Ethiopia had the highest growth rate in the world according to the World Economic Outlook – heritage preservation is not very high on the agenda of local decision-makers. On the

2 Among them was Princess Maryam Senna, Haile Selassie's granddaughter, who took on the patronage of this book.

Empress Zewditu I (between 1916–1930)

Emperor Haile Selassie I (1930)

contrary, heritage buildings are often regarded as an obstacle to development, for those buildings are often situated close to the city centres and occupy valuable land. It can be observed that it is a common strategy to deliberately leave heritage buildings unmaintained until they are dilapidated enough to have a good pretext for demolition. A drastic example is the demolition of the Asfaw Kebede Residence in January 2021 – an exquisite construction of early architecture in Addis.

However, in recent years, a slow shift in the appreciation of heritage can be observed. The government as well as private individuals have taken initiatives to preserve and restore historical buildings from the early times.

Most famously, the historical palace compound with the oldest and most interesting gems was converted into a public park by the federal government, which in this case understood the historical and economic value of this heritage. The *Ghebbi*, which means 'palace compound' in Amharic, became a major tourist attraction in Addis shortly after opening in 2019. But there is also a political notion to the so-called 'Unity Park', as heritage is instrumentalised to tell a specific story about the nation.

Furthermore, there have been private initiatives that made preservation possible in recent years. The restoration of the Ayalew Birru Residence by Ethiopian supermodel Liya Kebede is famous. At the moment, the 'Old Municipality' (formerly the H/Giorgis Agid Residence) is being restored by the famous Ethiopian actress Alemtsehay Wodajo. But still, these are exceptions. The majority of heritage buildings are in a rather bad condition and in light of the staggering urban development Addis is currently witnessing, saving these gems has become ever more difficult.

From an outsider's perspective, it seems contradictory that Ethiopians generally value their country's history so much, but when it comes to architecture, they are blind in one eye. Not only are heritage buildings being destroyed, but entire historic neighbourhoods are being cleared for new developments without context.

State of the Art

Up to now, only a few books and articles have been published about the early architecture of Addis Ababa. In *Old Tracks in the New Flower – A Historical Guide to Addis Ababa* released in 2004 by Milena Batistoni and Gian Paolo Chiari, the authors created seven itineraries along the seven historical paths that connected the *Ghebbi* with the different parts of the city. More than 130 buildings, often hidden in the contemporary Addis of the early twenty-first century, are described and documented in photographs. Additionally, through interviews with residents, the authors collected valuable background information about these buildings' stories. As the authors say: 'The purpose of [their] work is not scientific in that it does not have the pretension to attempt to analyse the architecture. On the contrary, it aims to document and, hopefully, communicate the fascination that stems from the syncretic[3] complexity of early Addis Ababa architecture'.

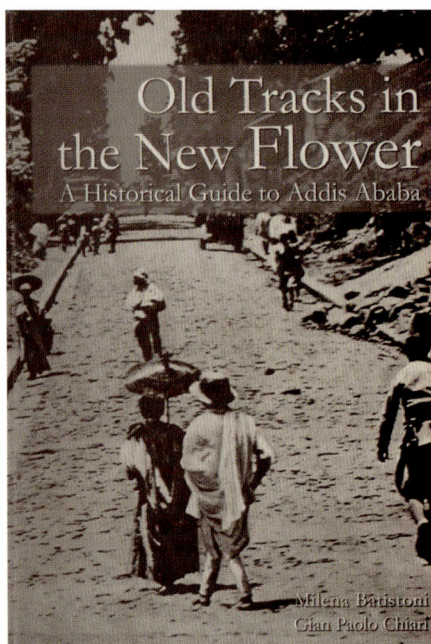 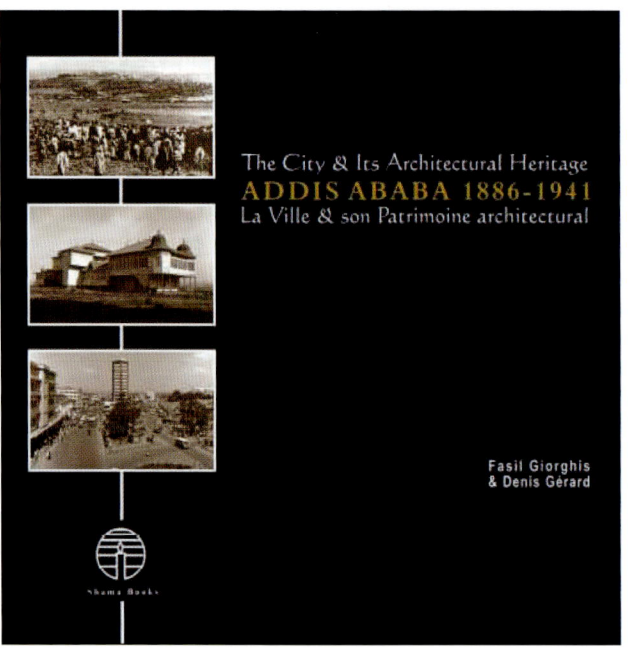

Batistoni & Chiari: *Old Tracks in the New Flower – A Historical Guide to Addis Ababa*

Giorghis & Gérard: *Addis Ababa 1886–1941 – The City & Its Architectural Heritage*

The work of Batistoni and Chiari was crucial for a systematic collection of 'Addis Ababa Urban Heritage' in a database that was produced in the following years by the German Agency for International Cooperation (GIZ) and the Ethiopian NGO 'Addis Woubet', which was co-founded by Princess Maryam Senna Asfa Wossen after her return from exile. (The database has never been made available to the public, but it was leaked and circulated among Ethiopian professionals.) The database systematically collected data for 173 historical buildings, including churches and monuments. For each building, the name, location, estimated year of construction, architect name, and current status in terms of physical condition and ownership were collected. One can say that this collection largely corresponds with the collection of Batistoni and Chiari.

About simultaneously in 2007, the Ethiopian architect Fasil Giorghis together with the French development professional Denis Gérard published a book called *Addis Ababa 1886–1941 – The City & Its Architectural Heritage*. Over almost 400 pages, the book, which was extended in 2019, contains an extensive account of historical photographs of Addis Ababa's early urban life, culture, and architecture and describes the economic and cultural forces that allowed the city to take shape. For the first time, the buildings are presented with complementary drawings and floorplans. Fasil Giorghis shows how the Ethiopian vernacular round hut has been incrementally transformed into a modern rectangular house. It sheds light on historical construction techniques as well as architectural details.

3 'Syncretic' retains the idea of coalition and appears in such contexts as 'syncretic religions', 'syncretic societies', and even 'syncretic music', all describing things influenced by two or more styles or traditions. The word also has a specific application in linguistics, where it refers to a fusion of grammatical forms. (www.merriam-webster.com)

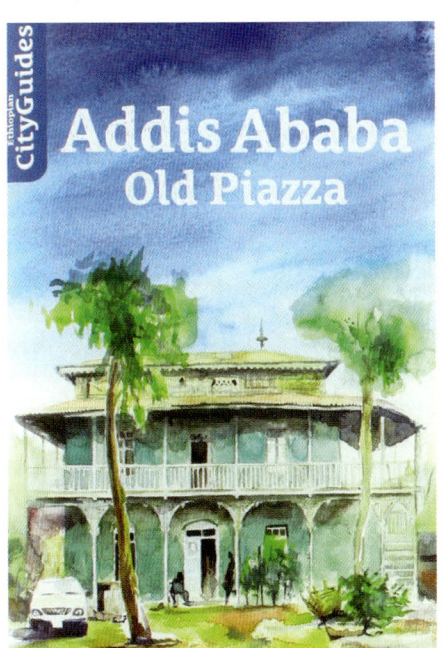

Harre: *Addis Ababa Old Piazza*

These two books, *Old Tracks* and *The City & Its Architectural Heritage*, have become classic accounts of the subject today, without any successors. It is worth mentioning the small book *Addis Ababa Old Piazza*, containing 'three self-guided tours' by Dominique Harre and published by the Centre Français des Études Éthiopiennes in 2017. It points to some of the main features of Addis Ababa Style architecture and is beautifully illustrated by Wondimagegn Gashaw.

While all these books contribute significantly to a description and documentation of the early architecture of Addis Ababa and a description of its main architectural features, it remains unanswered as to what architectural principles have had an agency in creating this unique architectural type. With this book, we attempt to look behind the surface of the architecture to reveal its somewhat mysterious DNA.

The Structure and Aim of this Book

The book is structured into three main chapters that go from the individual to the generic.
1. Phenotype: Case Studies
2. Genotype: Influence Analysis
3. Genes: Architectural Alphabet

In its terminology, it borrows a concept from biology and thus refers to architecture as organisms that are affected by an inner logic, DNA, and individual outer circumstances like environment, context, and people.

In that understanding, the 'genes' formulate an 'Architectural Alphabet' – a collection of design principles, whether in regard to construction materials, construction techniques, strategies for adapting to local climate, or organisational principles in the floorplan. The 'genes' are clustered in order to create complex and functional organisms. The different influences – be it physical influences such as the local climate and the local resources or cultural influences such as local or foreign building cultures – create the 'genotype' of the Addis Ababa House. In the individual buildings, the case studies, these clusters of influences have materialised as concrete, tangible expressions and thus can be seen as the 'phenotype' of the Addis Ababa House.

In our research, we had to reverse this logic. We started with the case studies as material containers of construction knowledge and then analysed the different influences that were at play in the specific historical context of the young capital. Finally, we synthesised the Architectural Alphabet, a collection of architectural principles that are beyond time and context.

The three chapters are flanked by introductory articles and an appendix. These two parts reflect the fate of urban heritage in light of the contemporary situation in which Addis Ababa has become a boom town for sometimes brutal urban development.

The five introductory articles are written by independent researchers and do not necessarily reflect the personal opinion of the editor. Fasil Giorghis historically classifies the emergence of the Addis Ababa Style and gives examples from his architectural practice of how to learn from it. Livio Sacchi gives insights into his restoration work in the *Ghebbi*, for which he was the responsible architect. Rumi Okazaki explains the urban formation of Addis Ababa and shows how ownership policies have affected heritage buildings. Piet Nieder follows situationist research methods to encounter heritage buildings and their present-day socio-cultural contexts. Tadesse Girmay sheds light on the conflict between preservation and urban development.

Learning from Heritage

This book hopes to raise awareness about architectural treasures of Ethiopia's urban past and witnesses of the heroic time of the Battle of Adua. The architecture is the result of a thriving African nation that is characterised by its openness towards other cultural influences without giving up on local traditional building knowledge. Traditional African ways of doing things met in a productive way with a modernity that did not mean the uniformisation of what urban life and culture can signify. Rather, the Addis Ababa House expresses a fresh desire for a new cosmopolitan urban African life.
Last but not least, this book hopes that the knowledge about architectural principles – from materials usage to smart and compatible design strategies right through to excellent crafting skills – can again become a reference for contemporary architectural practices in Ethiopian cities.

Influences and Transformations: Learning from the Addis Ababa Style

by Fasil Giorghis

A Brief History of the 'Addis Ababa Style'

From its foundation in 1886 up to the 1940s, Addis Ababa witnessed a distinct architectural style that developed as a result of the fusion between the local traditional construction and the influences that came from abroad. The period was marked by a gradual change from a predominantly agrarian society into an urban one. The opening up of the country to foreign traders facilitated the importation of commodities, new building materials, and construction techniques. This change was perceived as a process of 'modernisation', as it resulted in lifestyle changes and settlement patterns.

During the early days of the foundation of Addis Ababa, the level of local construction skills was rather limited due to the fact that permanent capitals ceased to exist after Gondar, which was the biggest city in the country during of the seventeenth and eighteenth centuries. For more than 180 years, Gondar supported a large urban population with consecutive kings who built castles, churches, bridges, and other structures in their territory. Following the collapse of the Gonderian dynasty, the continuous wars among regional rulers and the low esteem given to craftsmen negatively affected the development of architecture and construction know-how.

Eventually, as Addis Ababa started to take the shape of a permanent settlement, the nobility, rich merchants, and foreigners started to build large houses, at times with two or three levels. After the construction of the first Palace of Menelik in Addis Ababa, regional rulers were invited to come and reside in the new capital and given large tracts of land for their relatives and followers to settle. These dignitaries would normally build a large house on higher ground and their dependents continue to settle within the vicinity according to their social status and family relations. People living around parish churches founded by local dignitaries was another form of settlement pattern. Some areas, like the Somali Terra̧ or Shiro Meda, were dominated by people of a similar ethnic origin or trade. The influx of common people and the increasing number of nobles who resided in the capital after the imperial coronation in 1892 forced Menelik to modify traditional forms of land tenure and taxation in order to support the growing population of the capital. This type of settlement brought people of different classes into closer proximity, exposing people to urban ways of life. Here was a mixture of a wide variety of ethnic groups held together because of the dynamics of urban life of a new capital. This made Addis Ababa unique in Ethiopian history, with the diversity of its residents unconsciously leading to a plural society.

In those days, ordinary citizens still lived in circular houses made of wooden frames and plastered with earth mortar locally known as *tukuls*. The circular and oval

The many faces of Addis today:
The Mesob Tower is supposed to become 'Ethiopia's Eiffel Tower'.
Construction started in 2022.

houses are reminiscent of the Ethiopian traditional *tukul* form. The first houses built in Addis Ababa by the nobility followed this typology. Later, with the arrival of foreigners and new building materials, the same typology started to evolve in layout and external appearance.

The spatial organisation of the earliest houses ranges from a simple circular or oval plan to complicated geometric forms. The gradual change in typology, from the oval or round to the rectangular, reminds one of the continuous exposures to different cultures and the evolving lifestyle of the nobility of that period. In the construction of two-storey houses, stone masonry was used for the lower-level walls to support the upper floor, which was completed with clay plastered wooden frame walls. Wooden beams and joists carried the floor planks and upper part of the building. The first houses had a perimeter veranda wrapping around the house and supported by wooden posts. The roof covering material was initially thatch, but when corrugated iron sheet started to be imported via the port of Djibouti, it gradually replaced the local traditional material. Corrugated iron sheet roofing and its fascia decoration became a fashionable material that changed the appearance of larger and eventually all the houses in Addis Ababa.

The main foreign influences of that period were Indian and Armenian, which later included European styles through the works of Greek artisans and Italian contractors. Indian craftsmen from the Peshawar area were the most skilled builders who used carved wood for building front façades, balustrades, columns, and fascia boards. Despite being Muslims, Indian craftsmen were also employed to build churches. Armenian builders introduced their own types of arches, domes, and pyramidal roofs and contributed to the diversity of architecture in Addis Ababa. Dressed stone masonry buildings and decorations including plastered walls were introduced by European builders and used in public buildings, churches, and legations.

The houses and commercial buildings in and around Arada, the commercial centre of Addis Ababa, were covered with thatch and recycled tin roof that was made out of flattened recycled cans. Just before the coronation of Emperor Haile Selassie in 1930, the municipality was given orders to lend money to house owners to repair their buildings. Many houses were then covered with new corrugated iron sheets and whitewashed to give the city a better look during the coronation ceremony. Foreign traders such as Armenians, Indians, and Greeks owned a number of shops around the open stalls of the Ethiopians. These shops gradually increased in size and number, and the variety of goods for sale also grew. The arrival of the railway to Addis Ababa in 1917 increased the amount of imported goods. Different imported building materials such as corrugated iron sheet and glass found their way to the market. With the introduction of modern materials for construction, one notices the gradual change in the external appearance, finishing, and durability of traditional buildings. As the amount of imported goods and building materials increased, the open verandas were enclosed with glazed wooden curtain walls.

Dignitaries at a parade in Addis Ababa, 1934

Street scene in Addis Ababa, 1934

Street scene with the Imperial Palace in the background, 1934

It is this mixture of traditional forms and techniques with new ones coming from abroad that ended up producing what is popularly known as the 'Addis Ababa Style'. When Addis Ababa was captured as a result of fascist Italy's invasion of Ethiopia, a new urban and architectural development started to emerge. Buildings that were built from 1937 onwards were influenced by the architectural style of the occupation period. Even though the use of earth as a building material continued, the larger and more affluent residences and public buildings were constructed of concrete, stone, and brick. The Italian architects who designed buildings in Ethiopia introduced early rationalist and art deco styles. The Addis Ababa Style that had been popular earlier was no longer common as builders adopted the new construction system. Massive construction work took place during the five-year occupation period, which left its mark in most urban centres of Ethiopia. The Italian occupation period of the late 1930s and the international modern style of the 1960s replaced the local building tradition that was developing in the capital during the first two decades after its foundation.

Translating Traditions

Over the last 30 years since I started studying this style of architecture, I have observed the continuous loss of this heritage. The reasons for demolition are many, the most important being urban development. Some were removed due to the land value of the neighbourhood; others were pulled down due to deterioration and neglect. Even after some houses were listed, they could not escape demolition, as they were under one or other government institution. Private owners at times make drastic changes that render these heritage buildings unrecognisable.

Alliance Ethio-Francaise   Goethe Institute

My research and conservation work on the architectural heritage of Addis Ababa has influenced my architectural design work. Among the several buildings I designed, I want to discuss the Alliance Ethio-Francaise, the Goethe Institute, and the Ankobar Palace Lodge buildings in Addis Ababa and Ankobar as exemplary cases that were influenced by this style.

The Alliance Ethio-Francaise

The Alliance Ethio-Francaise, one of the oldest cultural centres in Addis Ababa, is a venue for French language courses, exhibitions, concerts, lectures, and film screenings. After it became the Alliance Ethio-Francaise, additional buildings were built to accommodate classrooms and administration facilities. The central and main structure remained as the initial and most significant building of the compound. This historic linear structure was built of stone masonry walls with verandas on the front and back side, which were later expanded and covered to accommodate a restaurant on the south side and an extension of the exhibition space on the front veranda side.
Some 20 years ago, the alliance decided to build new classroom blocks and additional administrative office spaces to serve the growing demand for French language training. The previous makeshift wooden barracks were removed to be replaced with new larger classrooms. The management together with the board had to select an architect who would translate the requirements into additional spaces while keeping the architectural character of the compound.
Based on my proposal of how I wanted to design the new blocks, I was selected as the architect for the new project. My proposal emphasised harmony between the existing historic building and the new blocks through the use of similar materials

Ankober Lodge

Inside Ankober Lodge

and features. Some of the main features I used were the original sheltered verandas as an access point to the classrooms. The dialogue between the two building blocks and landscaped courtyard was strengthened by the use of open verandas lined with wooden balustrades and built-in flower boxes. A half-hidden parking area was created under the classroom blocks by raising the buildings on pilotis and cutting the lower ground.

The buildings were built in brick with their corners lined and clad in stone, echoing the historic first building in the compound. Stone was also used to frame doors in line with the character of the historic building. Pitched roofs cover all the building blocks as a strategy to have good surface runoff and thermal insulation while continuing the earlier tradition. The wooden balustrade that runs along the veranda supporting the flower boxes is one of the main features of the two classroom buildings evoking the unmistakable Addis Ababa Style look.

The Goethe Institute

The design for the Goethe Institute, on the other hand, was primarily an adaptive reuse project of an early twentieth century villa that was the residence of the crown prince Asfa Wossen Haile Selassie. Even though the architect is not known yet, the villa clearly shows strong European influences. It is possible that it might have been designed by one of the European architects who resided in Addis Ababa in the 1920s and 1930s. This building served as a courthouse in the 1960s, as a political school during the *Derg* from 1978 to 1991, and later as an office space for Addis Ababa University's social science faculty.

Finally, after the change of government in Ethiopia, the possibility arose to combine the resources of the institute with the German foreign ministry, which was looking for a venue to house the works of the great contemporary Ethiopian artist Gebre Kirstos Desta. The then director of the institute asked me to find them a historic building that can accommodate the activities of the institute and display the works of Gebre Kirstos Desta in one location. As I was familiar with the majority of the heritage buildings in Addis Ababa, I took the director and his senior staff on a tour to visit the potential venues in the city. After this tour, the institute management selected the residence of the Crown Prince Asfa Wossen as the most suitable for their cultural activities and it was also not far from the previous location.

When I was tasked with preparing a restoration and adaptive reuse design, I started with the preparation of built drawings, condition analysis, and looking into possible ways of adapting the historic building to new uses and extending the facilities. After the study, my proposal was to use the imposing stone masonry villa as the main building for cultural activities, while adding a classroom block and a well-defined courtyard at the rear side. The bedrooms in the main structure were converted into offices for the director and administrative staff. An L-shaped classroom block was added at the back side without physically touching the main building. The transition between the old and the new blocks was made out of glass to accommodate a café with a terrace at the back. The large open terrace behind the main building facing east was transformed into a well-lit reading area. The kitchen wing next to the terrace became the bookstack area and audio-visual library. The new L-shaped classroom block was designed to define the open courtyard and accommodate the additional spaces for the institute. The classrooms in this wing are accessed via an open veranda similar to the old houses of the Addis Ababa Style. Along the new veranda, a continuous horizontal sun protection louvre is placed at the top part of the columns under the roof. The louvres are an echo of the wooden shutters of the main building and a typical feature of Addis Ababa Style houses. The central courtyard was created to have a well-defined external space that allows outdoor activities such as concerts, lunches, and cocktail receptions for the institute. The two parts of the institute and its outdoor spaces finally resulted in one whole architectural complex combining structures built more than 80 years apart and creating a dialogue between traditional and modern architecture.

The Ankober Lodge

The third building I want to discuss is the Ankober Lodge. When I was approached by its founder and owner, the late Ato Terefe Yeraswork, I was fascinated by the challenge of working on a historic site. Ankober was one of the earlier capitals of Emperor Menelik and a seat of government since his grandfather King Sahle Selassie of Shoa. It sits at the mountain ridge above the lowlands stretching up to the Red Sea. Some of the names of neighbourhoods in Ankober, such as Fit Ber and Arada, were later adopted in Addis Ababa.

The design brief consisted of a main restaurant-bar structure, which was going to stand in approximately the same location as the palace building, and some guest rooms along the steep mountainside. The authorities in the Ministry of Culture requested the main function of the building to be raised above ground level to allow future archaeological excavations and research to take place. This challenge was resolved by raising the restaurant with wooden pilotis, which resulted in the creation of a perimeter veranda and breathtaking views of the surrounding landscape. The lower level was used for storage and utilities as in traditional buildings.

I used this project to combine two experiments. The first was the reinterpretation of tradition for modern use, while the second was the possibility of using local artisans whose skills were no longer sought after. Age-old traditional building craftsmanship is gradually disappearing due to the fact that the building designs we produce nowadays are purely based on factory produced materials and imported skills and technology.

Conclusion

In my several years of experience in studying and working with heritage buildings in Addis Ababa, I have learned that there is a lot of knowledge that we have not properly understood. First of all, these buildings are mainly built of local resources such as stone, earth, and wood. Even the materials that used to be imported at the time are now being locally produced. Secondly, building parts such as verandas and pitched roofs are very well suited to the climate of Addis Ababa, whether it is in the dry or rainy season. The other important aspect is losing an age-old artisanal tradition that could be employed with some training for restoration works on historic buildings. Some might argue that these materials and skills are outdated for contemporary high-rise construction in our major cities, but we should not forget that more than 80 per cent of our population still needs this knowledge for shelter and related activities. If we commit ourselves to learn how to use these local materials and develop them to suit current needs, we will benefit a lot as a society, resulting in sustainable development and self-reliance.

Survey and Restoration of the Imperial Compound of Menelik II

by Livio Sacchi

The *Ghebbi* of Menelik II (*Ghebbi* is an Amharic word literally meaning 'compound fence') is the oldest imperial compound in Addis Ababa, with its foundation being practically coincident with the foundation of the city. It stretches over 400,000 sqm of land and is made of a series of eclectic pavilions. The fence is dotted by seven gates, each with a specific, historic function. The buildings, originally built with the help of quite a few foreign professionals and craftsmen, show the most various influences: from Arabia to the Ottoman Empire and from Armenia to India to European classicism. In those days, the Swiss Alfred Ilg (1854–1916), a talented engineer who also installed an ingenious water supply system pumped from the Entoto Mountains to the imperial compound, acted as a consultant for the entire complex. In 1905, electrical power was provided with the assistance of the German diplomat Friedrich Rosen (1856–1935). The old compound had to be partially rebuilt after a fire in 1892; during the reconstruction, two major pavilions were added: the Throne Hall and, a few years later in 1901, the Gibir Adarash or Banquet Hall. The last pavilion to be added was the small Council Building erected at the very beginning of the reign of Emperor Haile Selassie in the early 1930s.

The Survey and Restoration

The restoration of the *Ghebbi* has been an especially interesting and inspiring professional experience. The new job came to our office from an Ethiopian general contractor, Varnero Construction PLC (a third-generation, family-owned company of Italian origin), which had just been commissioned by the government to carry out the restoration and enhancement of the large historic complex. We had already had a similar experience with the same contractor in the city of Mekele in northern Ethiopia, with the restoration of the imperial compound of Yohannes IV, successfully completed shortly before this.
For the imperial compound in Addis Ababa, we were in charge of the architectural project; the structural project was entrusted to Dr. Messele Haile, an Ethiopian engineer with great experience and considerable sensibility for the built heritage. Our cooperation with Varnero Construction PLC was not limited to the architectural design; we also had to take care of the artistic direction of the entire work and provide full assistance in choosing and supplying materials as well as supervising the specialised workers brought in from Italy.
Over time, we were also asked to design a series of new buildings inside the compound: only the Visitors' Centre has actually been built following our project. The park has also finally been landscaped. It was renamed Unity Park and opened to the public in 2019.

Restoration of the onion-shaped dome of the Enqulal Bet

The State of the Site

We visited the compound for the first time in 2008. In those days, the *Ghebbi* could still be considered a 'well-kept secret', a mythical place known only to a privileged few. Though centrally located, the beautiful vegetation of the park sheltered its many buildings from the public streets all around; no visitors were usually allowed inside. Historic research, conducted in cooperation with the National Heritage and Research Authority in Addis Ababa, and an accurate survey of the entire *Ghebbi* site made us familiar with the surprising architectural qualities of its pavilions, realised in different decades with different functions and in very different styles. Some of these truly are masterpieces of their time and still constitute an amazing ensemble of unexpected architectural gems.

The entire complex was in bad condition in 2008: various military barracks and other minor service buildings were scattered here and there, some of them inhabited by garrisons. The timber structures had been seriously damaged by time and a lack of maintenance. The masonry walls also had major cracks, especially on the west side of the lower level of the Throne Hall, where a double system of reinforced concrete beams and tie rods had to be constructed some time ago. Many other wooden and finishing elements were either missing or badly damaged.

The Gems of the *Ghebbi*

The oldest nucleus of buildings includes the Prayer House or Enqulal Bet, the Emperor's Bedroom Building, the Empress's Bedroom Building, the Annex Building, the Servants' House, and a small Office Building used by the Minister of Defence. These pavilions, entirely made of wood with masonry inner cores, lavishly decorated with gracious, eclectic elements, all look fancy if not unique; they are ingeniously linked to one another with a system of raised, covered wooden walkways that allowed the family members not to have to walk on the ground if they did not wish to. Different craftsmen left a clearly recognisable and permanent sample of their stylistic choices and creative attitudes.

The Enqulal Bet (literally 'House of the Egg') – by far, and especially to European eyes, the most extraordinary artifact of the complex – is an octagonal, three-storey watchtower hiding a thick, round masonry pillar measuring 1.5 m in diameter at ground level. A picture taken in 1890 shows that the beautiful wooden loggias, the external wooden stairways, and the smaller, domed upper level were added in the late 1910s. The Oriental egg- or onion-shaped dome topping the building covers an internal wooden ceiling brilliantly decorated with colourful flower motifs. The eight cast iron railings protecting the external loggias of the first two levels are all different from one another. The room located on the second floor was used by the Emperor as a store for his precious books of prayers. The third floor contained the so-called 'telescope room': from the eight wooden and glass openings,

The Enqulal Bet during the restoration

Office Building of the Minister of Defence during the restoration

A side wing of the Coronation Hall during the restoration

the Emperor could gaze in any direction using his beloved telescope. From the second level of the Prayer House, a raised walkway, intertwined with a complex system of stairways, led to the Emperor's Bedroom Building. The two tiny booths on both sides of the stairway were specifically used to keep the household's only telephone – the first in Ethiopia.

The Emperor's Bedroom Building is a 15-metre-high square pavilion with cut-out corners that transform its plan into an irregular octagon – a fashionable geometry in Victorian times. The bedroom at the upper level is sheltered by a gabled roof, supported by four thin timber columns that in turn support the roof, and enclosed by an elegant, open loggia. Heavily decorated wooden doors are located at the ground floor, where the Emperor's parlour was located. False ceilings of no historic or artistic value had been added over time, hiding the original decorated ceilings.

The Annex or Elfign Adarash shows a corner loggia held by five groups of tetrastyle timber columns. Attached to the Annex is the building housing Empress Taitu's bedroom; another wooden raised walkway links it directly to the Emperor's apartment. Adjacent to the Empress's Bedroom Building is Empress Zweditu's Bedroom Building, with its beautiful woodwork stairway and loggias open to the view, curiously reminiscent of similar timber elements that can be found in distant places such as Japan or Southern California, all of them dating back to the early twentieth century.

A spacious Servants' House was the most damaged building of the entire complex. The pavilion housing the office of the Minister of Defence is a small, square, masonry one-storey building, lavishly decorated with the imperial crests, sheltered on the four sides by a light wooden loggia and covered by an elegant gabled roof. It looked very fragile and badly damaged. Not far from this stands another small building; at a slightly lower level is the imposing Throne Hall; at a still lower level is the Banquet Hall, the so-called Gibir Adarash, accessed through a monumental stone stairway. Finally, close to the Prayer House we have the Council Building.

The Throne (or Coronation or Reception) Hall, evidently designed under the influence of European classical architecture of the late nineteenth century, is an imposing, well proportioned, masterly built stone building. Two huge, symmetrical wood and glass wings were added on both sides during the Italian occupation in the second half of the 1930s, thus modifying the original aspect of the building. Some local experts suggested that these side wings should have been demolished in order to get back to the original volume: in agreement with other scholars and the Palace Administration, we considered them a meaningful part of the history of the building, thus suggesting to keep and restore them. The interior of these glass wings is also quite interesting: you simultaneously feel inside but also outside of the masonry building. The main entrance is through a double, imposing stone-clad stairway leading to an arched loggia. From this loggia you can enter the Throne Room, whose walls and ceiling are decorated with European-style gypsum and wooden panels, lavishly enriched by gilded details. Grand crystal chandeliers hang from the ceiling. Behind the Throne Room there is an elongated salon, used as a library, and some service areas. The lower level, accessed through side entrances from the garden, is supported by a powerful system of vaults propped up by heavy, lowered arches. Most historical sources report that this building was erected in 1889 for the coronation of Emperor Menelik II, but a picture taken in 1910 shows another edifice, known as the Clock Tower, standing on the Throne Hall site. An aerial view of 1929 clearly shows the present building. This means that it was created after the rule of Menelik II and only used for the coronation of Haile Selassie I in 1930.

The Gibir Adarash or Banquet Hall is an impressive, gigantic three-nave building with thick masonry-buttressed adobe plastered walls covered by a triple gabled roof with timber trusses supporting traditional pitches made of wood and reeds tied with leather thongs; an airy, open, wooden loggia runs on three sides of the building. The main entrance, located on the south-west façade, used to be guarded by armed soldiers and a cannon. Some 34 wooden columns in two rows separated the three aisles and supported the roof. They were later substituted with reinforced concrete pillars and beams. At the time of its construction (1901), the Gibir Adarash was considered the largest and finest hall in the entire country. According to sources, it could easily accommodate thousands of guests and hundreds of servants: conveniently, tea could be piped directly from a central brewery.

Indian craftsmen were largely employed during construction under the supervision of the aforementioned Alfred Ilg and Léon Chafneux.

The Council Building was finally realised at the very beginning of the reign of Emperor Haile Selassie I at the corner between the Prayer House and the Annex Building, not far from the wall now separating this part of the park from the private area of the compound presently used by the Prime Minister: a light blue lacquered wooden pavilion with an open porch, covered by a gabled roof, whose interiors are embellished by beautifully crafted natural wood panels.

Last but certainly not least, we have to mention that the park surrounding the buildings offers an incredible variety of trees and bushes, which all make up a luxuriant sub-equatorial mountain landscape. Its beauty is historically well known: many European fruit trees were planted there for the delight of the Empress.

The Restoration Work

During the years spent in Addis Ababa, our team established a friendly and fruitful professional partnership with the aforementioned Dr. Messele Haile and his office, MH Engineering PLC, and with the General Contractor. Ethiopian and Italian technicians, workmen, craftsmen, and decorators actively cooperated in order to achieve the best possible results.

The debate between the experts has always been interesting and fruitful: it forced us to mediate between the more rigorous positions of some of the Ethiopian scholars and technicians and our own opinion, softer in allowing the reintegration of missing or irremediably damaged parts.

We had to face quite a few technical challenges, and we also had to make some difficult choices, all of them taken with the Palace Administration and the Ethiopian scholars and experts that were frequently asked to give us their precious scientific and historic advice. We already mentioned the decision concerning the proposed demolition of the two side wings of the Throne Hall that in the end were kept and beautifully restored. Another interesting example is the double reinforced concrete structural system sustaining the triple gabled roof of the Banquet Hall, which divides the interior of the huge building into three naves. In this case, the challenge would have been the reconstruction of the original timber columns; unfortunately, we could not find any pictures or drawings showing what they looked like. In the end, we decided to keep the present structural system, just painting it red, thus making it visually more coherent with the beams and the surprisingly beautiful inner surface of the roof.

The final result we were looking for was an accurate restoration that would bring the different pavilions back to the most significant moment in their history, making the entire complex efficient and structurally safe; but as far as it would have been possible, we were also in search of the fascinating, original image of the *Ghebbi*.

Detail of the tetrastyle columns of the Annex Building

The Banquet Hall interior after the restoration

The buildings had to be open to the public and work as a museum in a park; some of them were also supposed to perform official functions such as receptions of foreign heads of state or official delegations. The pavilions therefore had to be brought back to the eclectic charm of the era in which they were built; their original, fancy decorations had to be brought to new light. The general image of the compound had to return to the glories of the past, but at the same time, it was necessary to prevent the entire complex from turning into a Disneyland for tourists, instead preserving the original imperial charm and gravity it once had.

Result and Outlook

The *Ghebbi*, as a whole, can be considered a cultural landscape – a combined work of nature and of the women and men of Ethiopia. It is still speaking of coronations, receptions, gatherings, official visits of foreign delegations, and also of a very comfortable domestic life. Clearly reminiscent of nineteenth century eclecticism, it narrates the end of an era.
In my opinion, because of its long history and unique position in the urban landscape of Addis Ababa, the imperial *Ghebbi* is of seminal importance for the collective psychological life of Ethiopia: a nation not only needs contemporary comforts, but also deep and meaningful cultural roots. The built heritage is the nation's soul; it physically represents its cultural spirit. No country is able to confidently look at

the future without respecting its past. But the *Ghebbi* also achieves outstanding universal values, transcending national boundaries with the specific illustration of a very special stage of Ethiopian architectural history.

The architectural restoration of the *Ghebbi* enhanced its historic and artistic values, but also allowed a reasonable and sustainable reuse of the entire compound. The opening to the public of most of the pavilions within the large and centrally located park, blessed with the already mentioned richness of the Ethiopian highlands flora, quickly transformed the *Ghebbi* into the active focus of the cultural, touristic, and political life of Addis Ababa. Eventually, displaying the lavish collections of the imperial memorabilia – kept in archives and warehouses – in the recently renovated venues will provide the noblest future for this magnificent architectural ensemble, made of buildings that truly are the silent witness to Ethiopian history.

Past and Future

Addis Ababa is now one of the significant African metropolises: the city also plays a symbolic role at the continental level, hosting the headquarters of the African Union. It has a rich architectural heritage from different periods of its long history. A complete and articulated programme of restoration and enhancement of traditional Ethiopian architecture, of the many buildings built during the Italian occupation, of those that were part of the imperial family estate, but also of those belonging to the modern period, to name just a few of the most interesting historical periods represented in the city, could substantially contribute to the overall urban regeneration of a capital that is running fast towards the future but must not forget its illustrious past.

Restoration of an entrance to the Banquet Hall

Map of Addis Ababa (hand-drawn, Italian labels)

- Piana di Salulta'
- M. Ullucc
- A Fiche
- A Debra Libanos
- Entoto
- Chiesa di Mariam
- Chiesa Roguel
- 2800
- Sorgente minerale Cascata
- Nuovo Quartiere delle Legazioni
- Leg. Francia
- Leg. G...
- Ponte
- Ex Leg. Germania
- Addis Alem
- Deg Burrù
- Deg. Ubbie'
- Ras Macconnen
- Ras. Micael
- Club Imperiale
- Campo delle Corse
- Osp...
- Quartiere Armeno
- 2450
- Chiesa di Ghiorghis
- Negad Ras
- Ponte di Ras Macconnen
- Deg. Ilosà
- Afa Negus
- Società Coloniale Italiana
- Dogana
- Abuna Mateos
- Chiesa di Sellasie
- Telegrafo
- Posta
- Granai
- Pizza Mercato
- 2460
- Ponte
- Zecca
- Ghebi Negus
- Strada Carrazz...
- Ambulanza Italiana
- 2450
- Indiani e Commercianti
- Hotel Taitu
- Scuole
- T. Gamela Uonz
- Finfinni
- Bank of Abyssinia
- Filoa Sorgente termale
- Ponte
- Licamocas Nado
- Deg. Tesamma
- Ras Uolde Ghiorghis
- Ras Tessamma
- Finfinni
- Ras Darghi
- Per Becciu Gallo e Piccolo Acaki
- T. Berchamo
- Via di Ada per...
- Pascoli
- Per Gambola e Gurghe
- 1950

Map of Addis Ababa, 1909, Regione di Gullelie-Addis Abeba (Finfinni) schizzo topografico, Bollettinodella Societa Geografica Italiana (hand-drawn copy)

Urban Formation and Architectural Heritage of Addis Ababa During the Ethiopian Imperial Period
by Rumi Okazaki

This text describes the urban formation and architectural heritage of Addis Ababa, a city that grew from a military camp only from the end of the nineteenth century. Addis Ababa's historical areas still preserve the spatial characteristics of the military encampment based on the topography, where the oldest architectural structures are found at the highest points.

1. Topographical Features of Ethiopian Settlements

The two capitals ruled by Emperor Menelik II before Addis Ababa, Ankober (2,770 m) and Entoto (2,800 m), were strategically located on the high plateau mainly for defensive reasons. While the church and residences of emperors were situated on hilltops, other residents often lived in houses with thatched conical roofs on the hillside, using the natural topography to show the hierarchical relationship. This type of topographical urban formation significantly influenced the planning of the new city of Addis Ababa. However, the altitude of Addis Ababa was relatively lower than the previous two cities because Empress Taitu, wife of Menelik II, preferred the slightly warmer climate around the area of the Filwoha thermal springs at the foot of the Entoto Mountains.

2. Urban Spatial Formation of Addis Ababa

By looking at a contour map of Addis Ababa, one can discover a miniature of the Ethiopian highland settlements. For example, the map created by De Castro in 1909 shows the position of residences of high-ranking nobilities and military officials based on topographic features. *Ghebbi*[1] *Negus* (king's palace, 2,445 m) is situated at the city's centre on a high mountain that overlooks the surrounding area. The residences of the noble class are also located on different mountains – most of them around 2,500 m high – in the northern part of the city,[2] separated by rank (such as the residence of *Ras* Makonnen, *Ras* Micael, *Afa Negus*, *Deg.* Burru, and *Deg.* Ubbie). In between, there were other residences, churches (*Chiesa di Ghiorghis, Chiesa di Selassie*), the archbishop's residence (*Abuna Mateos*), the foreign legation (*Ex. Leg. Germania, Leg. Francia*), modern public facilities (*Hotel Taitu, scuola, Bank of Abyssinia, Ponte di Ras Makonnen, etc.*), and foreign communities (*Indiani e commercianti, quartiere Armeno*) were formed. The city topography with elevation differences creates distinctive but loosely connected neighbourhoods. Some of these neighbourhoods, known as *sefer*, are named after prominent residents such as *Ras* Makonnen *Sefer* and *Ras* Birru *Sefer*. *Sefer* is not an administrative district unit, but rather a neighbourhood name used by the local people up until today.

1 *Ghebbi* is the Amharic word for 'palace'.
2 Some Ethiopian titles include *Negus, Ras, Afe Negus, Dejazmatch,* and *Kegnazmatch*.

Former residence of *Ras* Birru, currently used as the Addis Ababa Museum, 2020

Since the residences of high-ranking nobles and military officials were situated on top of hills, they are also well suited to becoming urban landmarks. *Ghebi Negus* became Unity Park. The former residential compound of *Ras* Makonnen, where Emperor Haile Selassie I built his palace, is currently the Ethnological Museum on Addis Ababa University's main campus. The former residence of *Dejazmatch* Birru became the Addis Ababa Museum. The former residence of *Dejazmatch* Wube now serves as Addis Ababa Restaurant. All these residences were urban landmarks and have become new public attractions after their conversion.

These buildings often have a large area of glazed windows or verandas that effectively create panoramic views from the interior. Since Addis Ababa has an altitude of more than 2,400 metres, the mountain-like weather is highly variable, with intense sunlight and chilly temperatures. Therefore, the rooms with glazed windows can also be used as sunrooms in order to adapt to weather variations.

Interior view, 2020

View of residential buildings in the Armenian *Sefer*, 2022

3. Tracing the Original Urbanscape of Addis Ababa: The Case of the Armenian *Sefer*

Many buildings near the Ras Makonnen Bridge have become a target for demolition due to the implementation of a redevelopment project called the Addis Ababa Riverside Green Project. However, the adjacent Armenian *Sefer*, an area between the neighbourhoods of Amst and Sidist Kilo, has almost been untouched. According to Takao Shiraishi's 2006 heritage database, at least 62 heritage houses were in this area. The author's literature reviews and interviews conducted in 2022 revealed that many of these houses once belonged to high-ranking nobilities, military officials, experts, and clergymen closely related to Emperor Haile Selassie I, who gave them land for their services. The descendants of these families still live in some of the compounds and have been passing on their legacy.

3-1. The State of Heritage Residential Buildings in the Armenian *Sefer*

Although these heritage residential buildings were once grandeur mansions, they suffered severe damage, especially after 1974 when surplus housing was confiscated and made into government or *kebele* housing by the *Derg* government. To investigate the actual state of these buildings, the author documented them and conducted interviews with their owners and residents. The following describes the actual status of architectural heritage in the study area for four types of ownership, with representative building examples.

Interior view with glazed windows and panoramic town view. The ceiling needs repair since pigeons started to live inside it, but there is no response or support from the *kebele*. Former residence of *Kegnazmatch* Wolde Yohanis, 2022

Portrait of *Kegnazmatch* Wolde Yohanis, collection of the family of *Kegnazmatch* Wolde Yohanis

3-1-1. Mixed Ownership

Mansions possessed by prominent personnel often fall into this category when descendants decide to stay and live with the surrounding community. One example is the residence of *Kegnazmatch* Wolde Yohanis[3], where his grandchildren currently live on the main building's ground floor, occupying about half of the floor. The rest of the building is used as *kebele* housing[4], with the other half of the first floor for two households and the upper floor for one household. Four households occupy the main building, but this is not the total number in the compound. There are 17 households besides those previously counted. Some are owned by the *kebele* and others are rented out by the family of *Kegnazmatch* Wolde Yohanis, as most of the renters are their relatives. The mixed ownership creates a harmonious community and has prevented high crime rates.

3-1-2. *Kebele*-owned Housing

The state of *kebele*-owned housing varies according to the residents. As mentioned above, it is not an easy process to receive funding support for the buildings' maintenance from the *kebele* or the government. Therefore, when people do not have ways to carry out repairs, they can only use the building as it is.

Fortunately, many residents in the area are older and knowledgeable about the historical background of their houses and have respect for the buildings. For example, the old couple who lives in the former residence of *Dejazmatch* Letti Yibelu

3 *Kegnazmatch* Wolde Yohanis was a military commander of the right wing under Haile Selassie's regime. He was also an engineer and is said to have designed his own house. One of the main streets inside the Armenian *Sefer* is named after him.

4 *Kebele* was formerly the smallest administrative unit in Addis Ababa. The role of *kebele* included the management of *kebele* houses. The *kebele* does not exist anymore and the management of the houses has been transferred to *woreda*, but the residents still use the term '*kebele* housing'. The *woreda* houses will be referred as '*kebele* housing' in this text.

Former residence of *Dejazmatch* Letti Yibelu, interior view of sunroom, 2022

Interior view of living room, with original furniture still in use, 2022

has been there for more than 50 years. They informed us that they used to rent the house from Tajesech Letti Yibelu, the daughter of *Dejazmatch* Letti Yibelu, before they rented the house from the *kebele*. However, as the house has become very old and severely damaged, there is not much they could repair on their own.

3-1-3. Government-owned Housing

On the other hand, when residents or institutions are capable and willing to pay for restoration and maintenance fee, the houses are well-conserved. This tendency was seen more in government-owned housing with a higher rental price than the *kebele* housing.

The Tesfa Addis Parents Childhood Cancer Organisation (TAPCCO) has been renting one of the heritage residential buildings from the government as their institutional facility for ten years. Twelve employees, 50 children with cancer, and their families spend time together in the compound during treatment. The main building is a shared residence for the children and parents, and behind it, there is a canteen and workshop space. The organisation mainly receives funding from the US and can fund the restoration of the building. When we visited the facility, the paint repair was going on. However, the thick paint may destroy the fine woodwork if used repeatedly over time.

3-1-4. Private Ownership

Regarding people who owned large mansions, the *Derg* government confiscated part of their buildings and turned them into *kebele-* or government-owned housing. For this reason, privately owned compounds or houses are not vast in size. An example found in the research area is shown on the opposite page (bottom image). Currently, two households with family ties share one compound. Their ancestors started to reside in this area before the Battle of Maychew in 1936. They had a successful beer-making business that the *Derg* government nationalised. The owner told us that the house has never been rebuilt and is almost 90 years of age.

4. Conclusion

The urban history of Addis Ababa only starts at the end of the nineteenth century. Despite the short period, architectural gems have flourished across the high plateau, creating a unique urban feature. However, the speed of development threatens the conservation of historical sites. Within the past decade, Addis Ababa has seen an unprecedented number of large-scale developments. Numerous heritage buildings and communities have been lost, and many residents have been displaced. For example, the district near the Ras Makonnen Bridge, just next to the Armenian *Sefer*, has been totally demolished as part of the 'Beautifying Sheger' River Development Project[5]. Project developers stress the importance of relocating residents from flood-prone riverbanks and creating a beautiful riverscape without paying much attention to one of the oldest community and heritage buildings within it.

As seen in the previous examples from the Armenian *Sefer*, most of the heritage buildings are owned by the *woreda* (previously the *kebele*) or the government. Many residents residing in the heritage buildings have lived in the area since the imperial period and have a deep attachment to the building and surrounding community. However, even if the residents wish to preserve the heritage buildings, if the government decides to redevelop the area, they have no choice but to relocate to another place. This fact has made heritage buildings vulnerable to demolition.

This is not unique to Ethiopia. Around the world, decaying historical sites have attracted informal residents and become a target for large-scale development. Only after development do authorities realise the value of historical sites when it is often too late, and almost only relics remain. Addis Ababa does not need to repeat the same mistake. Its traditional neighbourhoods, such as the Armenian *Sefer*, have grown organically and now embrace a diverse population encompassing many layers of history, community, nature, and economic activity. These neighbourhoods contain the seeds of future sustainable development that can integrate improvements without losing character. As globalisation progresses and cities become more homogenised, these neighbourhoods are the key differentiating element that gives Addis Ababa its character and future potential.

---

5 Details of the project can be found in the African Development Bank Group's 'Beautifying Sheger' River Development Project Investment Strategy and Infrastructure Plan, 2021.

Building used by TAPCCO under restoration, exterior view, 2022

Woodwork detail of the door, 2022

A privately owned building made of *chikka*, 2022

Agop Bagdasarian second residence

Overview of the four locations

Map of Dérive #1

Old Addis Dérive[1]

by Piet Nieder

Dérive #1 – in the Armenian Quarter

Coming from Sidist Kilo I, take Tewdros Street to get to the Armenian Quarter. I follow the map and arrive at the Agop Bagdasarian second residence, which today serves as the National Association of the Blind. A young woman stops me from taking photos, but Ato Sebsibe Yilma, Head of Office, kindly asks me to sit down on the deep sofa in his office. His suspicions quickly dissipated and he is delighted with my interest in the architecture. He explains that in earlier times, the Ministry of Finance was placed here and that it is a listed heritage building. It is owned by the municipality, which is also responsible for its maintenance. Regardless of that, there is a large crack on the side of the building, which looks worrying. Ato Sebsibe Yilma literally raves about the building. According to him, it is very pleasant to work in. Due to the generous room height, which allows a constant draft, and thanks to the thick clay walls, the room climate is very comfortable. Silently assuming the building is brick, I am amazed to find that the building is clad in sheet metal, imitating a brick wall. What a remarkable alienation effect! Ato Sebsibe Yilma explains that the red hue is original. After so many years, it still looks bright. Inside I notice that at that time, a variety of motifs were produced as sheet metal reliefs. This is also evident inside the building. The stairs and floor are made of wood. The walls are made of clay, about 60–70 cm thick on the ground floor and tapered to about 40 cm on the upper floor, plastered on the inside and covered with sheet metal on the outside. Only the pillars are made of stone. Ato Sebsibe Yilma raves about the building! His colleague, who I guess is also blind, shares his passion.

1 The term dérive – French for 'drift' – was a research strategy of the situationist movement. In 1956, Guy Debord defined the dérive as 'a mode of experimental behaviour linked to the conditions of urban society, in which participants drop their everyday relations and enter into spontaneous encounters and interactions'. It is an unplanned journey through a landscape, usually urban, in which participants 'let themselves be drawn by the attractions of the terrain and the encounters they find there'. (Guy Debord; June 1958). Translated by Ken Knabb. 'Definitions'. Internationale Situationniste. Paris (1).)

Page 221 of this book contains a QR code that leads to an interactive Google map. It shows the locations of the Addis Ababa Houses that were collected in the 'Urban Heritage Database'. For the dérives, I made use of the map on my smartphone.
If you are in Addis right now, try it out!

Introduction 45

Façade made from tin

Painted ceiling

The upper floor

Opposite is the *Grazmatch* Terle Residence. A younger man in a safety vest sits in a van on the side of the road and tells me through the window that there are more houses like this around here. He offers me his help and shows me a two-storey house one hundred metres further down Tewdros Street. He is Yilikal Fantanum, a graduate civil engineer, and it is obvious how much he appreciates these old houses.

The building he leads me to is the *Dej.* Letyibelu Gebre Residence. As we enter, a man invites me three times to taste his ingera and eat with him. The central interior is impressive: a large, dark, cool, very high ceiling. Everything seems soft and calm. Benches painted green are set up, with 10–12 men sitting and drinking Tej, the local honey wine. As I understand from Yilikal, the building previously functioned as a kind of courtroom. Letyibelu, he explains, was an important figure under the king. The rectangular room is 5 to 6 metres in height and about one quarter is divided by a slightly lower part with a wide wooden arch. Beautiful wooden pilasters support this arch. Light comes through the upper windows like a clerestory. The floor is made of wood, while the walls are made of clay and covered with wallpaper with floral motifs, which is certainly original. Yilikal is very enthusiastic about the constructive precision of the architecture. He particularly emphasises the perfect right angles, which is particularly remarkable for an earthen building. I estimate the surrounding spaces to be a room height of 3.2 m. The decorative gables act as ventilation outlets. The wooden roof construction remains visible. The partition walls are not pulled up to the roof, allowing further air circulation. Yilikal then shows me the basement, which can be reached via the inner courtyard. This is made of stone and apparently served as a prison for the accused. A man brewing Tej in the backyard is not happy with my presence. The Tej kitchen was added later. It is clearly visible that this building has not stood the test of time as well as the old building.

Ornamented tin panels at the staircase

Dej. Letyibelu Gebre Residence, now a *Tej-bet*

Gables help ventilate the room

Main room with a clear story

I continue into the Armenian Quarter. It is beautiful in its small scale, in its quiet bustle of people and animals. Urban agriculture can be seen everywhere. A sweet flower shop run by young men occupies a good portion of the sidewalk. The ground of the quarter is layered with dirt, plants, garbage, and bones. Whole skulls of larger ruminants lie here, rotting unhurriedly in the sun.

A man in a hooded sweatshirt is standing in front of a wonderful house that I was not previously aware of. It is a large, two-storey building, very nicely structured by the wooden construction, with many panelled windows. The man smiles and greets me. He has no cutting teeth and looks like quite a simple, ordinary man. Noticing my interest in the house, he tells me that he is the owner and that the builder was Yohannes Wolde Ab, his grandfather. Yohannes Wolde Ab worked for the City Council at the time and also had a 'Paris Citizenship'. The house is 150 years old and he lives here with his parents and children in a three-generation household. I tell him that I'd love to see inside, but he doesn't respond. I am happy to take photos of the outside.

I love the Armenian Quarter. It is so peaceful. An important finding for today is that people know about the qualities of these houses and appreciate them very much.

Keg. Wolde Yohanis Residence

The owner in front of his house, view from the south-east

Map of Dérive #2

Dérive #2 – in Piassa

The next day I cross Ras Mekonnen Bridge and walk up John Melly Street to find the 'Addis Ababa Culture and Tourism' bureau, but it does not seem to exist at the location that I assumed.

My attention is drawn towards an old, blue two-storey building with a prominent bay window. It has five slender stone columns and was built as an extension of another old stone building. This house, like the other building I will discover today, is not listed in the urban heritage database. Michael, a man under 30, lets me sit in his office behind a partition wall that has been added in recent years dividing the prominent bay window room. Michael operates a printing and postal office here. He says the building is 100 years old, and supposedly an Italian minister lived here. He does not know the details, but proposed to put me in touch with someone who does know.

On the other side of the street is the Hager Fikr Theatre (in Amharic: Country Love Theatre), the oldest theatre in Ethiopia (if you ignore the Asmari bet). As indicated on the plate on the façade, it was built in 1935 and renovated in 2002. A young man prohibits me from taking photos. I slowly continue walking in the compound and secretly enter the annex building. Strange metal bracings span across the big room, which has a fountain in the middle. Here I bump into a group of elegantly dressed people and am introduced to Ato Karim, the young director of the Hager Fikr Theatre. He leads me into the main hall, which is big enough for 600 people, and switches on the light for me to take pictures. He tells me that the building is made of concrete. The foyer has beautiful coloured glass art deco windows that remind me of Chagall.

I go deeper into the neighbourhood. I pass many relaxed people hanging out in the pleasing alley full of micro urban agriculture – even pigeons are kept here. Down

Building on John Melly Street (name unknown)

The upper floor

Inside the Hager Fikr Theatre

the street, I see another wonderful house. It looks almost like a prototype of an Addis Ababa House – in a modest version. What is especially amazing is the patchwork and repairs that have been done by residents over the years. The ground floor is more closed and seemingly serves mainly economic activities, while the upper floor shows residential purposes. As I try to take a photo, a woman strongly waves and calls to me. She comes towards me and we agree on 200 birrs for permission to take a few photos. It is a perfectly proportioned building, with simple details and an enjoyable degree of ornamentation – and it just belongs to its place. To me, it strongly creates a genius loci. The stone foundation forms stairs to the upper balcony, which leads to the different upper compartments. The wooden construction of the balcony is simple and efficient, with double columns and logical joints between the pieces. The wood used is slender, maybe a maximum of 12 × 12 cm. As I take the photos, many neighbours closely observe my activities and a woman continuously invites me to take a *bunna* (Ethiopian coffee) at her tiny street coffee shop. I urge her to be patient but she keeps on talking to me. I am happy to drink the *bunna* and a young woman who lives in the house tells me it is 'Italian'. They live with eight people in one of the compartments on the upper floor, of which there are about five or six. The balcony has a water tap, accommodates several satellite dishes, and also serves the drying of clothes. A woman indicates to me the beautiful view she has from the balcony over the historical neighbourhood, where the beautiful Azalech Gobena is visible in the distance.

Street life with unlisted heritage building in the back

The same street viewed from the north

Unlisted heritage building

The veranda on the upper floor

The Imperial Menelik Police Station, not listed

The Azalech Gobena crowns the area

It is one of my most important discoveries today that the Addis Ababa Style is not restricted to the listed buildings in the database, but rather it is a ubiquitous, living ingredient of the historic neighbourhood. People are very well aware of its aesthetic value and they are proud of it. It belongs to them in the sense of 'cultural ownership'. Everyone knows a little bit of history about it, but not many details – maybe also due to the language barrier.

At the corner of Eoen Street, a man points out the 'Imperial Menelik Police Station', which is 150 years old, as he explains. Here, as in many other old buildings, small sheds hosting tiny shops have been added at ground level. Interestingly, a contemporary police station can be found nearby on a big compound. Similar to the Gerichtssaal (*Tej-bet*) that I saw yesterday in Teeodros Street, functions seem to remain in their historical localities.

I enter the compound of the 'Old Municipality', a building we have studied in Berlin. The guard tells me 'Artist Alemtsehay Wogajo', maybe indicating the new owner of the property who is fundamentally renovating the (listed!) heritage building. The standards of conservation seem very worrying to me, as the roof is in parts completely removed, including the wooden support structure. In contrast to these parts that are drastically renewed, other parts of the building look very damaged, with a big hole in the wall that bares the big stones like flesh. Small trees grow from the top of the roof, surely causing much damage to the fabric. The famous tree, which was an iconic part of the building, lies in pieces in the dirt. It is touching and sad to see this living part of the city's history fading in a corner of a construction site – almost like a metaphor.

From Menelik Square I stroll down towards the Taitu Hotel. To me, the massive construction of the 'Adwa Victory Centre' is an incredibly brutal shift towards an urban design paradigm that has lost any sense of human scale.

The Old Municipality under restoration

The iconic tree in pieces

Opposite side with the huge construction of the 'Adwa Museum'

Map of Dérive #3

Dérive #3 – in Kebena

The taxi brings me to Balderas Condominiums. From here I walk to the *Ras* Abate Bwayalew Residence. This house is a lonely heritage building. Many big condos have been erected around it. The massive, sloped roof becomes visible behind fences from shining corrugated iron sheets. Only on the second view do I realise that there is a small opening to the compound. In the distance, I perceive a few women. They do not care about my presence as I remain standing at the fence opening for a while. The walls are high without many windows. I cannot guess how many stories the building has. The wattle and daub walls are not in good shape; one can see the substructure from woven wood and tied with ropes. As no one looks after me, which is quite unusual, I enter through the open door into an extremely high corridor. A woman suddenly comes out from the inside. I ask her if I can sneak inside and she say okay and cares no further about my presence. Strangely, the big corridor with a room height of 4 to 5 metres is completely empty. Old yellowish wallpaper is slowly loosening from the *chikka* walls. Doors and window frames are painted dark brown. I do not feel well knocking on doors. As I get out again, two old women are standing outside. They are not happy that I entered the building. I ask one if it is possible to walk around the building to see the other side, but she denies my request, which I accept right away.

I cross the river and continue my walk into the old Kebena neighbourhood. The very small alleys seem well-organised and liveable. Small shops and lots of urban agriculture in combination with a cobblestone paved road create a pleasant living environment. Some cats are around for hunting.

It's getting dark and I had already 'closed my day' with a fruit juice in Elizabeth Street and a sundowner cigarette. But somehow, I can't stop walking and as I am

Ras Abate Bwayalew Residence

already close to the *Afenigus* Nasibu Meskele Residence, I decide to have a little look at it. It lies on a hilltop with steep slopes and is situated at the end of a winding street, where it has a beautiful and strong presence. As I remain a distance from the compound and carefully take one or two first photos, the dwellers become aware of me. They indicate for me to come closer. As I approach and return their open smiles, the old woman asks me if I want to enter the house. I try not to appear too 'wanting', so I humbly accept the offer, following her up the ramp of old eucalyptus bracing. A teenage girl, her granddaughter, welcomes me with a smile. The upper walls seem to be built with brick or stone plastered with earth mortar. The wooden, filigree veranda had a pleasant width of maybe 1.8 metres. It is used for drying cloth and a small planting of kitchen herbs. It looks picturesque. They call the small annex in the front the 'telephone house'. I am invited for tea in their private room, which is extremely high. The old woman spreads her arms and looks up to the ceiling to express how much she loves this space. A partition wall of 2 metres in height divides the room into one part for living and one for cooking. The ceiling is covered with typical plastic tissue. As I drink the tea, a kitty sleeps on the backrest of the sofa just next to my head. The old woman shows me the *katma* she had just harvested. She proposes that I come back the next morning to take photos in the daylight.

On the following day, the lady and her granddaughter are not present but other residents are equally open to letting me visit the house. I am with about six to seven

Walls of *chikka* in the courtyard

Afenigus Nasibu Meskele Residence

Glazed gables from the inside

Veranda space

View from the north-east, the corner on the right is almost falling down

Wall construction on the ground floor

residents, and they enjoy the view from the back veranda. Eighteen families live in the house, 11 on the upper floor and seven at ground level. After a while, they ask me to join them in the backyard of the building. Here they show me how one corner is pending down dramatically. They explain that this damage happened two years ago after a fire. It looks extremely dangerous. It is in a part of the building where one of the women lives, and she has seven children. She is very concerned about her safety and complains that the *kebele* responsible for the building does not care about this damage, and it is forbidden for them to do any repairs themselves. In my eyes, it would be easily feasible to secure the structure in one day! Her friendly neighbour, Sisay, hopes my photos will find people that can take action.

Wall construction of Abate Bwayalew

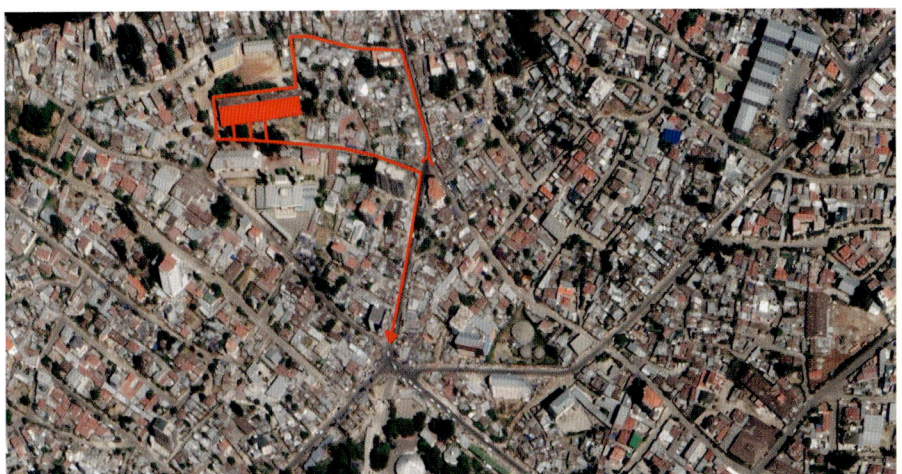

Map of Dérive #4

Dérive #4 – in Rufael

I arrive in Rufael. Suddenly the mountain chains that flank Addis appear so close. Rufael itself lies on a hill overlooking all of Addis. Most houses here are still single storey. Individual office buildings with four or five storeys sit among them. There is a small, beautiful market on the street. With the view of the mountain range, it is a perfect setting for living a decent life. A guy calls out to me, and as I decline to talk to him, he yells and follows me for several minutes. I turn into the small alley that leads me to the northern side of *Sheik* Ojele Residence, the largest of all Addis Ababa Houses.

There I find a young man and his wife washing their clothes in the backyard. As I slowly approach, he looks up at me and permits me to take a few photos. Lush vegetation and colourful clothes create a tranquil atmosphere. This eastern wing of the *Sheik* Ojele Residence is quite modest. There are few windows. The architecture has only few details, and even the door openings do not show much carpentry. '*Konsho bet, eidelem?*'[1] I ask, and the man nods, smiling. But they are quite occupied with their work. Kids come over to me as I continue. I perceive a row of households that occupy different parts of the long and vividly planted backyard. People of different ages work or play here. An old woman smiles at me but doesn't allow herself to be interrupted. As I reach the middle part of the building, the carpentry of the façade becomes very detailed and beautiful. The roof seems old but intact. Here, the perimeter terrasse that encircles the building is in much better condition than in the eastern part. Some men pass by and look at me, as I'm taking photos and speaking Amharic with a bunch of kids having great fun following me. The front part of the building overlooks a triangular open area and has a much more public feel. There are diverse commercial activities, with small shops (no coffee or

1 *Ferenji*-Amharic for: 'This house is beautiful. Do you think so, too?'

The backyard used by low income families

Sheik Ojele Residence

tea) and some big vehicles parked here. Big birds fly in the air, tirelessly claiming their realm. A few steps go up to the main entrance in the centre of the building. Three young men with beards stand in front of it.

One of them is Yosuf Almamun, who presents himself as the great-grandson of *Sheik* Ojele. He originated from Asosa, the capital of the Benishangul-Gumuz region in Western Ethiopia. 'I can show you the cellar,' says Yosuf and leads me towards the westernmost part that has grand verandas on both levels. This part had been an elementary school until recently; now 'this part is private'. Since a new school has been erected, the rooms are deserted and full of dust. Right away he leads me towards narrow, dark stairs – it is just a dark opening on the floor. He advances and I follow, a little nervously, and try to turn on the LED torch on my smartphone. The walls of the cellar are made from natural stone, with some earth mortar. The ceiling is made from strong wooden beams with an impressive span of more than 4 metres. Apparently, the cellar is only under the part that served as a school. We continue to visit the ground and upper floors. Yosuf shows a lot of patience but stays somewhat closed. I cannot read his thoughts or motivation for showing me around. Maybe he just wants to be kind. He will later also provide me with the phone number of his father (or uncle), who he says knows many details about the building. The woodworks of the veranda are most impressive in this part of the building. As seen in other Addis Ababa Houses, the columns are realised by double posts. Here they are joined together in a way that it appears as a single

Introduction 61

The upper floor of the former elementary school   The cellar

post. The kids are not allowed to play on the veranda unattended, as it might be too dangerous. I'm also not feeling extremely safe, but Yosuf tells me that nobody has ever crashed through the wooden floor. 'It's very stable!' The rooms are very high and generous in space. Doors formulate enfilades. They are placed in the middle of the walls. In the outer walls, their frames measure 20 cm in width. Windows are placed in a symmetrical sense, others even between rooms. Yosef is circa 1.8 metres tall, and he appears in my photos in a way that counteracts the impressive height of the rooms.

He receives a phone call that gives me permission to see the inside of their home, located in the central part of the building. I know that I am receiving special treatment because I am perceived as a tourist or a Western researcher. If an Ethiopian just showed up like me, he or she might face much more mistrust! Nevertheless, I am very happy to accept the invitation.

The middle part of the building is in very good shape. The descendants of *Sheik Ojele* obviously still live here. While they occupy the upper floors, the ground floor is rented out. Yosuf indicates that the wooden ornaments in this part need treatment. A three-flight staircase leads through an impressive space in green and brown paint. The space pushes out of the building, generating a volume with wooden mesh, which are ventilating the platform that is placed in front of the residence's entrance door. Here we leave our shoes, as they are Muslims. In fact, he tells me that it is not necessary, but I want to be as respectful as possible – I receive

Characteristic gables

The upper veranda of the former elementary school

Lantern room on the third floor

slippers. A lady sits on a big sofa watching TV. There is some sports equipment and the back of the room has a gathering place with an expensive carpet and cushions. I follow Yosuf up to the third floor to a lantern room with a kind of inner balcony that sits over the central room, which seems to have some representative function. Six elegant consoles support the balcony, which is perfectly squarish. It doesn't seem to be used that much. The lantern is entirely made of wood and glass, and the repetition of openable and fixed elements is nicely harmonious. The details are beautiful – every part is nicely proportioned and very well planned and executed. The combination of straight and diagonal lines with curvy balustrades make up an organised yet playful architecture. Again, a wooden mesh accompanies the stairs that lead up here in order to facilitate a constant exchange of air. These elements are in perfect shape, with no hint that they have already seen 100 years!

The kitchen is under the stairs. At the moment of my visit, it is the most lively room. Kids and young adults (a maid maybe) enjoy the relaxing feel of that space that is directly linked to the backyard-facing veranda. As seen in the western part of *Sheik Ojele*, the rooms are internally linked by windows.

The attitude the family shows towards me is similar to Yosuf's behaviour – friendly but distant. Even the kids do not care about me in the way kids in Ethiopia usually would. I assume that it is a rich, proud, and well-educated family. They have a comparably comfortable and non-precarious life thanks to the big house they inhabit. They have a computer and printer in the living room. In general, windows

Central room with a clear story

Living room

Remains of the original wallpaper

are covered, here but also in other old buildings I have visited. Ethiopians prefer their privacy and allow light to enter into the rooms via the door. It is quite an appropriate detail to have light coming from the upper end of a wall in combination with ventilation openings.

We leave the house and Yosuf shows me the so-called 'meeting room'. The huge room is located between the residence and the school part. I estimate the room to be 6 by 10 metres in size and 10 metres in height. Like the cellar, it is made from natural stone and mud mortar covered by adobe plaster. This room must have been a fortified storage room, as there are practically no openings apart from small windows at the very top of the walls – but there is one wooden door towards the backyard. A squat toilet is located here, as indicated to me by Yosuf.

I am already too full of impressions but Yosuf wants to show me one more detail: the remains of the original wallpaper are a bit hidden under the stairs. The wallpaper seems to be entirely hand-painted: black and yellow on a brown canvas. It shows a repetitive floral motive and is very generous and complex. The flowers bloom accompanied by half-opened offspring. Each of these groups is surrounded by an abstract floral pattern.

As I leave the compound heading for a taxi, the big birds are still making their circles through the highland air.

The so-called 'meeting room'

Reconcilable Longings:
Development and Heritage Conservation in Addis Ababa

by Tadesse Girmay Gebreegziabher

> *'Just like food and water, a cultural heritage is identified as an essential human right by UNESCO.'* (Lowenthal 1994).

1. Heritage Conservation and the Current Urban Development Paradigm

Heritage is a crucial asset of urban centres that represents an intricate reflection of the historical, social, cultural, economic, and political aspects of the centres and their residents. For this reason, heritage conservation has become an indispensable part of urban development. The success of heritage conservation in the current era is, however, increasingly dependent on reconciling it with expanding urban development needs and transformative projects. While cities must undergo endless changes in order to adapt to the needs and aspirations of their residents, the pressures on historic structures and spaces bring developers into conflict with heritage conservationists. Such conflict can be seen as emanating from the mismatch between the capacity of the environment to allow more development while keeping the existing ones.

Many researchers have emphasised the unique place heritage has in the sustainable development of societies today. Some have specifically associated such roles of heritage with more local systems in terms of the conservation and evolution of skills, technologies, and cultural systems. Others focus more on the place of heritage in attracting tourism. In either case, ensuring the perpetuity of efficient local knowledge management and income generation, respectively, requires careful consideration. Due to the complex relationships between heritage conservation and urban development, various stakeholders are now starting to appreciate the fact that these aspects cannot be treated in isolation from each other, hence the need for relevant integrated policies and project plans.

The lack of sufficient understanding of heritage and conservation issues not only affects development policies but also brings such plans in conflict with the conservation needs of residents and heritage experts. At the grassroots level, the brunt of ill-planned development projects is borne by the poorest of the poor, who are increasingly excluded from the new urban development schemes. Such issues are rampant in developing countries where dissenting voices are often ignored, if not suppressed, by powerful government agencies. Such challenges have been tackled in developed countries by the adoption of collaborative and communicative practices, including advocacies and pressure groups. These practices work in sync with the approach of integrated heritage conservation and management, since the collaborative and communicative principles promote negotiated solutions that guarantee heritage sustainability.

As the capital of one of Africa's most populous and historic nations, Addis Ababa houses a plethora of historical, socio-cultural, political, and economic heritage attractions. Yet, owing mainly to the lack of clear knowledge and conservation policies, inefficient implementations, and strong inertia from developers and government offices, the city represents one in which the heritage conservation and urban development needs are in serious conflict.

The aim of this essay is to identify the current conundrum of heritage conservation and urban development in Addis Ababa and to then suggest reconciliation approaches between the city's needs for rapid growth and the sustainable conservation of its heritage.

2. A Legacy of Neglect

Many of the monumental heritage resources of Addis Ababa were built during the imperial regime (mainly during the reign of Emperor Menelik II and later Haile Selassie I). These are often made of worked stone and mud mortar and combine wooden gables and balconies. Some were built as the residences of famous figures (e.g., governors, ranked military officers, members of the royal family, ministers, etc.) who had played major roles in Ethiopian history. As a result, the architectural designs of some of these residential buildings are unique.

The brief occupation of Addis Ababa by Italy added yet another unique architectural touch to the city's monumental heritage. Specifically, the buildings of government offices and the residences of important colonial officers – including the viceroy – introduced Fascist-style structures, themselves a reflection of the mix of influence from the 1920s rationalist movement in Italy and Roman-era designs. This gave Addis Ababa several buildings with massive appearances, but with edifices exhibiting simple designs, to accentuate the absolutism of the administration (e.g., the National Museum old building, which was the Viceroy's residence and chancery; and the Immigration and Nationality Affairs building, to mention a few).

The birth of the Organisation of African Unity (now the African Union) in the early 1960s, with Addis Ababa selected as its seat, presented the opportunity to further develop the city with a more modern look. Emperor Haile Selassie I particularly advocated a facelift that would give Addis Ababa the look of a modern city and with that, the reflection of Ethiopia as a modern state. Such national vision allowed more construction to be conducted, adding to the existing unique collection of residential buildings in the city. It was particularly necessary for the Emperor to depict his state's modernity via trendy physical structures and to renew his place as the architect of the nation's modernisation after returning from exile in 1941. Consequently, the government demanded the creation of new institutions requiring new buildings and building types. This would later influence the architectural trend in the country, both in terms of quality and quantity. With that came gradually an increasing departure from the traditional styles and the predominance of more

View of Churchill Avenue from Lagare towards the north

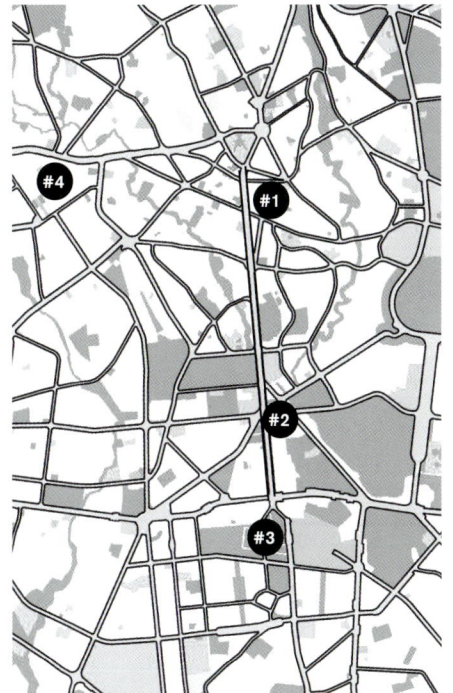

Map showing the four study areas along Churchill Avenue: #1 Ghandi Street/ #2 Beherawi/ #3 Lagare/ #4 Merkato

nuanced styles. That craze of image building by successive governments defining their own ideology through new institutions and buildings has been seen to affect heritage over many decades, mainly through neglect of the past and emphasis on the current ideology.

The culture of nineteenth and twentieth-century modernism seen in Addis Ababa was shaped in relation to contemporary changes in social, political, philosophical, and artistic views that revolutionised lifestyles. Building technology and architecture also maintained the characteristics of the period and operated as a milieu of contemporary experiences. Hence, except for several praiseworthy examples, the idea of reflecting the cultural heritage assets and their values was not given much attention. As a result, Addis Ababa's most iconic historical buildings of the early twentieth century were progressively neglected from the time of Emperor Haile Selassie I (reign 1930–1974) to the *Derg* regime (1974–1991). The neglect took different forms but was mainly manifested by allowing multiple families to live in such historical buildings designed for single-family occupancy. The adverse views toward relicts of the preceding regimes also meant that the new multifamily residents were not informed about the unique architectural and historical values of such buildings and the need to conserve them.

Ghandi Street: Minimum changes in the façades of the buildings (left), some (top) and considerable (bottom) change in the façades

3. Four Exemplary Sites in Addis Ababa

In this section, different scenarios in four selected historical sites of the city are considered in order to illustrate the level of conflict between heritage conservation and urban development. The selection of sites was made based on their age, history, function, and sensitivity. For the sake of a balanced comparison and representativeness, two sites – one before and another after the Italian occupation period – are considered.[1]

#1: GHANDI STREET. Possibly the most historic quarter of the city, one of the rare neighbourhoods where conservation has been 'successful', in general terms, i.e., the overall building volumes are in place (in terms of scale, bulk wall, and height). Otherwise, the details of almost all the buildings along both sides of this street have already been changed to a level that the authenticity is significantly affected.

#2: NATIONAL THEATRE AREA (BEHERAWI). Since the old days, people used to come here for the cinema, business meetings, banking, health services, sports,

[1] To examine the conflict, the researcher used his experience of the areas over the past 20 years; compared Google Maps in 2002 and 2022; and interviewed people of different age groups (35 to 65) who had lived and worked in the areas for many years and carried out discussions with heritage professionals of authorities and advocacy groups (ARCCH, AACTB, Heritage Watch, and kirs baladera). The selected sites are in the historic centre of Addis, are also expensive development areas, and aged between 86 and 136 years.

Yebegoadragot building in the demolition process

Yebegoadragot building before demolition, with the commercial Bank of Ethiopia headquarters building in the background

driving lessons, schooling, and many more activities. As a result, most people (whom I asked about their feelings) were not happy to see dramatic changes in the area. One manifestation of this dissidence is the futile effort to save the recent demolition of the Charity building (Ye-Begoadragot hintsa), which made way for high-rise development. The building was among the first in history to serve mixed-use functions for the city, making the area vibrant for more than half a century. The historical building was demolished in August 2022.

#3: LAGARE. The area is among the first developments in the city, marking the main office and central station of the Djibouti-Addis Ababa railway (built c. 1897–1917). The historic quarter and the railway compound, despite its current non-operational status, stayed intact for more than a century until the recent political change in the country (2018), which attracted developers from the UAE to start a massive real estate project for high-end users. Though the development will benefit the city somehow, it has disadvantages in terms of the erasure of public memory, demolition of well-designed and successfully built structures, and the total isolation of the

Lagare – overlap of the new proposal by Eagle Hills over the urban layout in 2018   Poster of the Eagle Hills

area from its context due to its design and target groups of high-income society. The map overlaps show that the new real estate development proposal totally disregarded the historic Lagare. This implies that the developers are either unaware of the importance of Lagare or want to deliberately densify the site considering the value of urban land in their investment, with full permission and support from the government.

#4: MERKATO. It was considered the largest open-air market in Africa. However, today, most parts of this open market are transformed into incoherent multi-storey buildings housing the previous functions on single storeys in new vertical stalks. This has changed the characteristics of the environment from a totally open, less congested, local material usage – human friendly and visually interactive – to closed, more congested buildings, imported materials – unfriendly, highly congested vehicular movement with inadequate parking areas in proportion to the much more functional floor areas created of the building blocks. It was also noticed on Sunday, 23 January 2023, that the building in the foreground is in the process of demolition to give way to another possible multi-storey building.

4. Conclusion

The historical buildings of Addis Ababa are the result of the vernacular architecture, local invention, and foreign influence. Some of the domestic architectural designs are unique. These building heritages are witness to the city's culture, architecture, civilisation, and history at large. Hence, they constitute different values: aesthetic, historic, economic, scientific, social, and spiritual for past, present, and future generations. They are to be conserved with the highest values and efforts.

To conclude my view on a more positive note, I ask whether and why we should have an urban development project that will create a city devoid of history. While there is no question that Addis Ababa should be a city that embraces modernity and is suitable for the transformations of the age, it should also equally showcase its beautiful past – its colourful heritage. I argue that the existence of one should not be seen as a threat to the other, but rather as a more meaningful entity.

An urban development that leaves enough room for heritage conservation promotes a far greater sense of belonging by its residents and attracts local and international visitors. On the contrary, one that has no regard for the centre's heritage will not only erase the very fabric of its history and rich socio-cultural, political, and economic dynamics but also call for the same doom on its tomorrow. As an optimist, I argue for the former and strongly believe that the development and heritage conservation longings of the city are perfectly reconcilable – through genuine negotiations, an appreciation of the value of heritage, and a common vision for a brighter tomorrow.

A building block in Merkato is in the process of demolition to give way to another possible multi-storey building

Model by Victor Girardet

2

Phenotype
The Case Studies

View from the south

External staircase as a connection

Cast iron ornaments

Masonry core with Indian ornamentation

Wooden veranda

Enqulal Bet (Egg House)

The pavilion was built between 1890 and 1910 as part of the imperial residence of Menelik II (Sacchi 2021: 55). Located on a prominent hill, it overlooks the entire city. The pavilion was one of the first constructions that marked the foundation of a new capital. Probably designed by Luigi Cappuci in 1889 (Batistoni and Chiari 2004: 28) and erected by Indian craftsmen, it was originally built as a two-storey complex with a rather traditionally-styled thatched roof and a masonry core, as is visible in an old photo from the late 1890s. The smaller third floor as well as the external wooden staircase and the metal dome were later additions realised by 1909. These features enhance the unique character of the building and contribute to its popular nickname, 'Enqulal Bet' – Amharic for 'Egg House' (Batistoni and Chiari 2004: 29). Since 2019, the Prayer House has been preserved and reused as a museum in the public Unity Park.

The building consists of three octagonal volumes that are placed in a vertically aligned manner. It has a diameter of around 11.5 metres at the bottom and 6.2 metres at the top. The total height of the structure is 18 metres. Each floor holds

Hand-drawn ceiling paintings

Ceiling of the upper floor

Interior view of the dome

Interior view of the upper floor

an individual structure, as they differ in height and dimension. All sides of the three octagons are proportional, which is emphasised by centred and aligned openings. Connected through external wooden verandas and staircases, each floor consists of one room with its own function. Through a raised wooden covered walkway, the pavilion simultaneously serves as one of the access points to Menelik's bedroom. The entrances are located southwest of the tower, while two small niches on each side of the staircase hold a telephone booth. It is retrospectively known to have held Ethiopia's first telephone.

The prayer room can be found on the bottom floor. Measuring 1.5 metres in diameter at ground level, the room is reinforced by thick, round masonry columns that serve as the foundation of the entire structure. In contrast to the upper floors, there are only a few small openings that contribute to a much darker room alignment. The exterior walls are decorated with floral elements, embodying and emphasising portals as seen in many Indian prayer houses and tombs. The heavy core is surrounded by a wooden veranda with a wooden support structure. Towards the upper storeys, all walls and ceilings

The dome and entrance show Indian influences

Side view of the pavilion

View from the top floor towards the staircase

are made of light wood and glass. The load is transferred via the wooden supports and wall panels.

The second floor has the bright archive and study of the Emperor. This floor is covered in richly decorated window panels flagging the sides. The windows lead the eyes toward a suspended ceiling that is colourfully painted with florals, fruits, and Indian ornaments. The attached veranda is also made from wood and catches the corrugated iron roof with decorated wooden pillars. Occasionally the wooden balustrade is replaced by flat ornamented metal sheet parts.

On the top floor, there is the watchtower or telescope room. The viewpoint has glass openings from which you can look out in all directions. The top floor is connected to the other floors via a corded telephone (Sacchi 2021: 55).

A bulbous, double-walled metal dome, which was added when the Prayer House had to be rebuilt after a fire, covers the entire upper structure and is panelled as well as decorated with floral motifs. The veranda is held in place by a wooden structure that extends through all floors and is covered with a corrugated iron roof. With this choice of materials and

The Case Studies 79

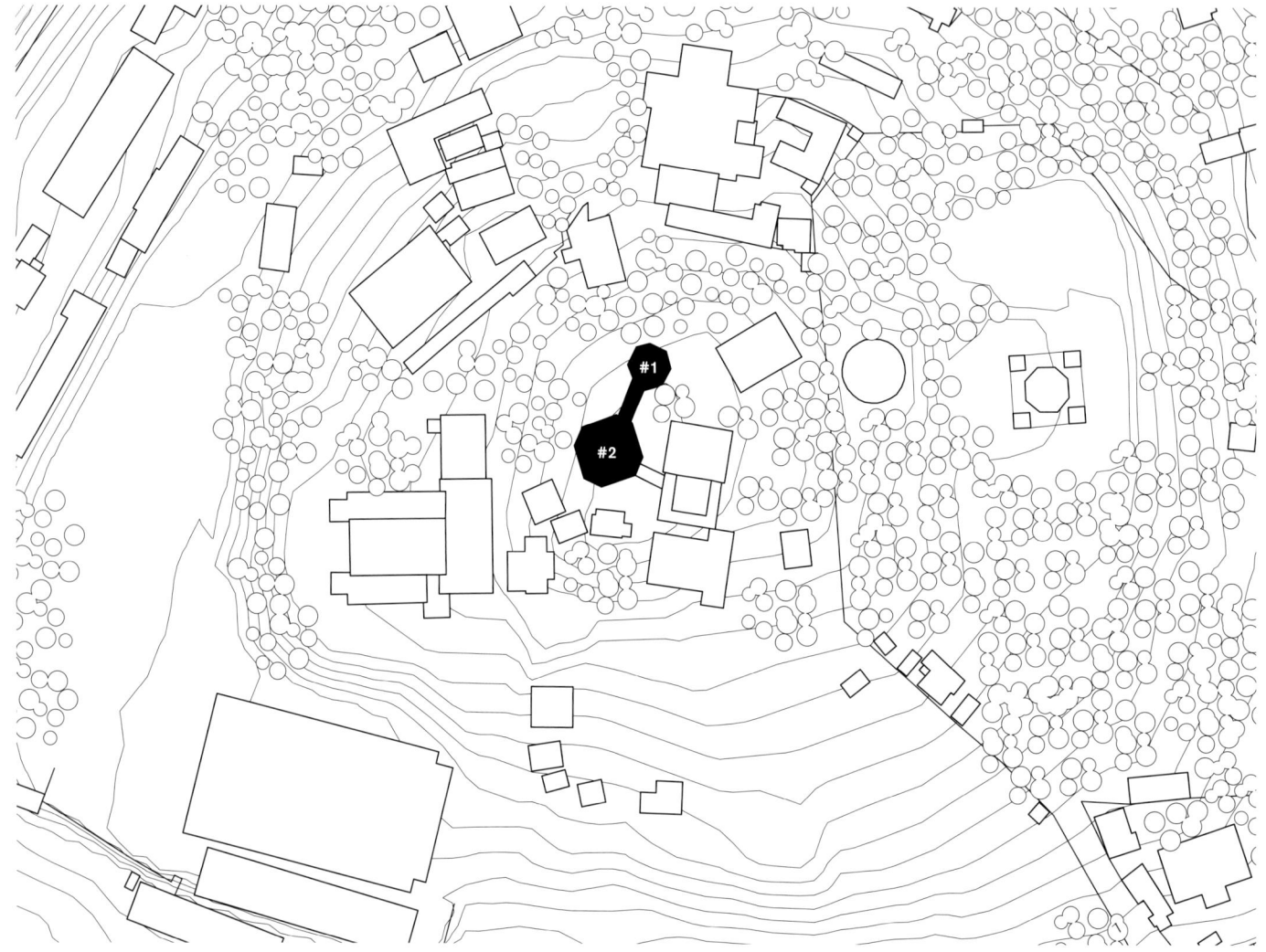

Site plan 1: 2000 (#1 Enqulal Bet / #2 Elfiñ)

ingenious placement of the exterior structure, the pavilion not only protects against climatic conditions such as rain, but also enables constant air circulation.

Each floor has its own style of ornaments and decorations. Floral and geometrical elements on stone enhance the portal on the first floor. Painted floral elements on the ceiling as well as flat metal sheets are on the second floor, as well as carved wood panelling with big windows. The craftsmen of the building, who were most likely Indians, left characteristic attributes on the Enqulal Bet. Lavishly decorated wood carvings on verandas and beams as well as roof finials and ornaments on the eaves are key elements. Furthermore, an abundance of colours on painted murals and wood carvings represents important features of Indian architecture (Batistoni and Chiari 2004: 21).

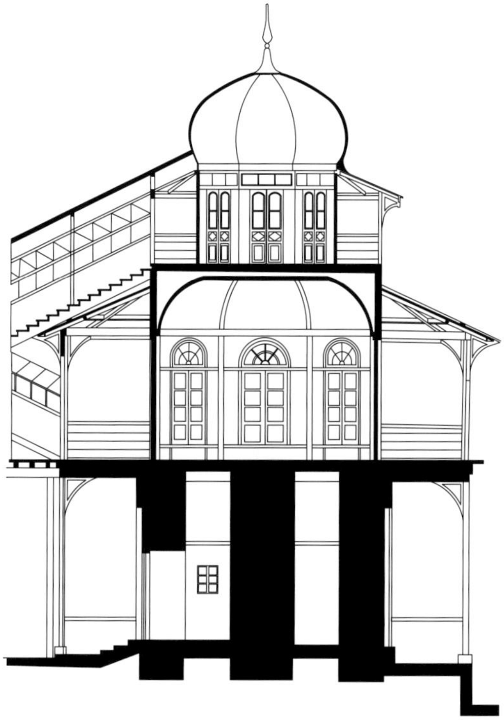

Section

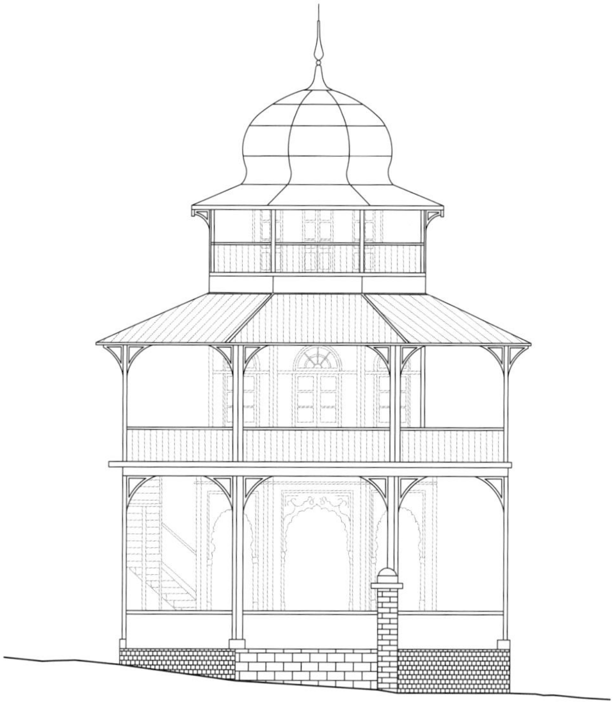

Elevation

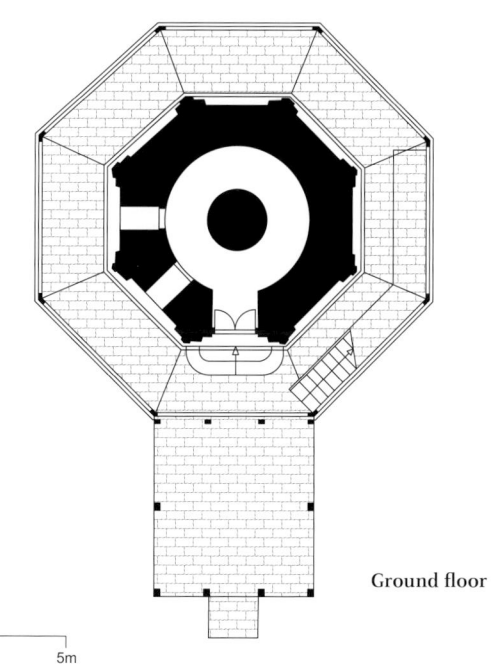

Ground floor

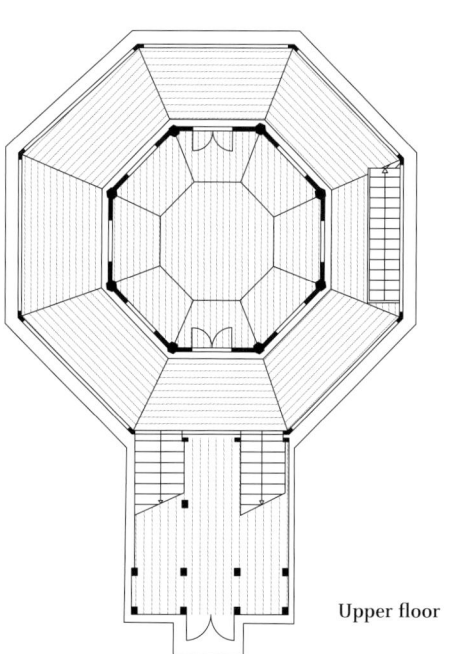

Upper floor

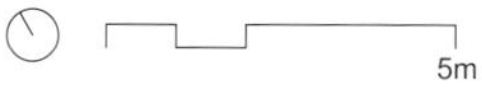

5m

The Case Studies 81

View from the north

View from the Enqulal Bet

Wooden roof ornaments

View from the north-east

Roofed bridge: view towards the Enqulal Bet

Elfiñ (Imperial Residence)

When the Elfiñ, the Imperial Residence, was erected, Menelik's capital was still on the Entoto Mountains. The structure served initially as a sort of holiday home for Menelik and his wife Taitu when they visited the hot springs of Filwoha in the plains of Finfinni. Therefore, one can say that the erection of this building is at the very origin of Addis Ababa itself. The construction of Menelik's *Ghebbi* – which means 'imperial compound' – started in 1886–1887. The Elfiñ was built in the very centre of the compound on a hilltop to have a better view over the vast landscape. It was only in 1891 that the capital officially moved from Entoto to Addis Ababa, the 'new flower'.

The Elfiñ has two storeys and a height of 15 metres. It has a square plan with cut-out corners. There are three entrances to the building from north, south, and west. Both levels have the same number of openings, but the lower level takes less light than the upper level. The two storeys are connected by an external staircase that is inserted into the perimeter veranda in front of the southeastern façade. The upper veranda merges into two roofed bridges that on one side connect the

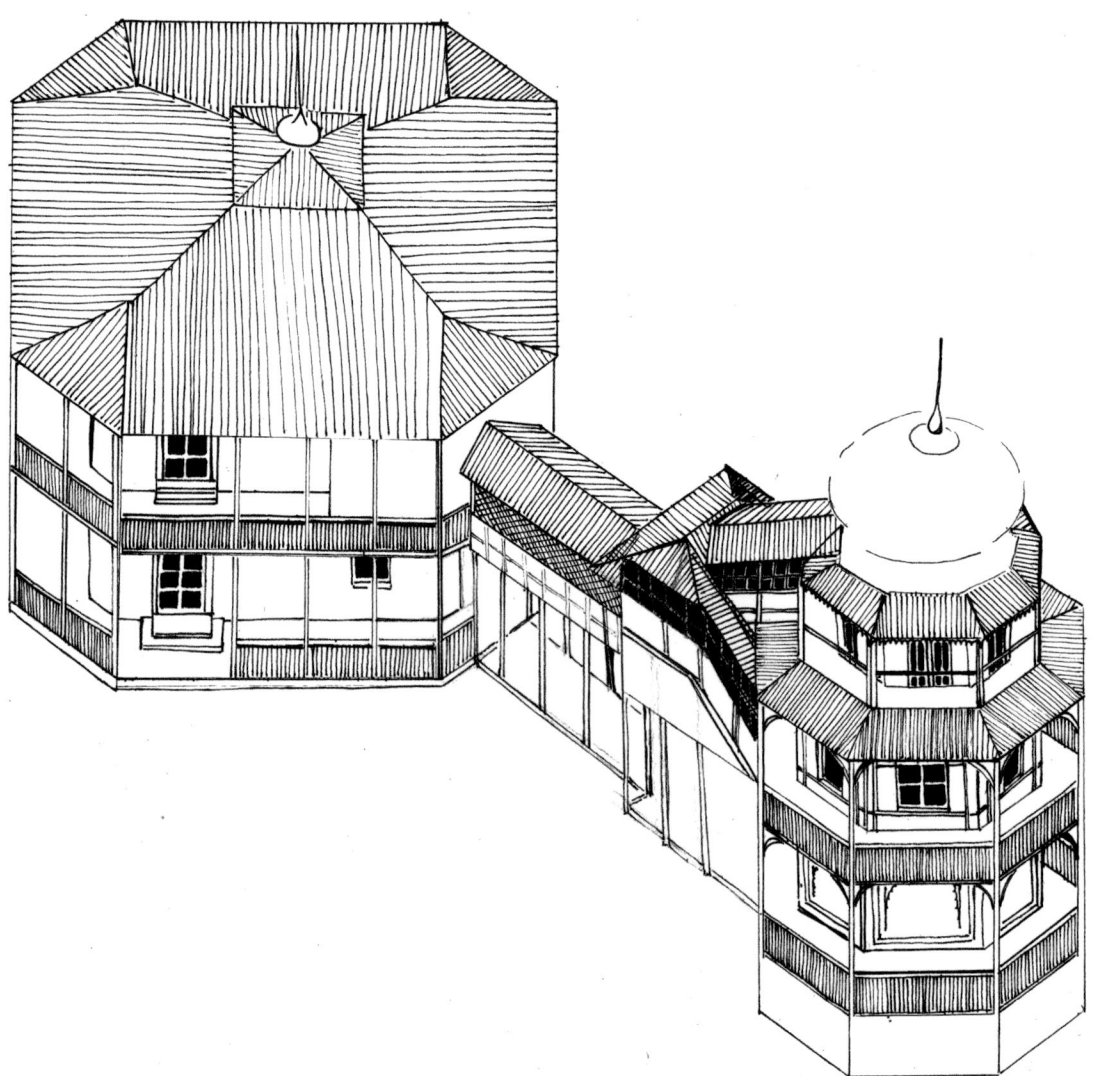

Axonometry

building with the private quarters of the Empress Taitu in the east, and on the other side with the Enqual Bet in the north, which Menelik used for praying and studying. The western side of this bridge is covered up by a wooden mesh to give shelter from the prevailing winds. The building is sheltered by a gable roof that sits on the masonry walls and is additionally supported by four filigree timber columns.

Like many old buildings in Addis Ababa, the building has a raised main entrance and a heavily decorated wooden door on the north façade. The main volume is surrounded by open loggia supported by a thin wooden structure on the perimeter of the building. The lower level served as a reception hall for Menelik's guests (Giorghis and Gerard 2007: 216). The reception hall with a room height of approximately 4.6 metres is enclosed by stone masonry walls of about 1 metre thickness. The four squarish wooden columns have a diameter of 27 centimetres and a height of 4.2 metres.

The upper floor contained Menelik's private room for sleeping and resting (Giorghis and Gerard 2007: 216). The space is 5 metres high at the lowest point and 7.6 metres

Open loggia, first floor Main entrance

Wooden ornaments on the main entrance door Detail of a wooden ornament

at the highest. Again, there are four columns structuring the space as support for the roof structure, and with only 20 centimetres of diameter and a height of 6.6 metres, they appear very elegant. There are entrances to the main space from every façade of the building, providing lighting from each side. The building consists of a single, main space on both floors and there are no interior corridors. With a width of 2.6 metres, the perimeter veranda is very generous and as in many old buildings of Addis Ababa, provides space for social interaction (Fasil Giorghis, Talks on Local Building Types: The Addis Ababa House, TU Berlin, 18 May 2021). Additionally, the perimeter veranda allows the Emperor to communicate in all directions with his followers and observe the surrounding. It is known that the Emperor took great pleasure in using his telescope to observe the city, which started at almost zero when the Elfiñ was constructed and successively became the vibrant capital of a united Ethiopian Empire by the time of Menelik's death in 1913 (Batistoni and Chiari 2004: 28). A water pipe that was installed by the Swiss engineer Alfred Ilg was used to irrigate the Elfiñ's vegetable and flower garden.

The Case Studies 85

Visible structure of the roof

Menelik's private room

Decorated ceiling with ornaments

Menelik's reception hall

Light-filled upper floor with staircase

Main entrance of the north façade

The Elfiñ has many Indian influences with regard to decorative elements. Also, most of the builders of the building were Indian (Pankhurst 1995: 13). They were most skilled in using carved wood for front façades, balustrades, columns, and fascias along the eaves.

There are low relief carvings on the main entrance door consisting of flowers, plants, and animals, leading to the living room of the Emperor. The ceiling and the interior are not decorated as in the Enqulal Bet, but there is elaborate wooden panelling in the interior. The last distinctive feature of the Addis Ababa Style that one can find in the Elfiñ is the finial at the apex of the roof. Finials originally symbolised the background of each family for Indians; but it is also part of Ethiopian building traditions (Fasil Giorghis, Talks on Local Building Types: The Addis Ababa House, TU Berlin, 18 May 2021).

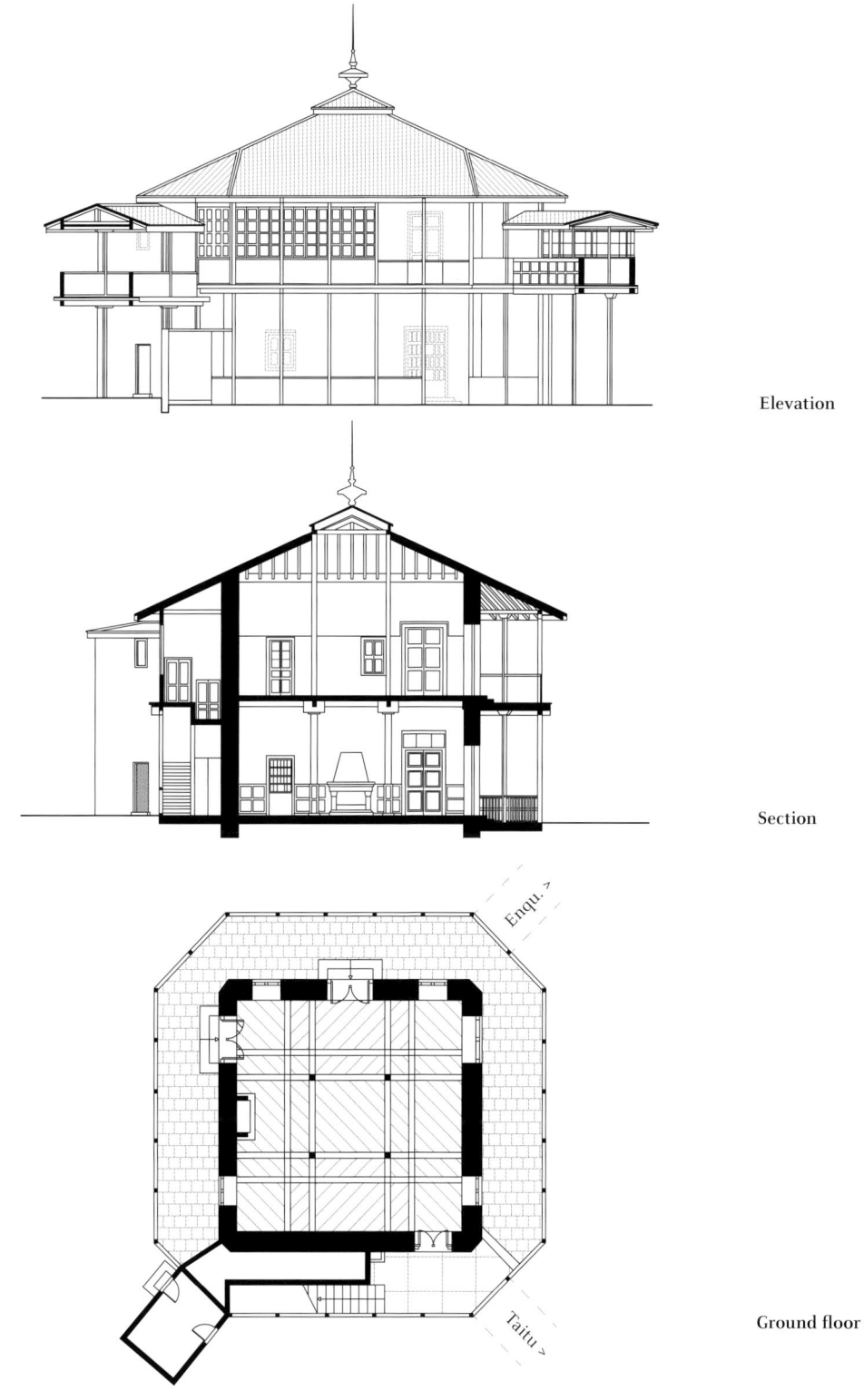

Elevation

Section

Ground floor

The Case Studies 87

View from the east

Curtain wall

Roof structure

Main room

Dej. Wube H / Mariam Residence (Addis Ababa Restaurant)

The former residence of *Dejazmatch* Wube Haile Mariam is situated towards the north of Arada. In the map of the Italian geographical society from 1909, it is marked 'Deg. Ubbiè' House. At the time of its construction, the house and its wider compound followed the typical, traditional settlement pattern of the young capital. The house marked the centre of the plot of land, situated on a hilltop and hosting the aristocrat's family and their followers. Still today, the historical neighbourhood is named '*Dejach* Wube *Sefer*'. During a period of one century, the area was intensely densified, mostly with low-rise construction that maintains a glimpse of the historical layout of the neighbourhood.

Dejazmatch Wube Haile Mariam was a nobleman of Menelik's court. His residence was built between the last decade of the nineteenth century and the first decade of the twentieth century (gtz, 2009).

One approaches the building from Benin Street. The building has only one storey and consists of a circular main volume and an adjoined rectangular structure. The entrance on the eastern side of the building is elevated about 1 metre from

Elevation of the circle wall with window

Compartment rooms

Terracotta floor tiles, 10 × 10

the ground. The composition of the elevation is divided into three horizontal components. The base foundation is made from natural stone, the curtain walls are made from wood with many small glass panels, and the impressive roof was initially made from thatch. Today, many smaller additions have been realised to extend the number of rooms. The floorplan on the following page shows its current plan layout.

This building reflects many local building traditions. The remarkable circular main volume with its high pinched roof resembles to some extent an upscaled *tukul*. Its diameter measures more than 15 metres. The central room is round as well and has a diameter of more than 10 metres. A quite complex wooden structure allows an impressive room without columns. As shown in the hand sketches, it has one main truss and three additional trusses with an angle of 45 degrees between the trusses. The beautiful structural framework that supports the roof has a strong ornamental quality that gives the main room a generous and interesting atmosphere.

The thatch that originally covered the round building has been replaced by corrugated iron sheet. Another transformation that

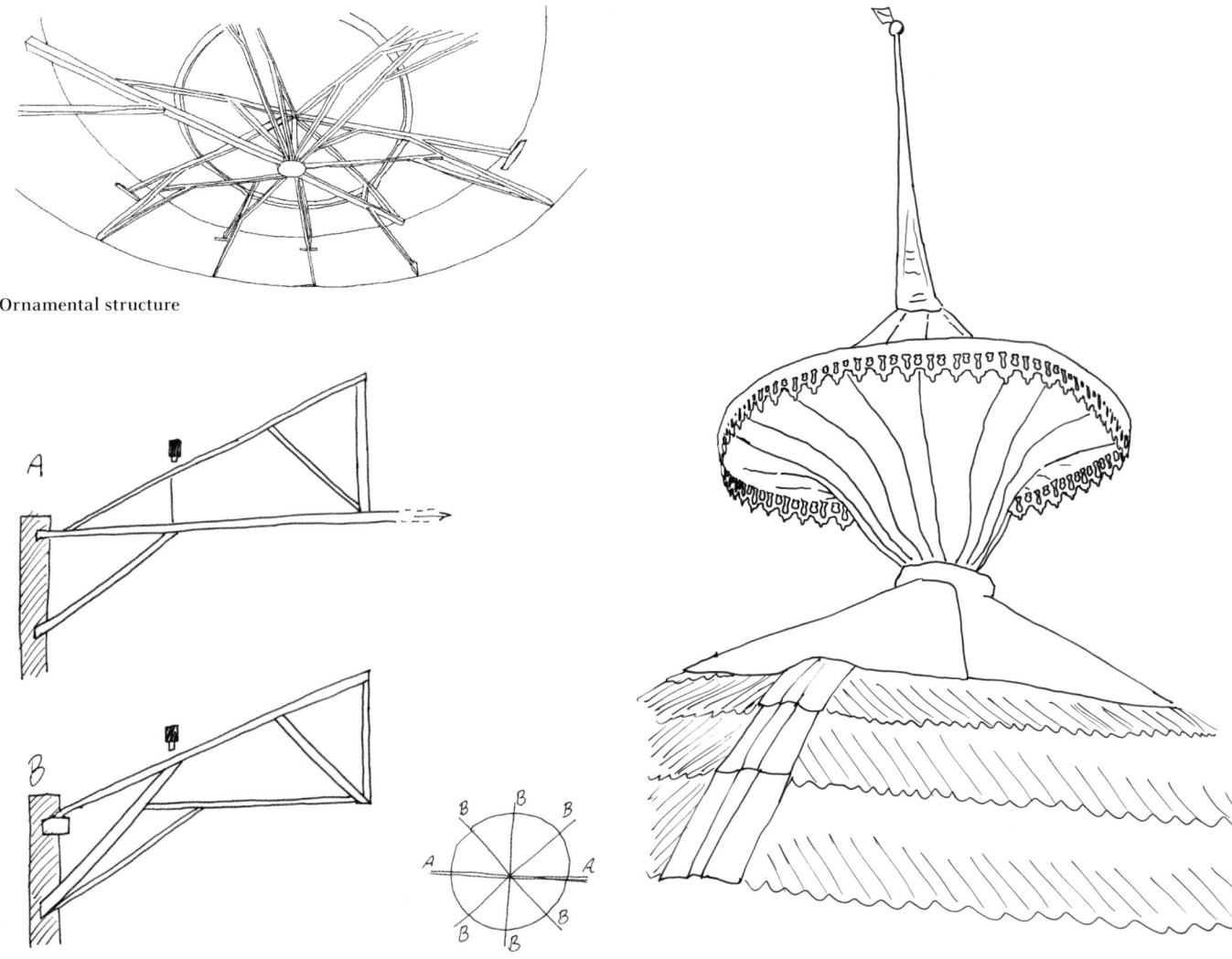

Ornamental structure

Two principles of wooden trusses

Indian roof finial

the building has seen is the closing of the formerly open veranda that went all around the building. One can still see the wooden columns towards the edges of the roof – now part of the wooden envelope of the perimetrical rooms. The result is an onion-shaped floorplan with smaller compartment rooms that are grouped around the main room. Several windows in the main room still witness this transformation. The floor of the main room consists of wooden planks, while the perimetrical rooms have terracotta flooring. This might also be the case because these spaces were initially open to the weather.

The main room has three doors and four windows that show into the adjacent compartment rooms. Together with the 14 blind panels, the encircling wall consists of 21 irregular segments. Historically, there might have been a suspended ceiling covering the wooden structure, as seen in other Addis Ababa Houses such as the *Sheik* Ojele. When consulted on restoration works at the 'Addis Ababa Restaurant', Fasil Giorghis proposed to leave the structure visible.

On the one hand, it is said to have Indian influences (gtz, 2009), such as the roof finial, the decoration on the eves, and

The Case Studies 91

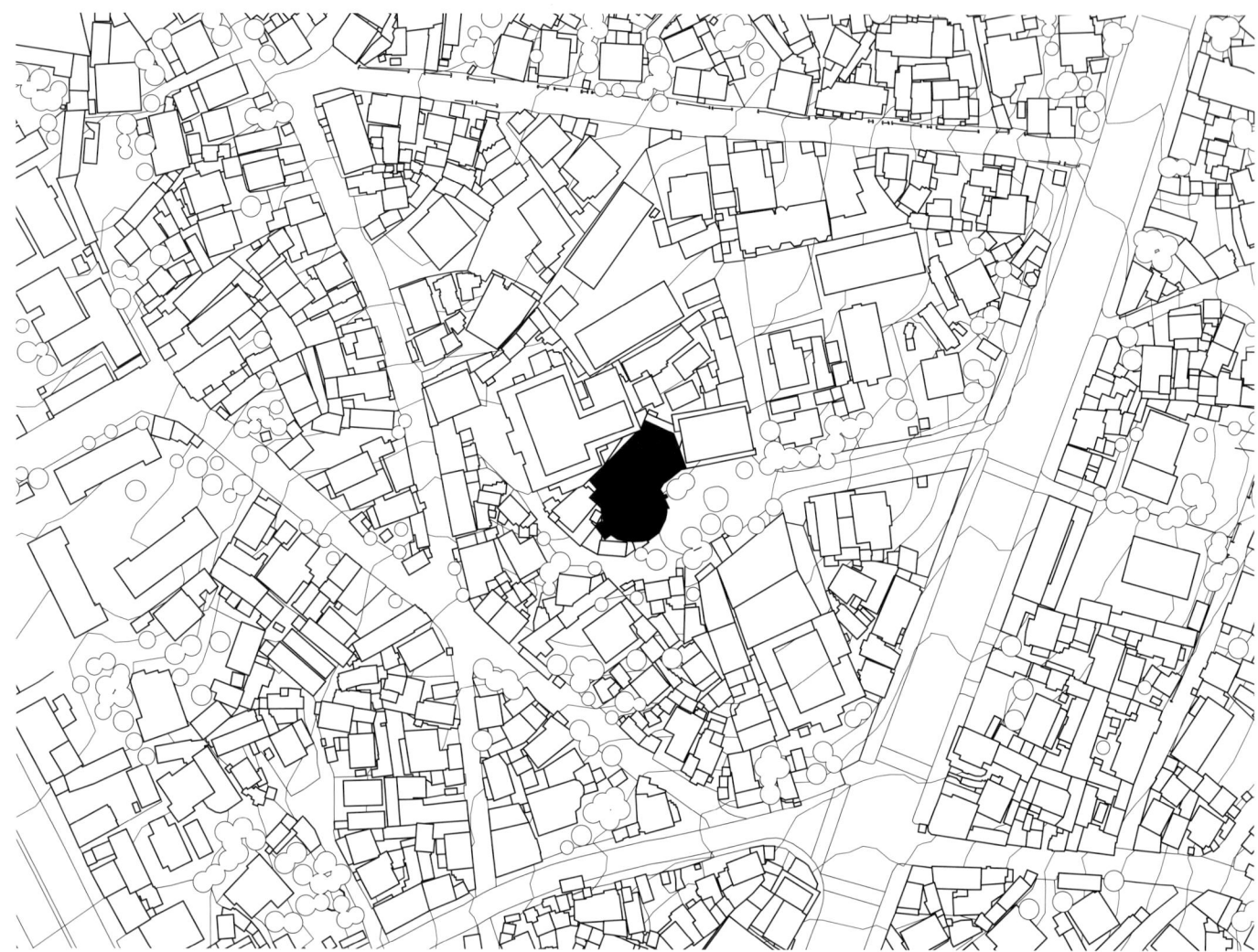

Site plan 1:2000

the gable entrance. On the other, the local influences cannot be overlooked, as there are no round housing types in India. As Fasil Giorghis states, the round shape of traditional buildings in Ethiopia has to be understood in relation to local living, and especially eating, culture. Tables are always round and the Ingera, the traditional Ethiopian food, is round in shape. It is known that Queen Victoria brought a big round table and a high mirror as a present on the occasion of the wedding of *Dejazmatch* Wube with Princess Zewditu in 1891. During the Italian occupation, the house was used as a political office (Giorghis and Gerard 2019: 256).

Today the residence of *Dejazmatch* Wube hosts a formidable traditional restaurant, thus it is possible for members of the public to visit.

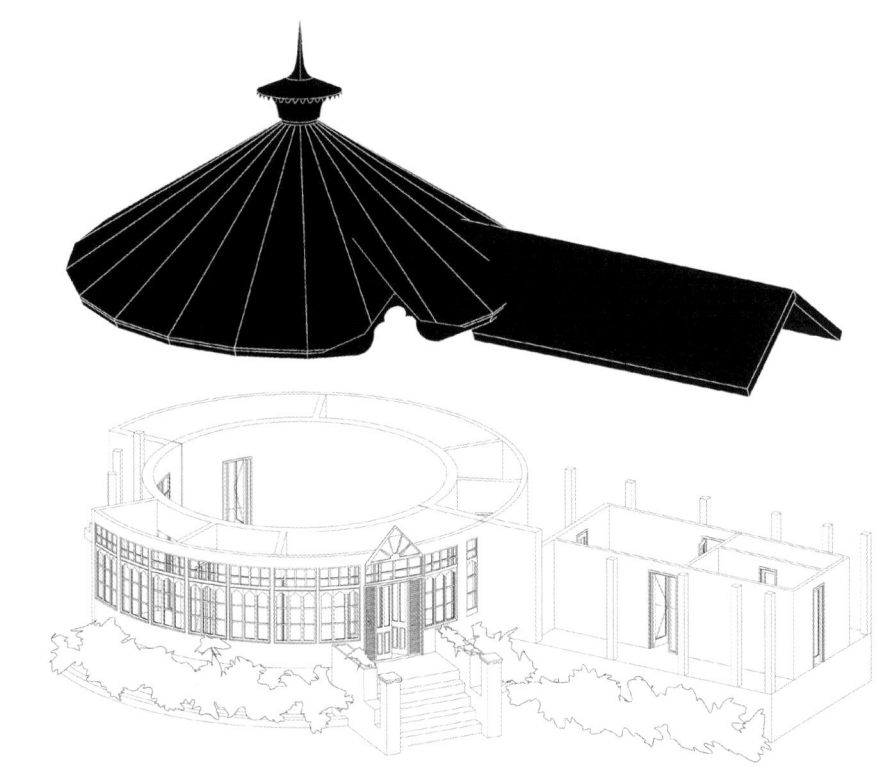

Axonometry

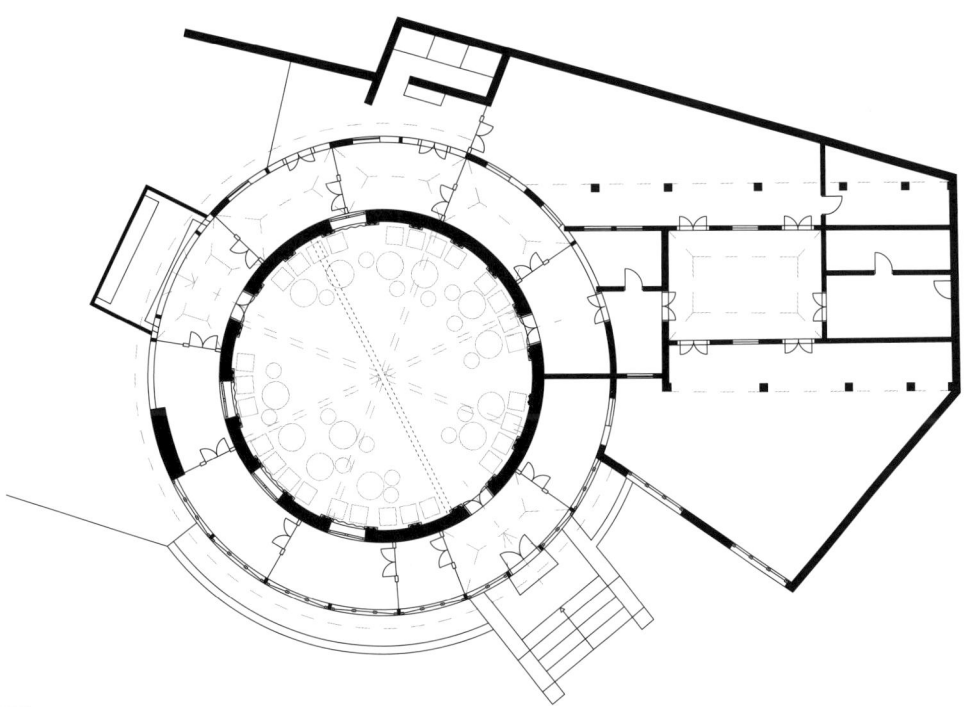

Ground floor

The Case Studies 93

View from the south

Urban context in 2022

Stone and clay construction

Decorative wallpaper

The surrounding porch provides shade

Living room

Alfred Ilg House

Alfred Ilg, an educated engineer from Switzerland, was a close advisor of Menelik for 29 years from 1872 to 1901, first for technical tasks and later increasingly for foreign policy. Ilg already served Menelik in the times of the former capitals of Ankober and Entoto. The house that is known as Alfred Ilg's residence is situated on one of the oldest roads of Addis Ababa, halfway between the *Ghebbi*, the political nucleus of the city, and the Arada market, the economic nucleus. The house itself is constructed on a slope, having a direct view of the imperial compound. After Ilg left Ethiopia in 1901, the house became a public school, one of the first under Menelik's reign. The young *Ras* Tafari is said to have learned French in this school. It is now state-owned low-cost housing and currently hosts a young accountant who migrated to Addis. The house itself follows the traditional oval shape, typical for the North Shewa houses that Ilg was familiar with from Entoto. It has a single storey with a generous room height of approximately 3.2 metres. The house is erected on a foundation of natural stone that rises approximately 1 metre above the terrain. The uppermost stones are carefully cut to

View from the south | Hallway | Construction of the roof | Veranda on stone walls

Elevation

create a surface and base for the filigree wooden veranda posts. The sloped oval roof is built in the traditional manner of weaving. A layer of slender strips of endemic wood, which was split by hand and not sawed, creates the tensile base for the thatch to be knotted on. The gaps between the wooden strips allow the knotting of the cover from thatch against a counter-layer of resilient plant fibres. This roofing technique can be applied to round and oval shapes but not rectangular designs (see p. 186).

The walls are made from crude natural stone with mortar from earth and straw and finished with lime plaster. It is known that Alfred Ilg imported furniture and even wallpaper from Switzerland. The wallpaper found inside the house in 2022 is indeed remarkable and certainly old. However, given the many transformations in terms of use and structure that the building has seen, it is doubtful that it is the original that Ilg installed.

The transformation of the plan seen on the right has been proposed by Abnet Gezahegn Berhe.

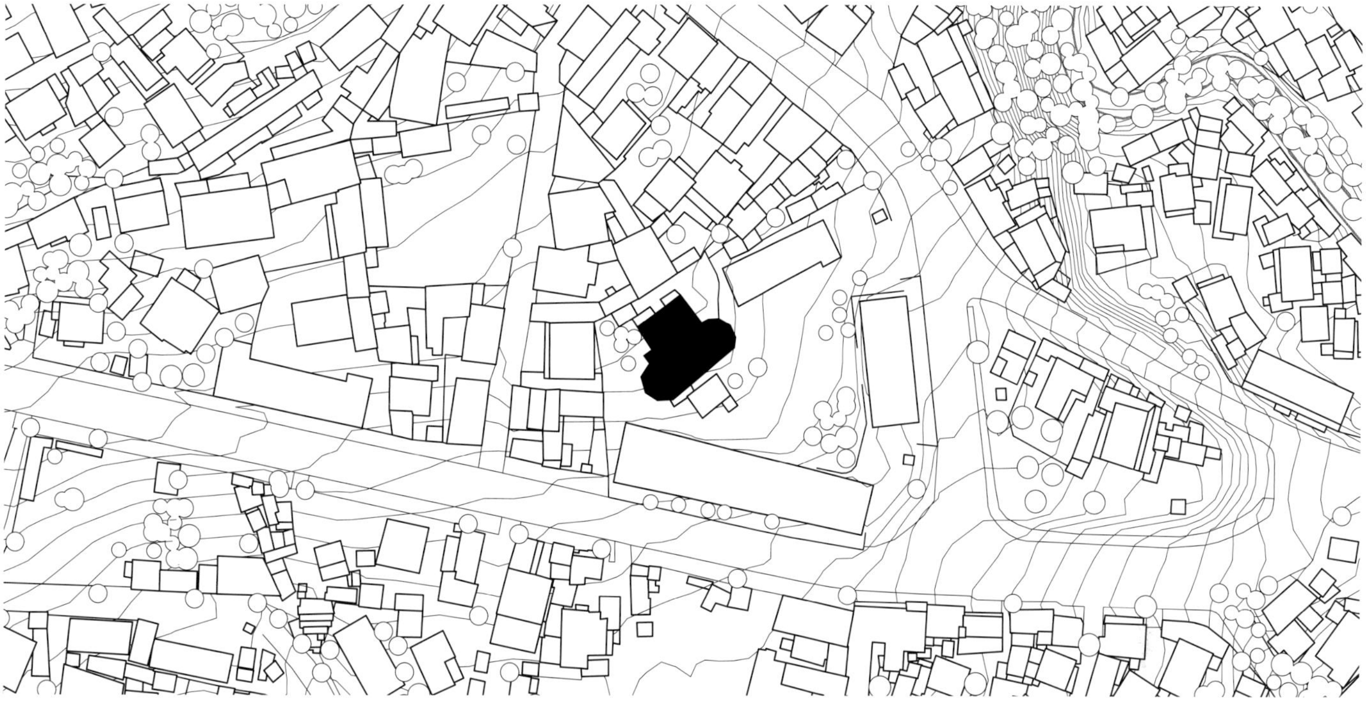

Site plan 1:2000

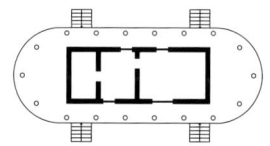

Alfred Ilg's plan in the 1890s

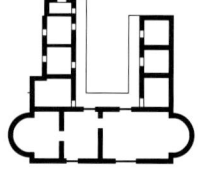

Rectangular additions in 1935

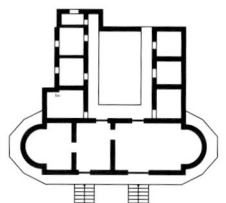

Cover of the courtyard in 1974

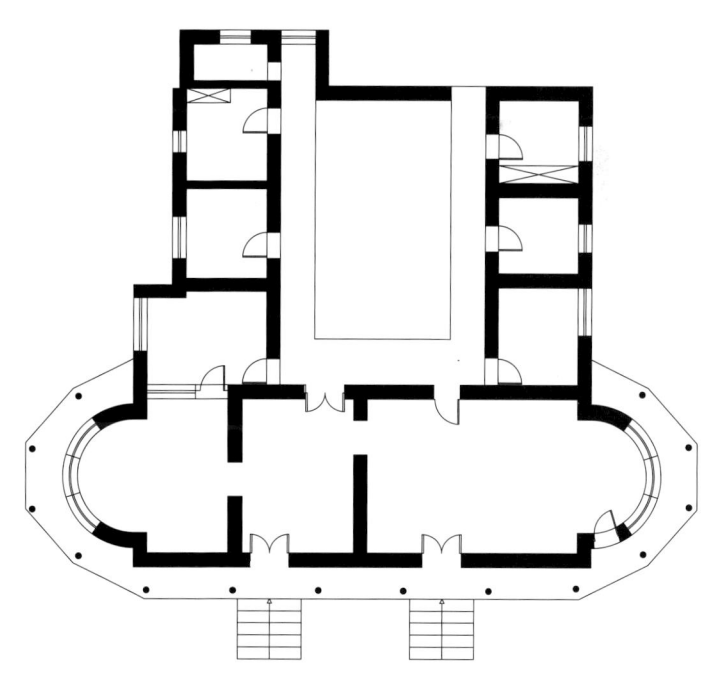

Current plan

5m

The Case Studies 97

View from the north

Extension section 1:50

Mohamed Ali House

Long before the founding of Addis Ababa, Indian merchants settled in the eastern city of Harar. As Menelik wanted to make his new capital the commercial centre of Ethiopia, Indian trading companies set up stores in Addis Ababa, where they introduced the new typology of the residence-store (Harre 2015a: 8).

The most powerful company was G. M. Mohammedally. The company owner himself, Mohamed Ali Shaikh Sharafaly, was a representative of the Indian community at the imperial court (Batistoni and Chiari 2004: 72).

The site of the Mohamed Ali residence is located in Arada near present-day Cunningham Street. It is marked as 'Indiani e Commercianti' on the 1909 map, and its location can be seen near the historic market of Arada (Societa geografica italiana 1909). The complex includes several notable buildings, including stores, offices, and warehouses, with one of the more recent buildings being designed by Armenian Minas Kerbekian in 1920 (gtz, 2009).

The Mohamed Ali residence was built in the early years of the century by an unknown architect. The core volume is

View from the south

very simple. It consists of a two-storey rectangular building with a floorplan of approximately 18 × 10 metres and single-storey additions to the east and west of an additional 3 metres in depth. It is likely that the first floor was used for storage, while the upper floor was the home of Mohamed Ali and his family.

The components that make this building so remarkable are the northern and southern additions, which are light, wooden structures that seem to be glued to the main volume. This combination of elements gives the building its remarkable, almost eclectic appearance and a certain spatial complexity. These two components are functionally part of the living area on the upper floor.

On the north elevation, usually referred to as the primary façade, is a strikingly unique addition elevated on slender wood posts with delicate wood spandrels and a gable roof of corrugated metal and delicate trim at the eaves. The elevated space is glazed on all three sides and resembles a *Jharokha* – a classical Indian component from the Rajasthan region, where it was used by householders to show off in their

Symmetrical composition

Ornamentation of the eaves

Wooden railings

Complex composition

courts. A secondary roof, which cantilevers about 1.7 metres, provides shade for the glass surfaces. The triangle of the gable contains beautifully crafted fixed ventilation louvers. The space under the *Jharokha* proves to be a comfortable, shaded area that is still popular today.

The south side of the Mohamed Ali residence, however, tells its own story. It is dominated by the symmetrical double staircase covered by a canopy on slender wooden posts. The truss roof that is supported by columns was especially found to provide shade and water protection for the stairs and the entrance and wooden construction below. The two staircases meet on a landing 3 metres above ground. From there they pierce into the building's volume between two sort of identical towers, where they lead to the upper floor at 4.5 metres above the ground. The two small towers are crowned by pitched roofs. The stone walls reach a height of approximately 7.5 metres. Above the gable is filed by wooden planks. This construction makes the use of a stone lantern unnecessary.

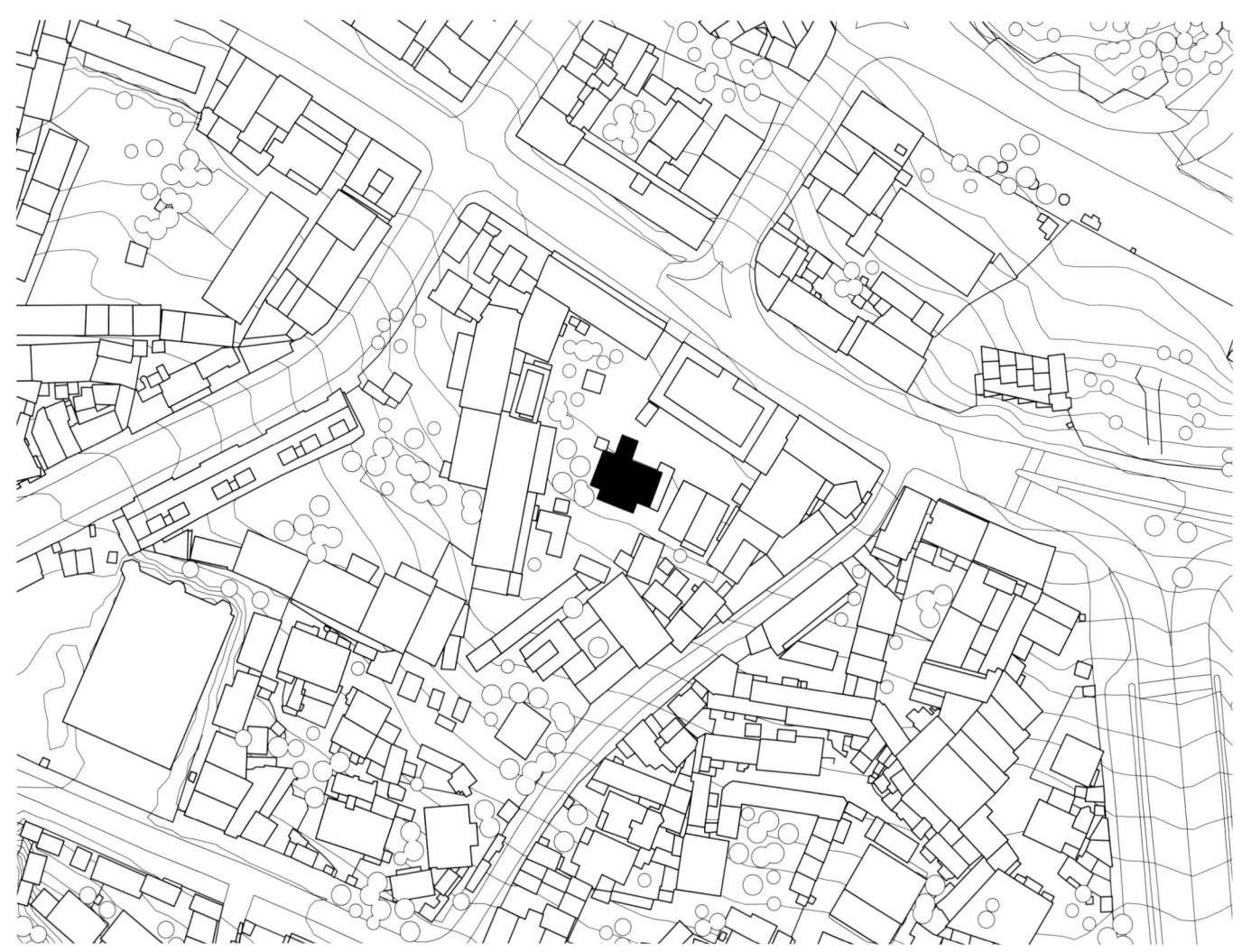
Site plan 1:2000

The walls from crudely hammered natural stone are covered with a thick adobe plaster, leaving visible the precisely cut corner stones as well as the framings of the openings. All wooden elements are painted in a light shade of green. The roof from corrugated iron sheet is supported by a wooden truss system. The edges of the roof are decorated by fascias from tin. Wooden planks are used for flooring and the construction of the staircases.

Three types of arches are found in the building, with these arch structures located on doors, windows, and canopies.

At the beginning of the twenty-first century, there were some attempts to renovate the building and to establish the office of a preservation organisation in it. Only the commitment of preservationists saved the building from collapse. However, the building is currently empty and looks very dilapidated. A steel scaffolding holds the wooden ceiling of the upper floor and a huge crack is visible under the *Jharokha* room on the north side of the building.

The Mohamed Ali House partly collapsed in May 2023.

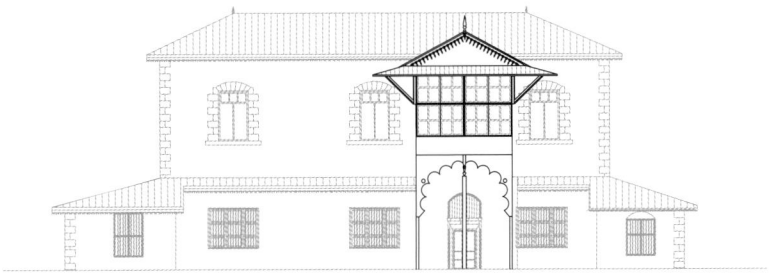

Elevation north

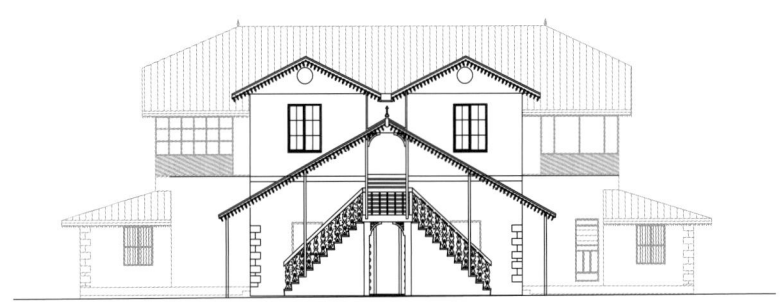

Elevation south

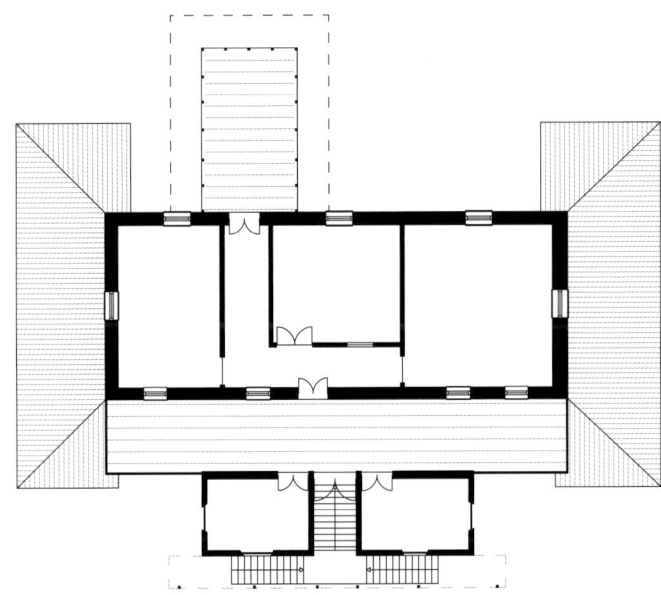

Upper floor

The Case Studies 103

The former elementary school, view from the west

Decorated architrave Wooden knob Ceiling, ground floor Ceiling, upper floor

Two-flight staircase Enfilade, upper floor

Sheik Ojele House

Nestled in the north-western part of Addis Ababa close to St. Rufael Church, this outstanding example of early architecture in Addis Ababa is the one remaining building from the previous three buildings in the compound. Measuring more than 90 metres in length, *Sheik* Ojele House is the largest private palace from the times of Menelik. Built in the first years of the twentieth century, it is considered to be one of the earliest palaces of the nobility to be built in the capital (Giorghis and Gerard 2019: 244).

Ojele Al-Hasan was a very wealthy man. Under the lead of *Ras* Makonnen, he was part of conquering the Beni Shangul, a peripheral region in the west of Ethiopia close to the Sudanese border, in 1897–1898. He subsequently became the regional ruler in Asosa at the beginning of the twentieth century. As the historian Bahru Zewde wrote, Ojele was confined in Addis Ababa for some time together with other Muslim leaders, as he was found guilty of making contact with the British in Sudan (Batistoni and Chiari 2004: 99). It is said that he refused the title of *Ras* that

Central part with residence in the two upper floors

Menelik offered to him in favour of being named a *Sheik* (Giorghis and Gerard 2019: 244).

The rectangular volume measures more than 90 × 25.5 metres. The room heights are also impressive: one on the ground floor measures 5.6 metres, while on the upper floor one measures 4.2 metres. In its linear arrangement, four different parts can be distinguished that in material terms create an organic unity, while with regard to functions, the respective architectural refinement and orchestration of roof shapes are very differentiated.

1) In the centre, the proper residence is situated on the second and third floor. Today, descendants of *Sheik* Ojele's family live here. 2) The westernmost part, which has two storeys and a cellar, presumably served different representative functions. For many years it served as a primary school, but today it remains unused since a new school building was erected in the neighbourhood. It is known that the cellar served as a store for the *Sheik's* gold. 3) The very large parts in between appear to have been used as dwellings for the *Sheik's* followers and commercial

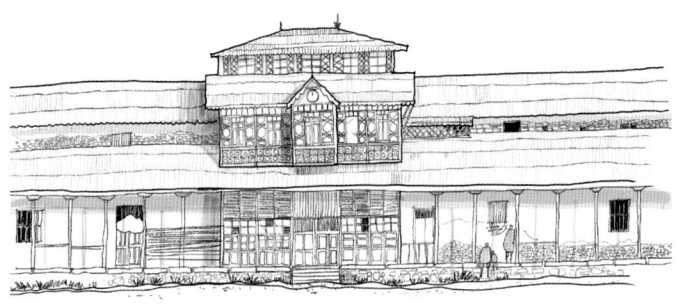

Elevation central part

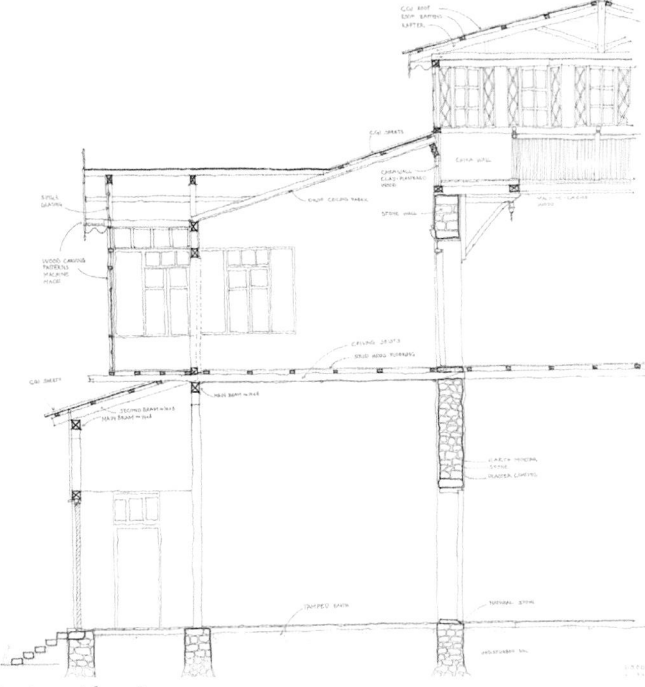

Section with atrium

Elevation detail

activities such as storage. As Batistoni and Chiari point out, it is also known that he was involved in slave trading. The very high rooms found in the building's spine (one of which is called 'meeting room' and has a pit latrine) might also have served to confine slaves (4). The part towards the east of the residence measures 34 metres in length and is constructed in a much simpler way than the rest of the building. Today, this part is managed by the municipality and rented out to low-income families who use the beautiful backyard for urban agriculture.

Ojele employed Indian craftsmen for the woodwork and local masons to construct the thick stone masonry walls (Giorghis and Gerard 2019: 244). The entire building sits on a 75-centimetre plinth from natural stone covered with a generous perimeter veranda. The veranda shows beautiful carpentry that reflects the prevailing Indo-Islamic decorative influences, recalling architecture from Massawa (Batistoni and Chiari 2004:99). In the part of the former school, the veranda goes over two storeys and is enriched by four balcony-like extensions with gabled roofs. These balconies

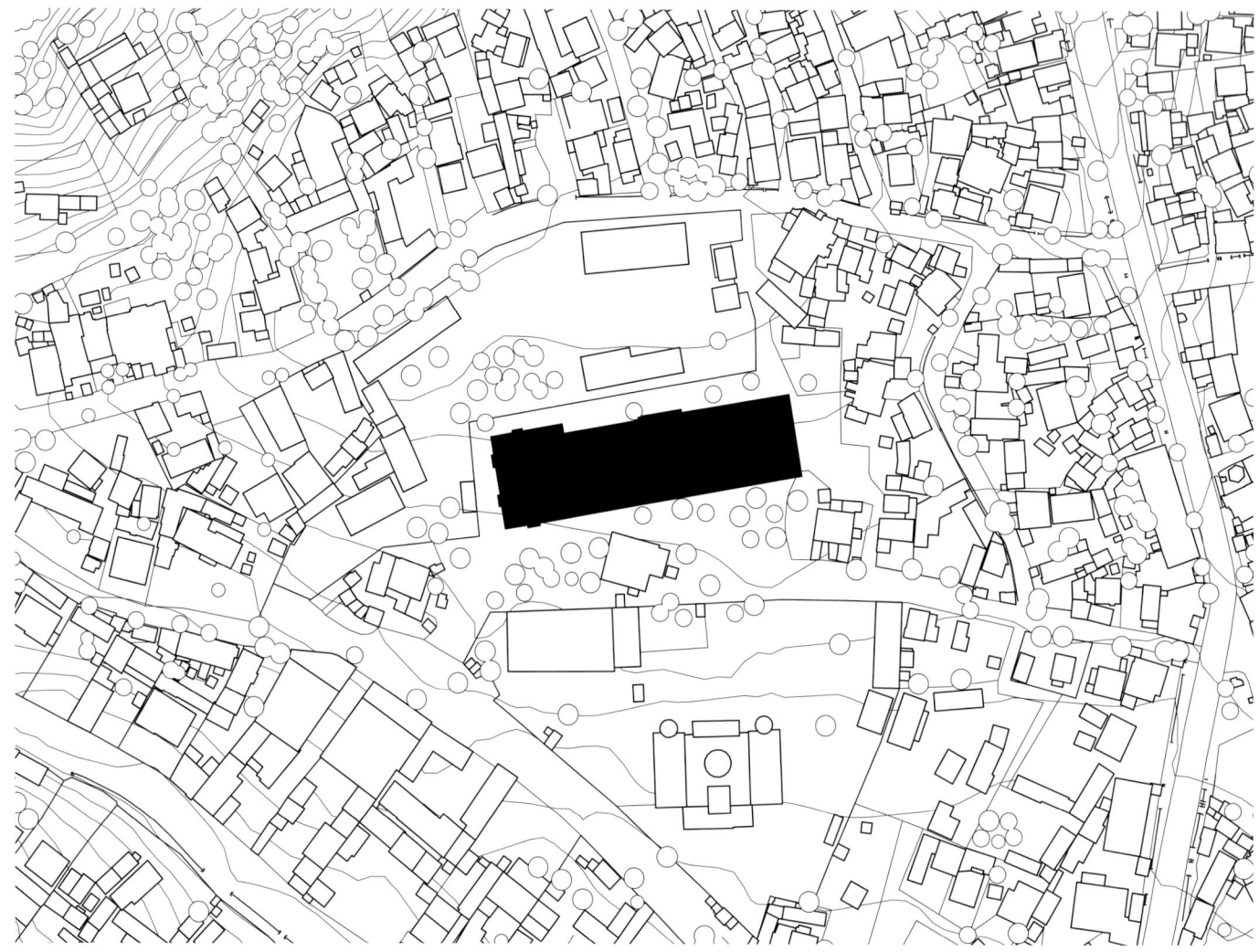

Site plan 1:2000

possibly served as *Jharokha*. Well protected from the rain, the thick walls of approximately 60 centimetres are made from crude stone with earth mortar and adobe plaster. The quality of the adobe finishes differs greatly. The construction appears strikingly crude in the huge storage rooms in the spine of the building, with room heights of more than 10 metres.

When it comes to the central part, where the residence is situated, the different crafting techniques as well as the architectural language becomes even richer than in the school building (photos of this part can be found on page 64–65). Walls are partly realised with machine-carved wooden panels. The residence is reached by an impressive three-flight staircase topped by wooden *mashrabiya* for constant ventilation. The living room on the southern side of the building has a sort of *Jharokha* with coloured glass fillings. Doors and windows show highly elaborate carving techniques. The most remarkable feature, though, is the nicely lit and ventilated double-storey atrium in the middle of the flat. Towards the northern side adjacent to the kitchen, the residence opens towards the northern backyard with another generous veranda.

Elevation south

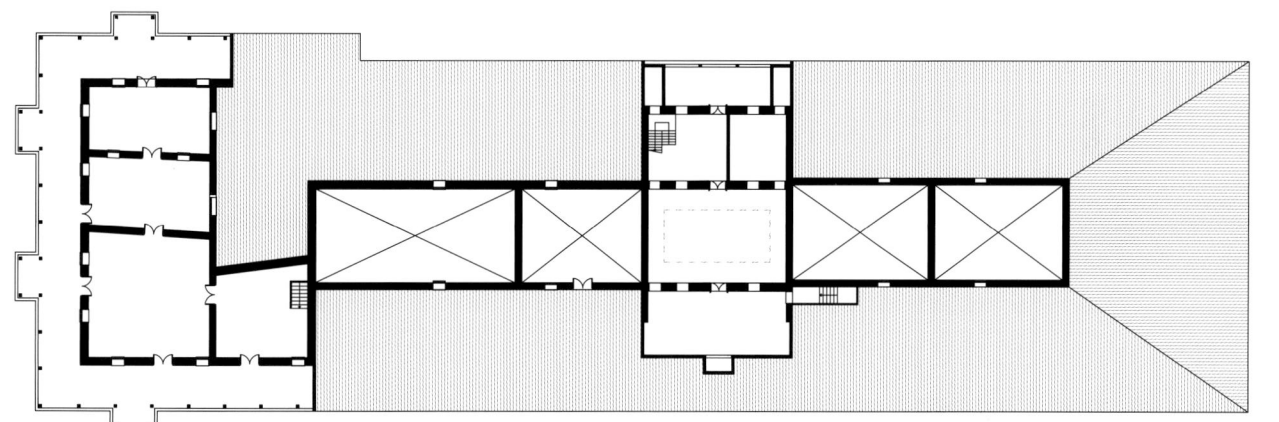

Upper floor

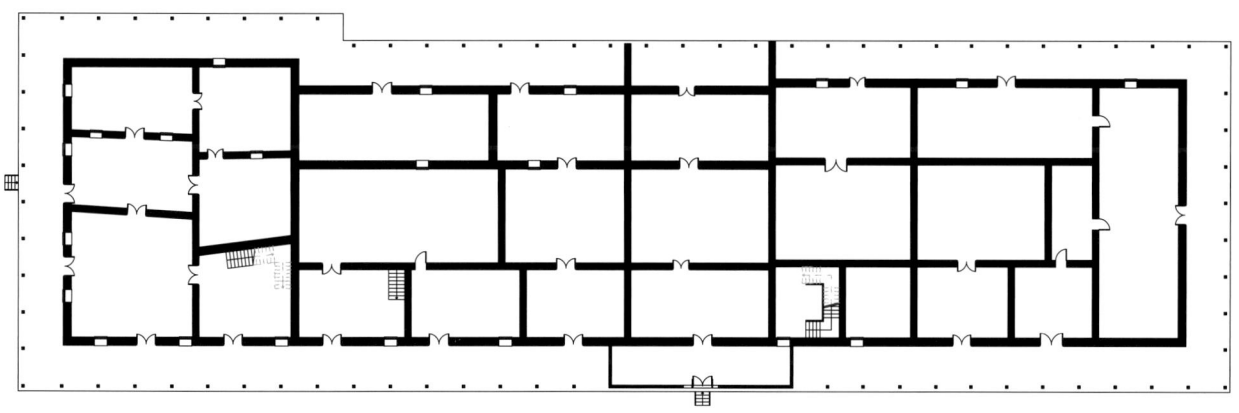

Ground floor

5m

The Case Studies 109

Open perimeter veranda

Passerelle on the second floor

View from the west, photo from the 1980s

Stair veranda connection

Beams above veranda

Outside door type

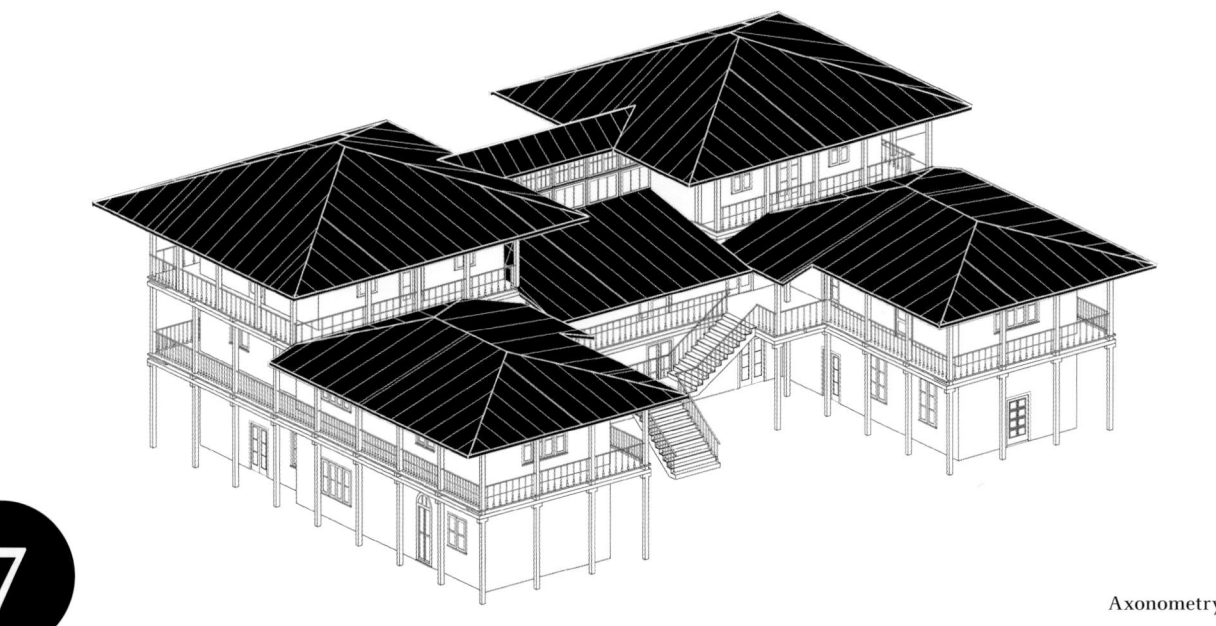
Axonometry

7

Negadras H / Giorghis Residence (Old Municipality)

Under the reign of Menelik, this building was until 1916 the residence of *Negadras* Haile Giorghis, the head of merchants' (who later received the title of *Bitwoded* because of his close relations to the royal family). At the time, Haile Giorghis was the richest man in the empire (Giorghis and Gerard 2019: 240). After *Ras* Tafari took power, the owner was deprived of his residence, which subsequently served as the Municipality of Addis Ababa until 1964 and was later used as Addis Ababa Supreme Court until 2008. During a period of 15 years when it was unused, the building decayed rapidly. Driven by the personal initiative of well-known Ethiopian artist Alemtsehay Wedajo, the building is currently undergoing a general restauration process, which explains why it was not possible to take accurate photos for this book (see p. 54).

The importance this building played in the history of the city cannot be underestimated. This fact already becomes apparent due to its very central and strategic position close to the historical Arada Market and opposite St. George's Cathedral. Towards the east is a direct view to the *Ghebbi*, which

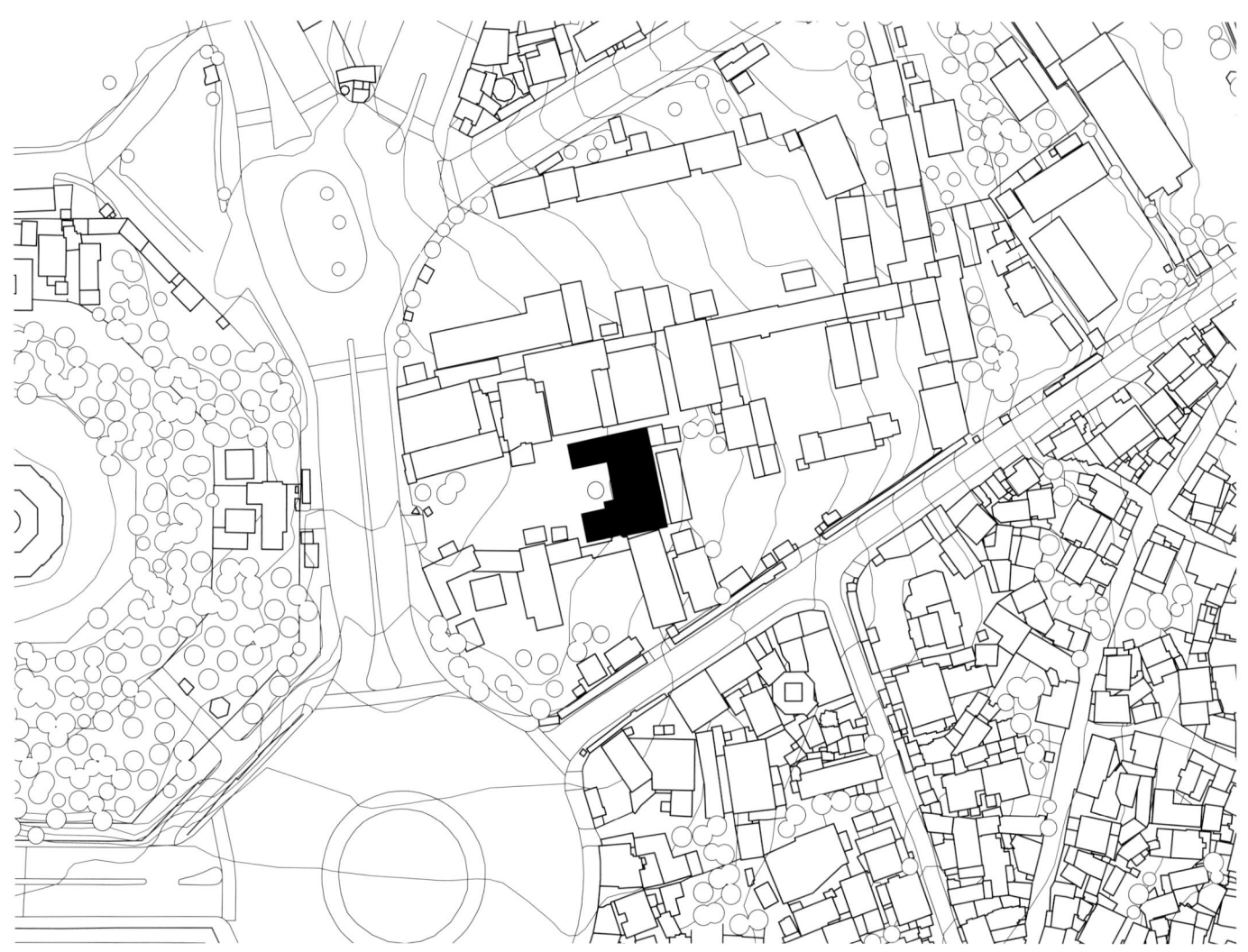

Site plan 1:2000

allowed the house owner to decipher the signals the Emperor used to send to his courtiers by semaphore (Giorghis and Gerard 2019: 240). In the 1909 map, it is marked 'Negad Ras' (Societa geografica italiana 1909).

From an architectural point of view, the quality of the *Negadras* Haile Giorghis Residence lies more in its composition and the functionality of the volumes rather than in its stylistic elements or details. It consists of three storeys formulating a U-shape that opens towards St. Giorghis Cathedral. The first two storeys are built from 70-centimetre-thick crude masonry plastered with lime mortar. The second floor is entirely encircled by a covered wooden veranda as the main circulation, reached by a prominent T-shaped staircase in the centre of the courtyard. A photo from 1936 shows that originally there were two very long one-flight staircases on both sides of the courtyard, of which the two landings are recognisable in the current plan. The two volumes of the third floor sit like corner towers on the eastern part of the buildings, slightly shifted towards each other and connected by a 7-metre-long wooden bridge that sits on top of the roof.

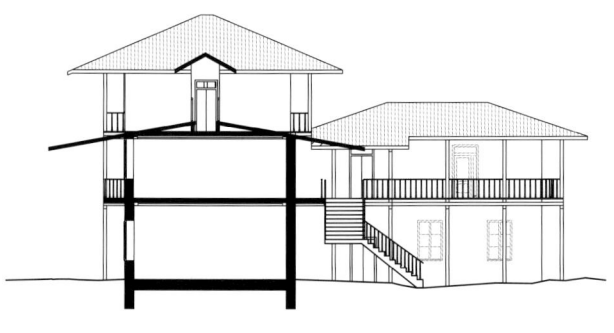

Section

Elevation west

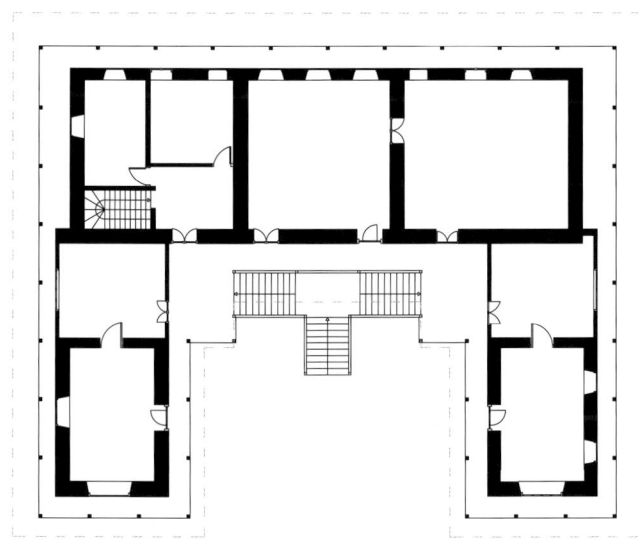

First upper floor

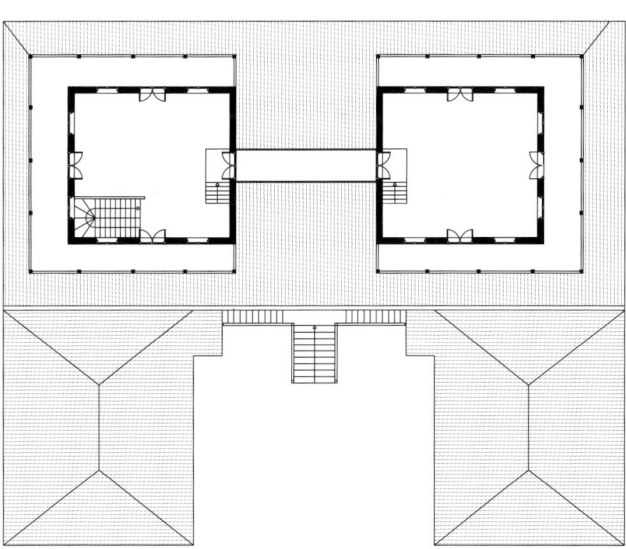

Second upper floor

5m

The Case Studies 113

View from the south

View from the west

Office Building of the Minister of Defence

The *Ghebbi* was closed to the public for decades and re-opened only in 2019 as Unity Park. Therefore, earlier researchers did not have access to the historical buildings located there. This explains why this small but noteworthy pavilion was not documented before 2012. It is neither mentioned in *Old Tracks* nor in the gte database. However, Livio Sacchi published a book about his restoration works in Ethiopia and it contains drawings of the pavilion.

The building served as an office for the Minister of Defence, who was also called 'Minister of Pen' because he was responsible for writing official documents. Presumably, the Emperor was not literate. The documents were written in Amharic, English, French, or sometimes Arabic. Many of the documents that were written by the Minister of Defence are well-kept in the archives of Addis Ababa (Livio Sacchi, Talks on Local Building Types: The Addis Ababa House, TU Berlin, 1 June 2021). In 2010, when an extensive heritage survey was made at the *Ghebbi*, the fragile pavilion was in a terrible state, almost collapsing. Fortunately, it was rehabilitated.

Decorative wooden panels for shading

The Office Building of the Ministry of Defence was built around the 1890s. It consists of only one storey with a square plan measuring 6 × 6 metres. A porch that goes all around the building with a constant width of 1.5 metres is defined by 12 very skinny wooden posts measuring only 12 × 12 centimetres. Those posts carry the expressive roof, which has a pyramidal form and is accentuated by delicate pointed gables in the middle of each of the four eaves.

A finial with an abstract, floral shape sits on each of the gables.

A fifth finial, which is bigger and realised in a round manner, sits on the centre of the roof.

The building as a whole can almost be seen as an archetype of an Addis Ababa House, as it illustrates a few repeating principles. It consists of a core made from a heavy material, such as stone or bricks, and a lighter, wooden envelope that formulates a spatial layer all around the building. The wooden structure of the envelope merges with the wooden structure of the roof it carries.

Ornamental decoration in the form of an arch

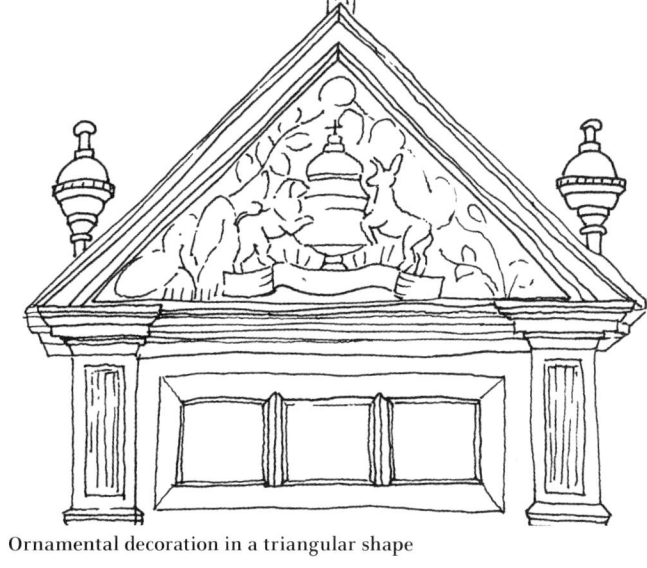
Ornamental decoration in a triangular shape

Decorative pilasters

Wooden windows

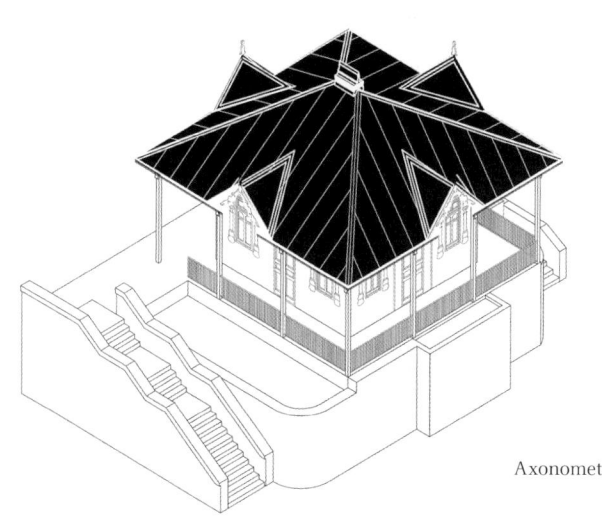
Axonometry

In general, the pavilion seems to be symmetrical towards all sides, but by taking a closer look, one sees a few deviations that produce a certain hierarchy and orientation of the building. This is the case because of the following two aspects of the building. A) Each of the four walls has two windows on both sides, but only three of them also have a door in the middle. The fourth wall – the one that shows towards the west – is blind and shows a niche at the place where the door would be otherwise. B) Towards the east and the façade that shows in the direction of the Elfiñ, there is a sort of wooden curtain hanging below the roof, supported by beautiful wooden consoles. Supposedly, this indicates the façade that contains the main entrance. As it is opposite to the blind wall, one can imagine that the minister was sitting in front of the niche in the blind wall.

This pavilion is very simple in its composition and does not seem to need to follow many functional requirements in its architecture. For that reason, the pavilion is more interesting for its many decorations, which are described below.

The 40-centimetre-thick outer walls are made of bricks and

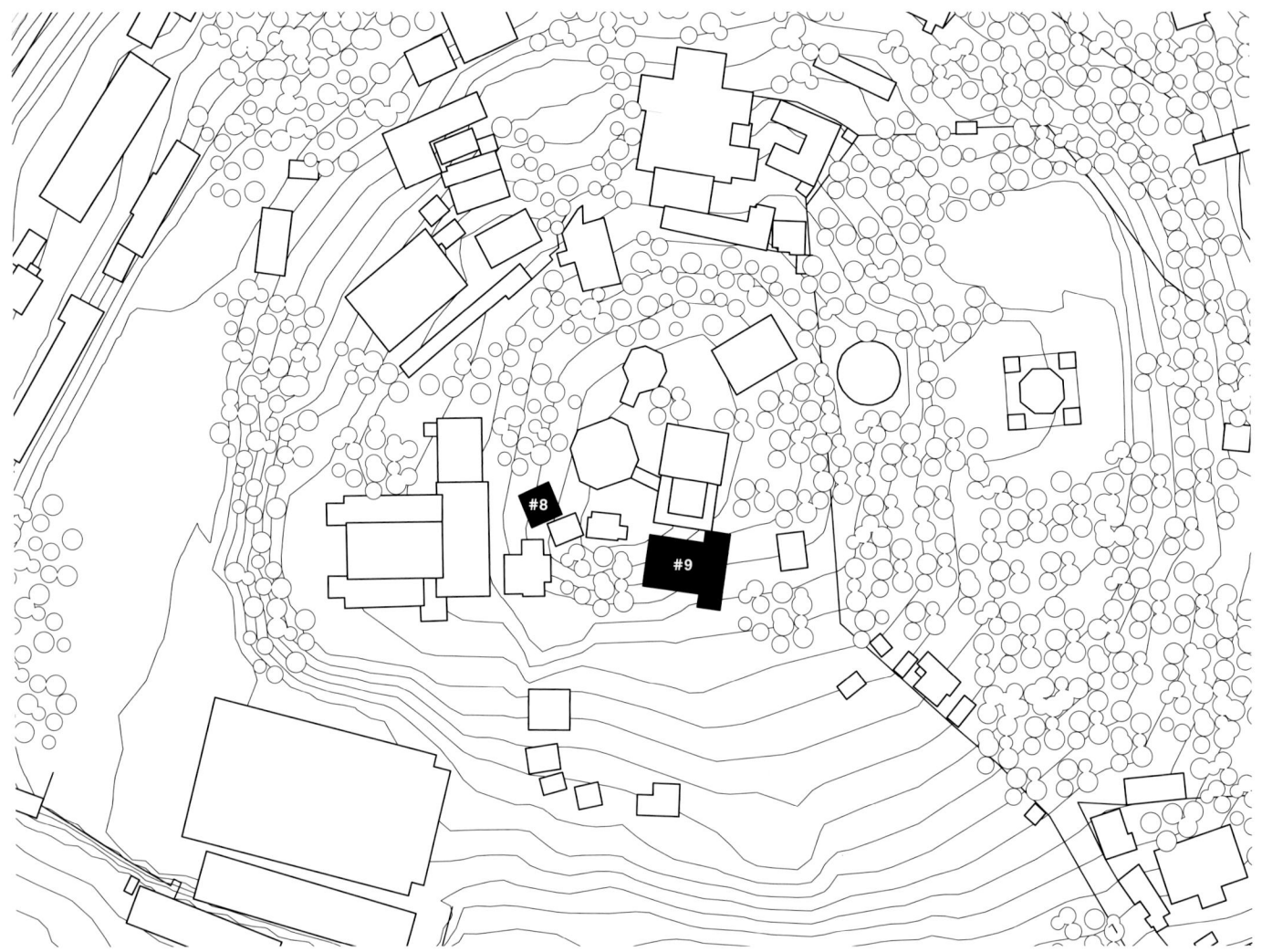

Site plan 1:2000 (#8 Minister of Defence / #9 Empress Zewditu Residence)

finished with lime plaster. The window and door frames show very elaborate ornamentation, supposedly influenced by Armenian and/or Indian craftsmen. These ornaments seem to be made out of gypsum and are integrated into the lime plaster. Next to elaborate pilasters that flank each window, there is a decorative pediment in the form of a triangular gable or in the form of a round arch. Similar to Renaissance architecture, triangular gables and round arches are alternate along the façade, thus the gables are placed over the windows on the east and west, while they are placed over the doors on the south and north side of the pavilion. Hexagonal terracotta tiles are used for the interior floor covering. Fascias along the eaves are made from wood and partly from tin, which shows that the choice of material was sometimes secondary and more a question of availability.

As photos from 2010 show, the walls were painted light blue, while the decorations were painted brown, yellow, and green. These colours are the original ones from the feudal times of Ethiopia, which ended in 1974. Today the walls are painted light yellow for conservation reasons.

Elevation

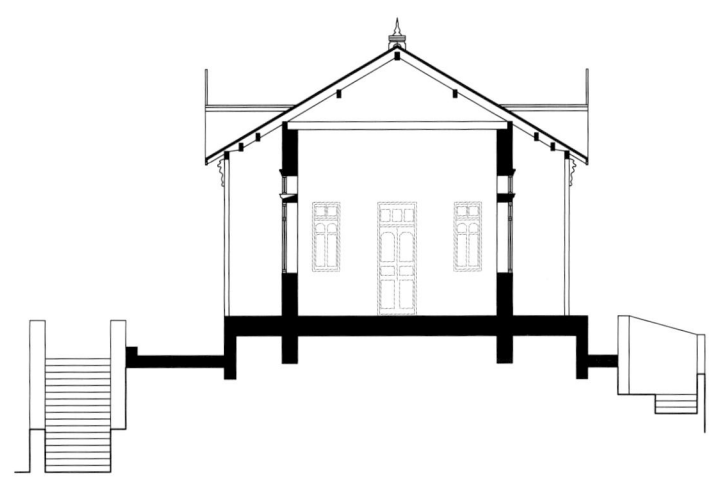

Section

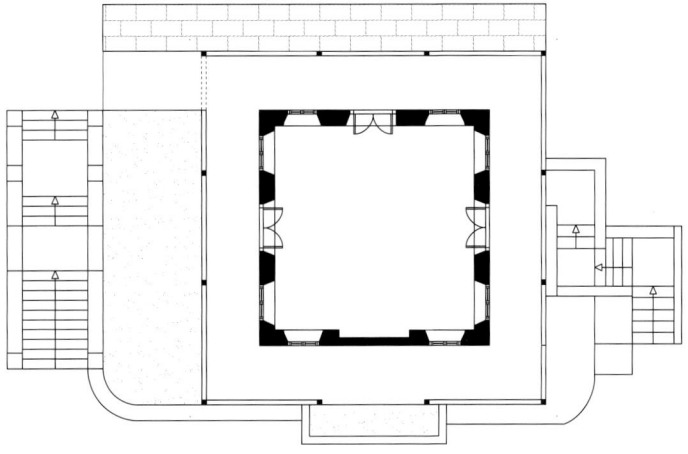

Ground floor

5m

The Case Studies 119

View from the south

Roofed bridge connects the buildings of Empresses Taitu and Zewditu

Geometric woodwork decorating the loggia's railing

View from the south-west

Sunroom on the upper floor

Empress Zewditu Residence

Princess Zewditu was Menelik's daughter. Her mother was a noblewoman of Wollo and a brief companion of Menelik. From 1916 to 1930, Zewditu was the Empress of Ethiopia and the first female head of an internationally recognised country in modern African history.

The building is on the steep side of the *Ghebbi*'s hill, which made it necessary to erect a massive retaining wall of 3.5 metres in height against the terrain. The residence is the southernmost building of the imperial residence, which consists of individual edifices that are interconnected by roofed bridges. As the *Ghebbi* at the time was usually quite crowded by many Addis Ababaens, the bridges facilitated a certain degree of privacy for the imperial family. One of the roofed bridges connects the Zewditu building with Taitu's residence. However, Zewditu's building is accessible from different sides.

It was built between 1907 and 1910 and has a T-shaped floor plan consisting of a squarish building in the west and a longer building in the east. The building is made of two floors and a smaller basement floor with service rooms. The south-facing wooden veranda might be the most noteworthy part

Elevation south

of the building. The elegant loggia is characterised by its fine wooden details. Here, the two upper floors are connected by an elegant outside staircase that bridges the 4.4-metre height difference. The top floor offers a fantastic view of the city.

Livio Sacchi proposes that the balustrades are inspired by architecture found in Japan in the same period. 'You find similar kinds of façades in very distant parts of the world' (Livio Sacchi, Talks on Local Building Types: The Addis Ababa House, TU Berlin, 1 June 2021). Originally there were free-hanging curtains for shading on the upper part of the loggia. The loggia leads to a sunroom characterised by its wooden curtain wall of 190 glazings and its sliding windows. During the restoration in 2012, some parts of the building that had been added over the decades were demolished in order to bring the building back to its original state.

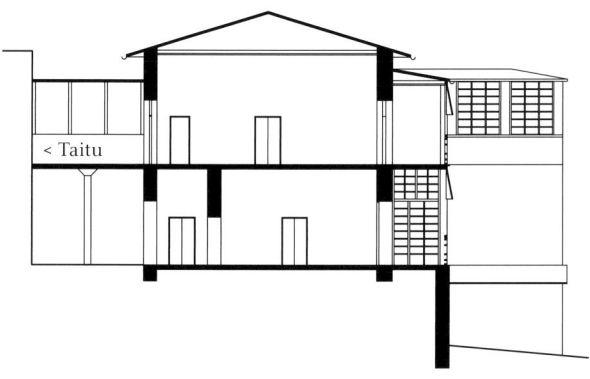

Section

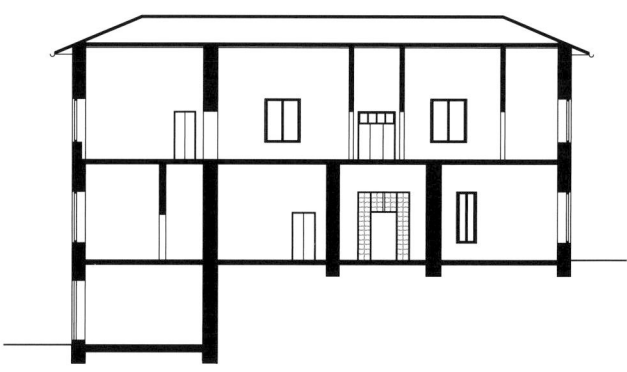

Section

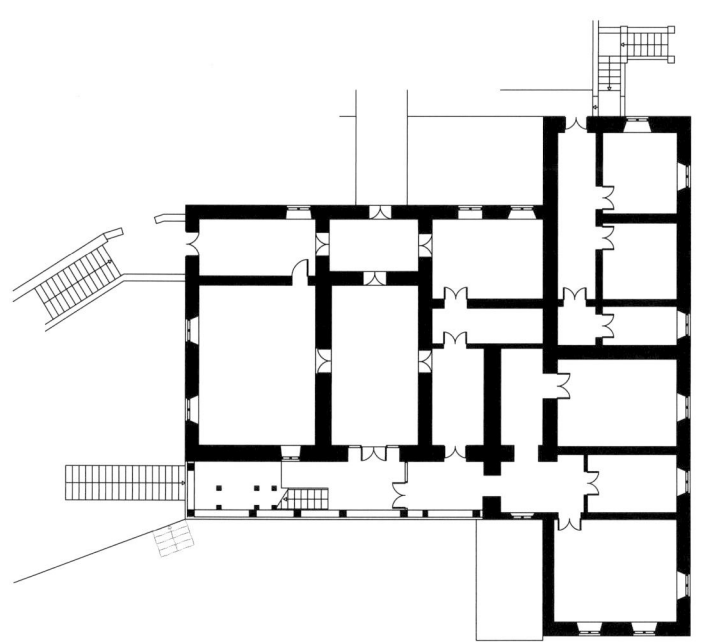

Ground floor

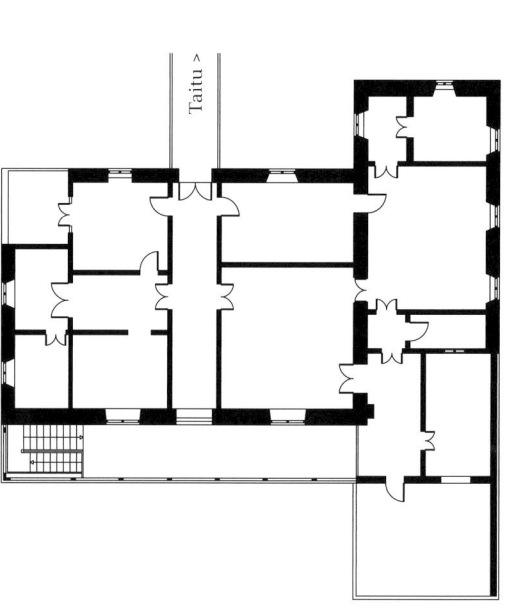

Upper floor

View from the north-east (photo retouched)

Window detail

Former main entrance on the south

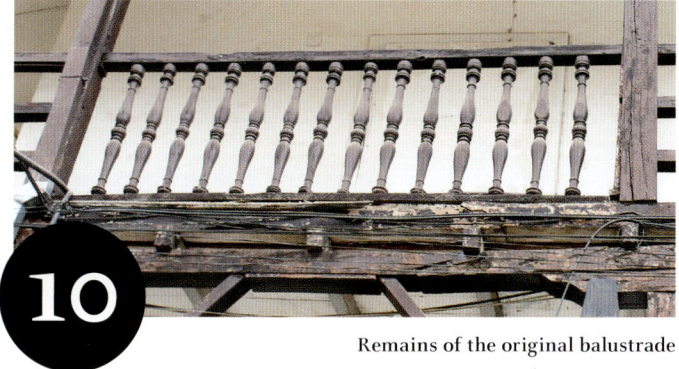

10

Remains of the original balustrade

Vertical evolution of the wooden structure

Taitu Hotel

The Taitu Hotel, allegedly the first hotel in Addis Ababa, was built in 1907 on the initiative of Empress Taitu. It was designed by the Armenian Minas Kerbekian and managed by the Greek Bollolakos since the 1910s (Batistoni and Chiari 2004: 68). The Taitu Hotel accommodated mostly Ethiopian dignitaries, diplomats, and foreigners, as room prices were much too high for most Ethiopians. The words that Empress Taitu is said to have put over the entrance illustrate the ambition that might have guided her: 'People coming from the sea, do you believe Abyssinia is one of the last countries in the world? Here you can sleep and eat according to your customs.' Until she reached old age, she used to send strawberries cultivated in the Elfiñ's garden to the hotel's customers (Batistoni and Chiari 2004: 68). The Taitu Hotel is situated in the Arada area on top of a south-facing hill. The main entrance was originally situated on the south façade and overlooked the plains of Finfinnee.

The Taitu Hotel is a two-storey building on a rectangular plan of approximately 34 × 22 metres. The building is symmetrical on the longitudinal axis and the transverse axis and crowned

The Case Studies 125

Art deco railing

Art deco door handle

Access to the veranda

Pyramidal ceiling

Enfilade on the ground floor

Main room on the upper floor

by a two-tear roof covered with corrugated iron sheets and exposing a ring of rectangular windows in the tier. The entire building is erected on top of a generous plinth of natural stone that extends towards the south, formulating a generous, almost landscape-like staircase. Perimetrical verandas go all around the building on both levels. Wooden posts are placed with bays of over 3 metres. While there are double columns with a height of 3.6 metres on the ground floor, there are single wooden posts on the upper floor carrying the roof measuring 3.1 metres in height. The construction of the wooden elements follows a tectonic logic with great readability. In addition, the vertical evolution of the wooden capitals is remarkable, as they create wooden arches on the upper level that ensure the stiffness of the construction. The walls of both storeys are made from natural stone and plastered with clay. They measure 70 centimetres on the ground floor and 50 centimetres on the upper floor. Many internal walls on the ground floor have generous rectangular openings with a span of over 4 metres and are held by wooden lintels. On the other hand, the outside walls show different

Scetch of upper floor

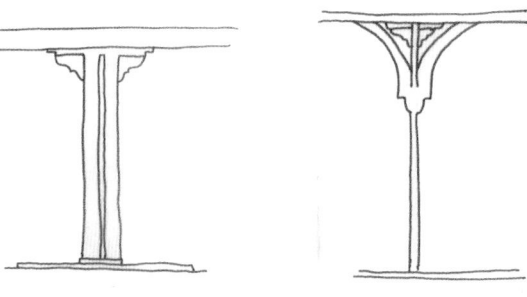

Pillar typologies

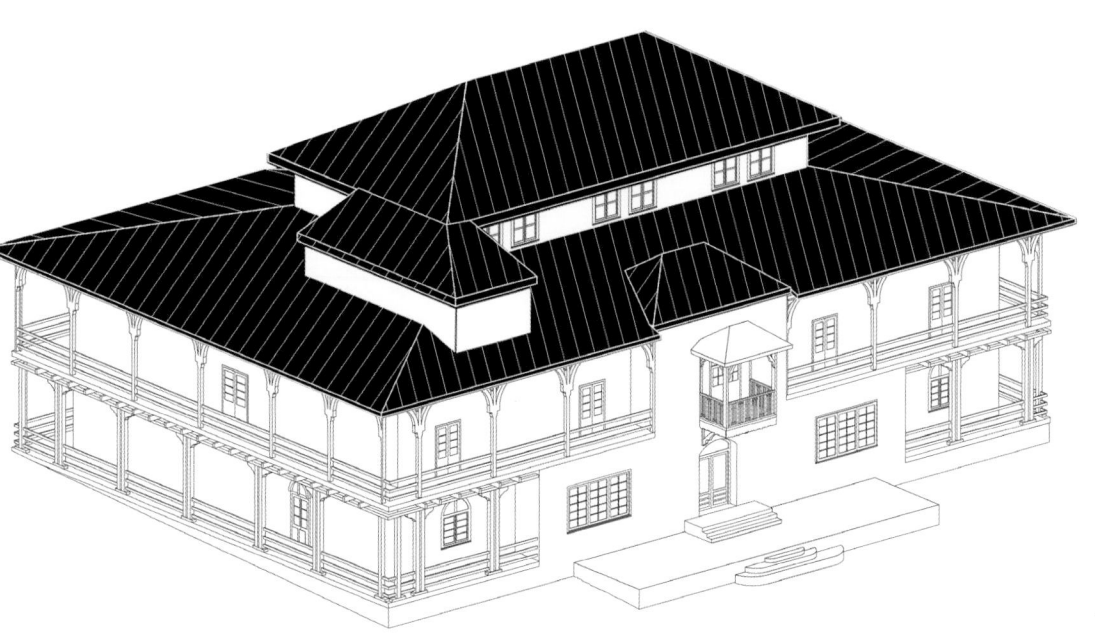

Axonometry

forms of masonry arches in various spans. On the ground floor, many of the round-arched openings create niches that widen towards the inside to allow more light to get into the rooms. Most internal doors are glazed and create interesting view connections to the various spaces of the lobby and the restaurant. In the design of the windows, Kerbekian was obviously inspired by the art deco movement in Europe.

On the upper floor, the stone walls formulate two impressive round arches spanning about 4–5 metres. The private hotel rooms are square-shaped, with each having private access to the veranda space and a pyramidal ceiling made from thick fabric. The beautiful art deco two-flight staircase that connects the two storeys in a spatially interesting manner is highly noteworthy, as it guides the visitor from the ground floor's transverse axis to the upper floor's longitudinal axis. The design of the balustrade is realised with great mastery of shape and functionality.

The occupying Italians changed the name to 'Imperial Hotel', thereby pointing towards Mussolini, of course, rather than Empress Taitu. During the time of the occupation, the building

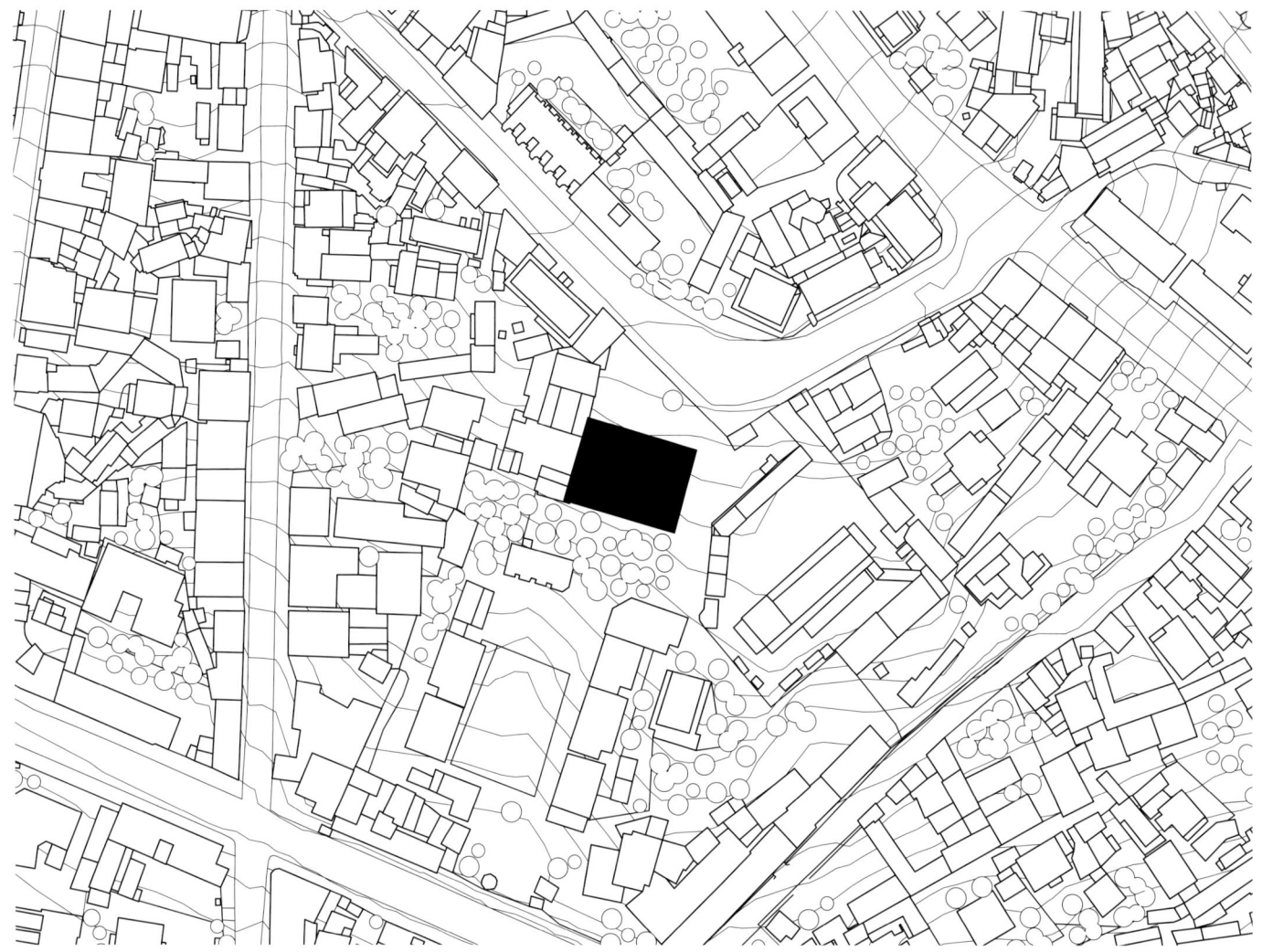

Site plan 1:2000

and the compound saw some major modifications, such as the integration of a wooden ceiling on the upper floor. Thus, the clear story that Kerbekian had designed was closed at a room height of 4.4 metres. The Italians opened the so-called 'officers club' in the room that was created under the roof and reached by a narrow staircase on the southwest of the building. Several annex buildings were also built during that time. The original nicely carved vertical balustrades were replaced by much simpler horizontal timber beams. The main entrance was transferred to the north façade, which is accessible by car. Historical photos show that similar to other old houses in Addis Ababa, the Taitu Hotel had a bridge connection to a small two-storey tower to the west on the spot where the famous Jazzamba would later be found. In 2014, a fire destroyed the Jazzamba-Club. It speaks volumes that even in 2022, it is possible to see a large amount of unfinished repair work that is exposing the building's valuable fabric to dirt and rain.

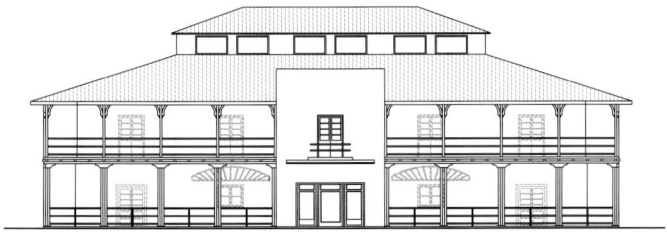

Elevation north

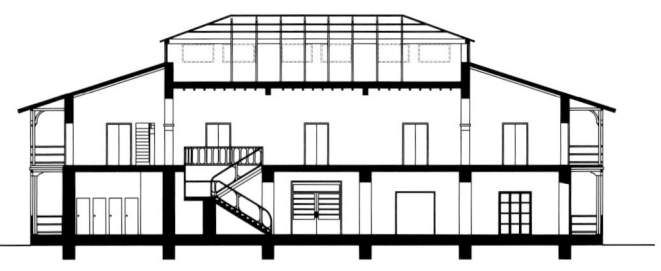

Section

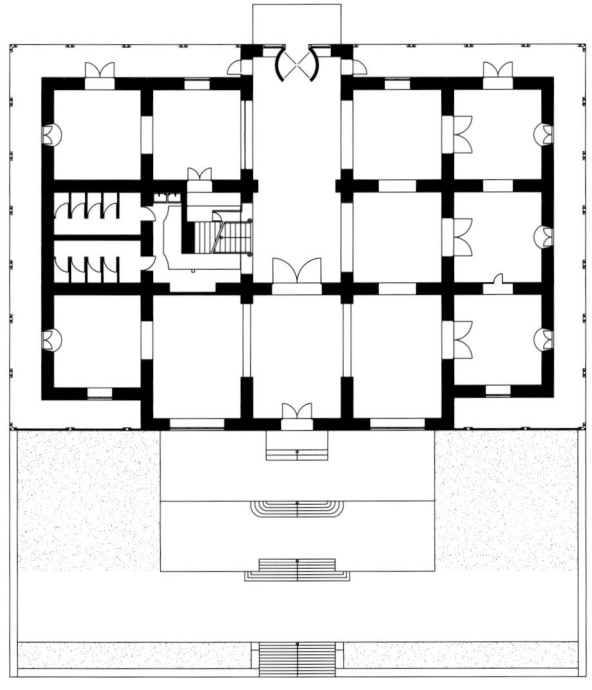

Ground floor

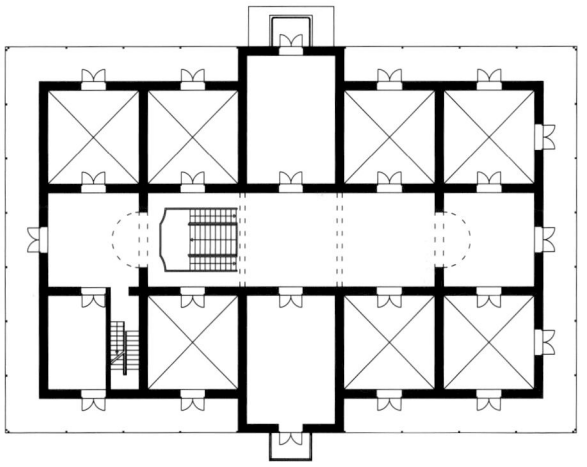

Upper floor

5m

The Case Studies 129

View from the north

Façade modules of the veranda   Veranda space

Afenigus Nasibu Meskele Residence

Afenigus Nasibu Meskele's residence is a two-storey building located near Sandford International School. Its prime location on a hilltop with a direct view connection to the *Ghebbi* is characteristic of the old houses of Addis Ababa and bears witness to the social status of the owner. For about 16 years, *Afenigus* Nasibu was Chief Justice under the reign of Menelik and his sentences were feared by his defeatists. An Italian traveller from the first decade of the twentieth century described him as a terrible yet just man that strictly followed his duty as an infallible organ of the state: the 'Negus' mouth' as his title, *Afenigus*, says (Batistoni and Chiari 2004: 139). His residence was built in the years between the nineteenth and twentieth centuries, and certainly not after 1908, the year *Afenigus* Nasibu died (Batistoni and Chiari 2004: 139).

The *Afe* Nasibu residence is a two-storey building with a rectangular floorplan and is approached from the north. The site is characterised by a slight inclination of the ground. The composition of the elevation consists of three horizontal layers: stone walls with *chikka* plaster at the bottom, filigree woodwork in the middle, and metal sheets on the top

Roof overhang with fascias

Dilapidated state of the building

Wooden carvings on the former main entrance

Glazed gable with a diamond pattern from the inside

level. The two storeys of the building differ a lot in the way they are constructed. The lower floor appears very massive, as it hardly has any openings. It was built in stone masonry and plastered with a mixture of lime and sand. Supposedly it was used mainly for storage, as the lack of openings and windows suggests, but maybe also as a prison. Different families live here today, and informal structures lean onto the walls (Giorghis and Gerard 2019: 260). In contrast, the upper level is characterised by an accurately fabricated wooden perimeter veranda. This floor is mainly used for living.

The well-designed curtain wall consists of modules that are found on both the northeast as well as the northwest façade. It has a closed wooden balustrade at the bottom, a wooden, multi-glazed curtain in the middle, and fixed louvers at its top. The centre of each module, which measure approximately 2.6 metres in width and 3.5 metres in height, feature openable windows integrated into the curtain wall. Today almost all of the glass panels are damaged or missing.

The veranda goes almost all around the building but is also connected to a corridor that separates the floorplan into a

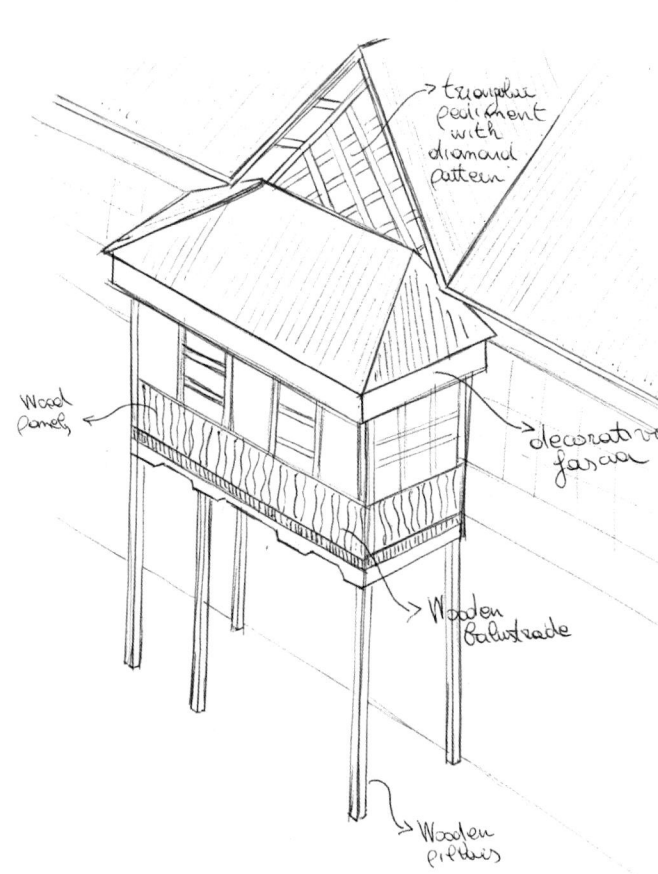

Addition analysis

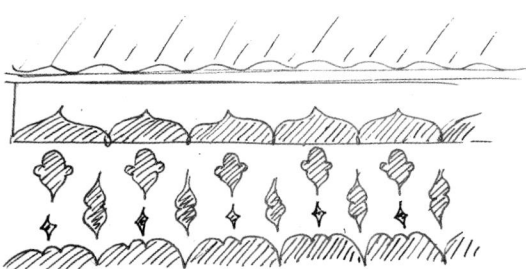

Ornament analysis

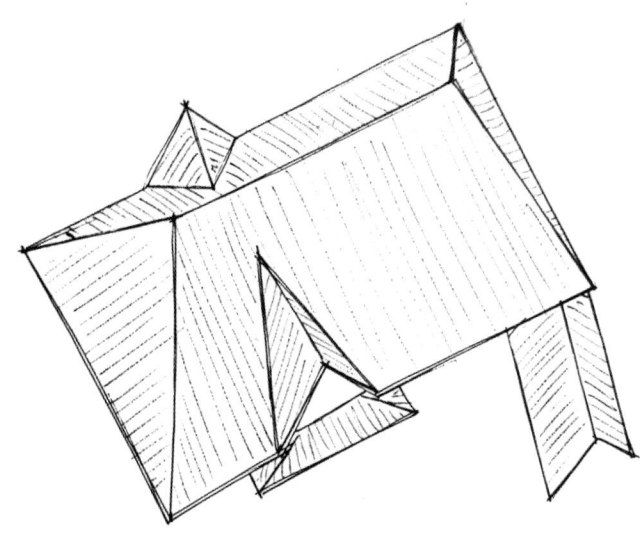

Roof shape analysis

more representative part on the north and bedrooms towards the south (Giorghis und Gerard 2019: 261). With its generous size of about 2 metres, the veranda space has a multi-functional purpose, such as circulation, recreation, and social interaction.

The upper floor is crowned by the pitched roof of corrugated iron sheets with a wide overhang. The roof structure is made of thin wooden beams onto which the corrugated iron sheets are placed. The roof is modulated with two gables on each of the longer sides, both of which form an equilateral triangle in the elevation. These triangles, characterised by diamond-patterned fenestration, are aligned with the perpendicular inner corridor and thus allow light to reach the interior of the building.

As far as the decorative elements are concerned, a metallic ornamental fascia that adorns the entire perimeter of the roof is noteworthy. It is probably of Indian influence.

The simple rectangular form of the volume is modulated by two small yet noteworthy additions. Firstly, there is a hanging balcony on the southern side that characterises the main

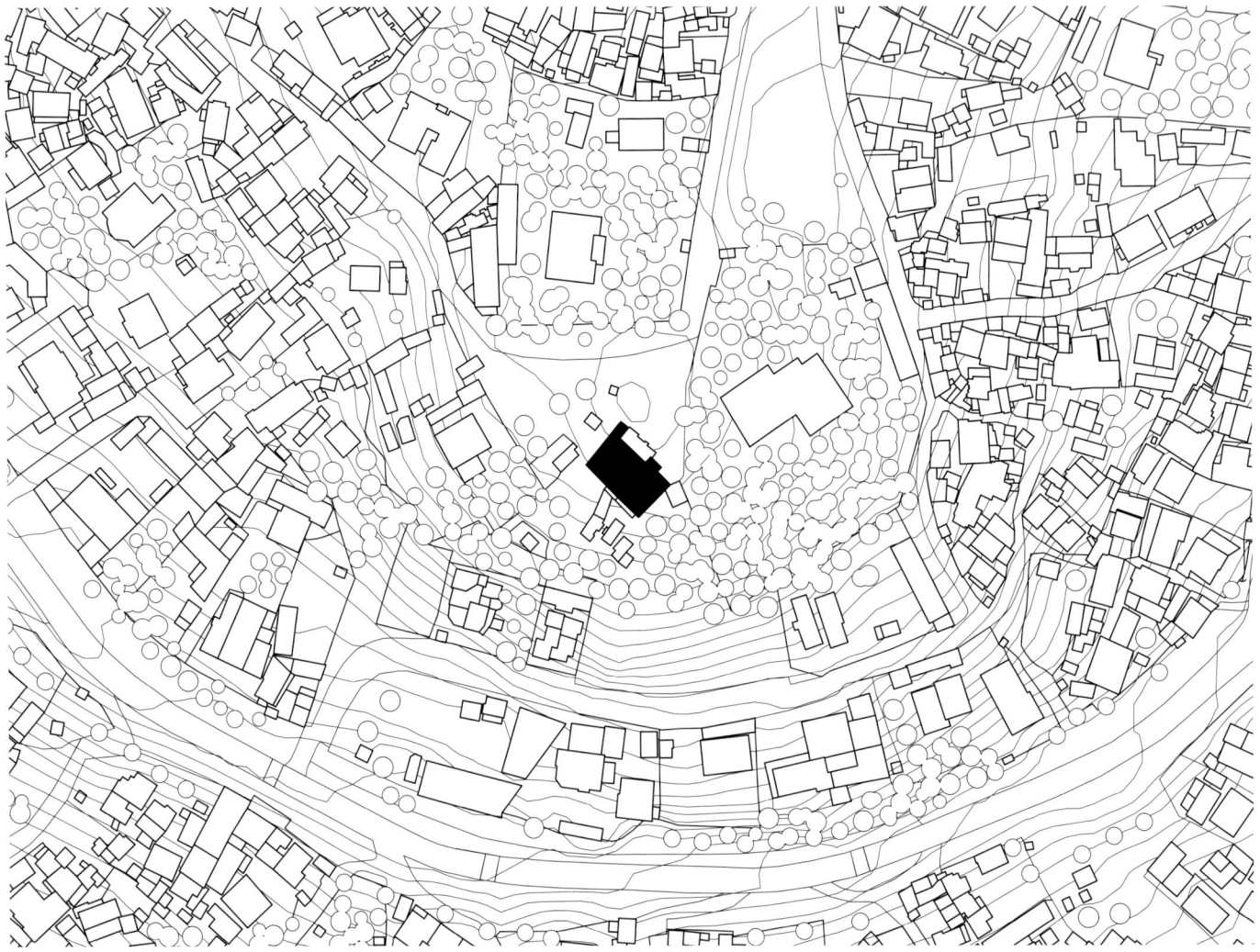

Site plan 1:2000

façade. This element, supported by thin wooden columns, has its own roof, added below the volume of the main roof. Moreover, it takes up the composition of the curtain wall, although distinguished by the presence of decorative elements in the lower band. These elements suggest a balustrade and therefore an originally open balcony. The balcony creates a shaded entrance below. The entrance door shows the most elaborate wooden carvings in the entire building and it can be assumed to have originally been the main entrance.

Secondly, there is a roofed, L-shaped staircase on the northern part of the front façade that leads to the upper floor. While the lower part of the staircase is made from stone, the upper part consists of a wooden structure. This access was supposedly added later on when the number of households living in the building increased after 1974 when the building was converted into a multi-family house.

The structural simplicity on one side and the refined details on the other make this building a magnificent example of early architecture in Addis Ababa.

Elevation northeast

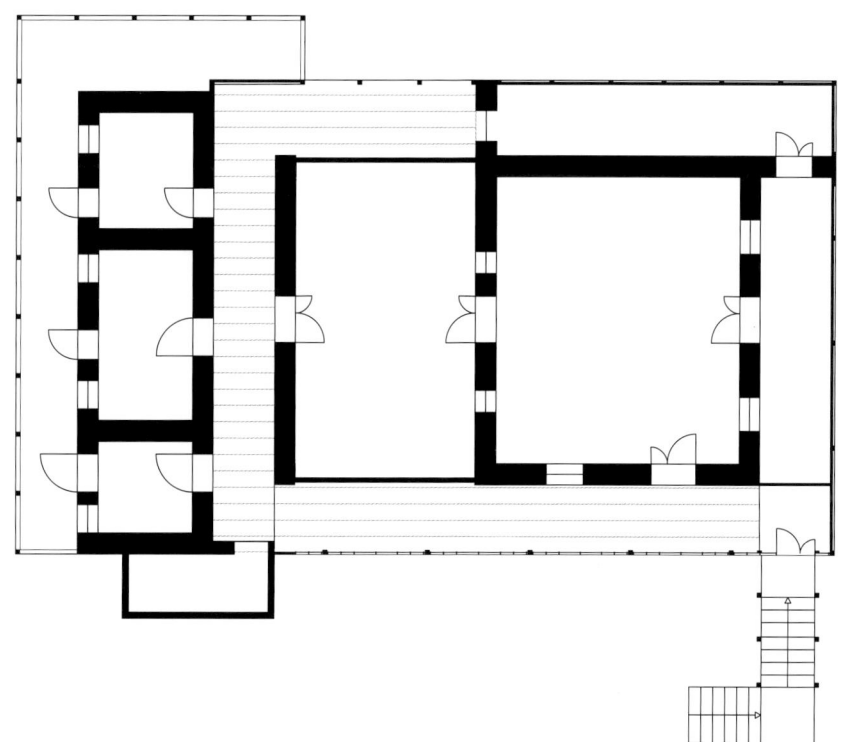

Upper floor

5m

The Case Studies 135

Today the building is hidden in lush greenery

Entrance seen from the west   Staircase detail

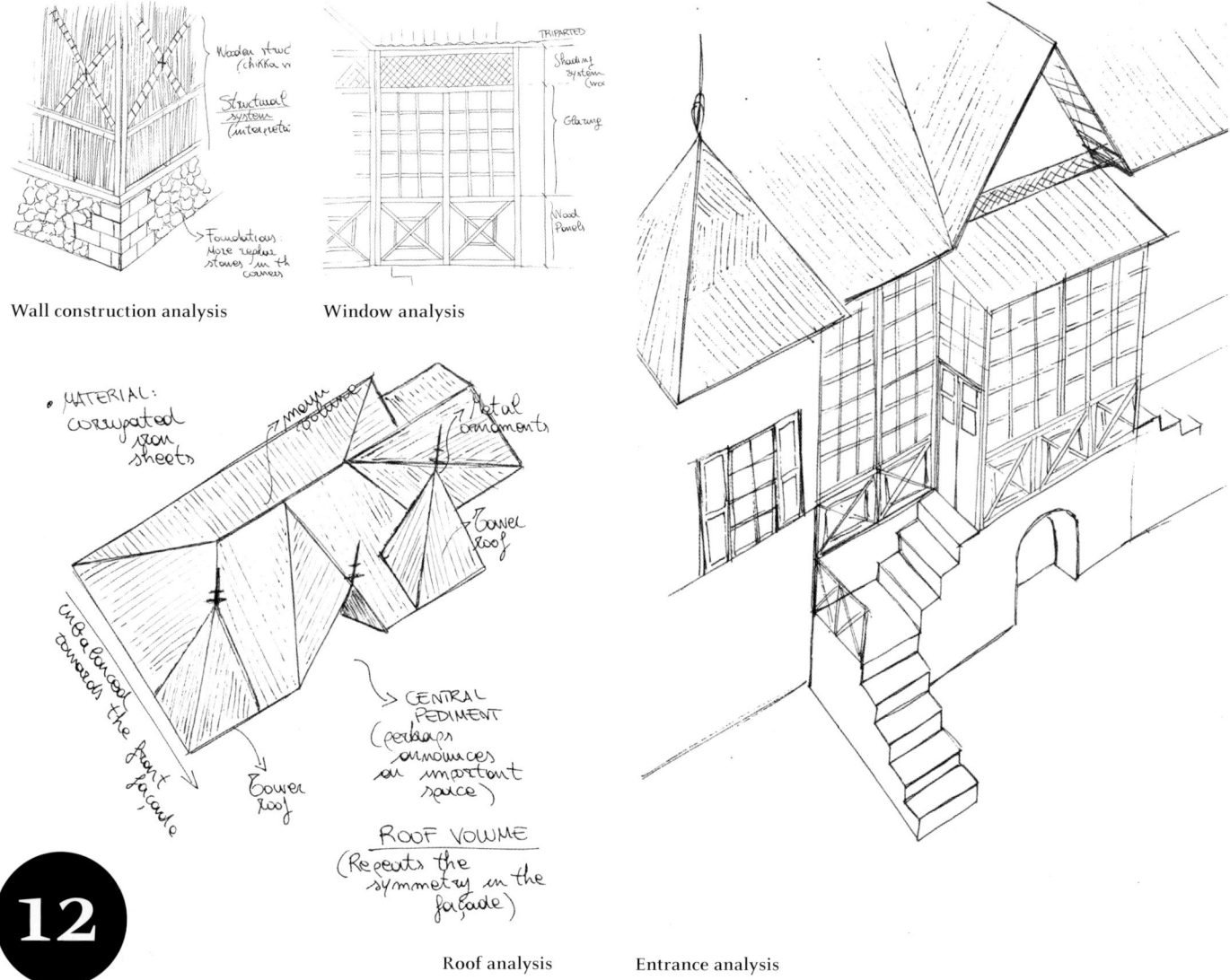

Wall construction analysis

Window analysis

Roof analysis

Entrance analysis

Balambaras G / Medhin Residence[1]

The small and picturesque residence is situated at Wolete Yohannes Street in the heart of the Armenian quarter. It is a remarkable example of the Addis Ababa Style. Due to its dilapidated state it can be assumed that the building is now used as a multi-family, low-rent *kebele* house.

The single-storey volume of the building is divided into three horizontal layers. At the bottom is a strong stone foundation that levels the slope of the terrain and rises on the south-west side a good 1.5 metres from the ground. Above the foundation sit the walls, which are 3.5–4 metres in height and made of *chikka*. The lower part of these walls is plastered with a lime mortar. Wooden windows with shutters are placed in the middle of the *chikka* walls and right on top of the lime mortar line. Both on the front, facing south-west, and on the back, facing north-east, these walls are interrupted by elegant curtain walls of wood and glass that extend over the entire height of the building. Finally, the expressively shaped roof of corrugated iron sheets sits on top. Two towers are accentuated by pyramidal roofs topped by finials. The entrance is also accentuated by a pointed gable.

Unmaintained *chikka* wall

View from the north

Wooden window in *chikka* wall

Curtain wall on the rear façade

The ground plan of the building is rectangular, with a small rectangular extension on the south side. With the exception of this extension, the building appears absolutely symmetrical. This can be seen on the façades and can probably also be transferred to the floor plan (which was not available for this research).

The symmetrical front façade is the most interesting part of the building. The construction of the monolithic foundation continues into the two stone staircases. These staircases are placed to the left and right of the entrance. Both consist of eight steps. The direction of travel is turned 90 degrees after four steps, so that the entrance to the building is reached on the side walls of the curtain wall, which forms a bay window at this point.

The modular curtain walls (both at the front and at the rear) are also divided into three horizontal levels. The bottom section has wooden panels stabilised by diagonal struts. Above these are the modules of fine wooden struts and glass panels, into which window or door openings are integrated. Finally, the upper section has a wooden mesh for ventilation.

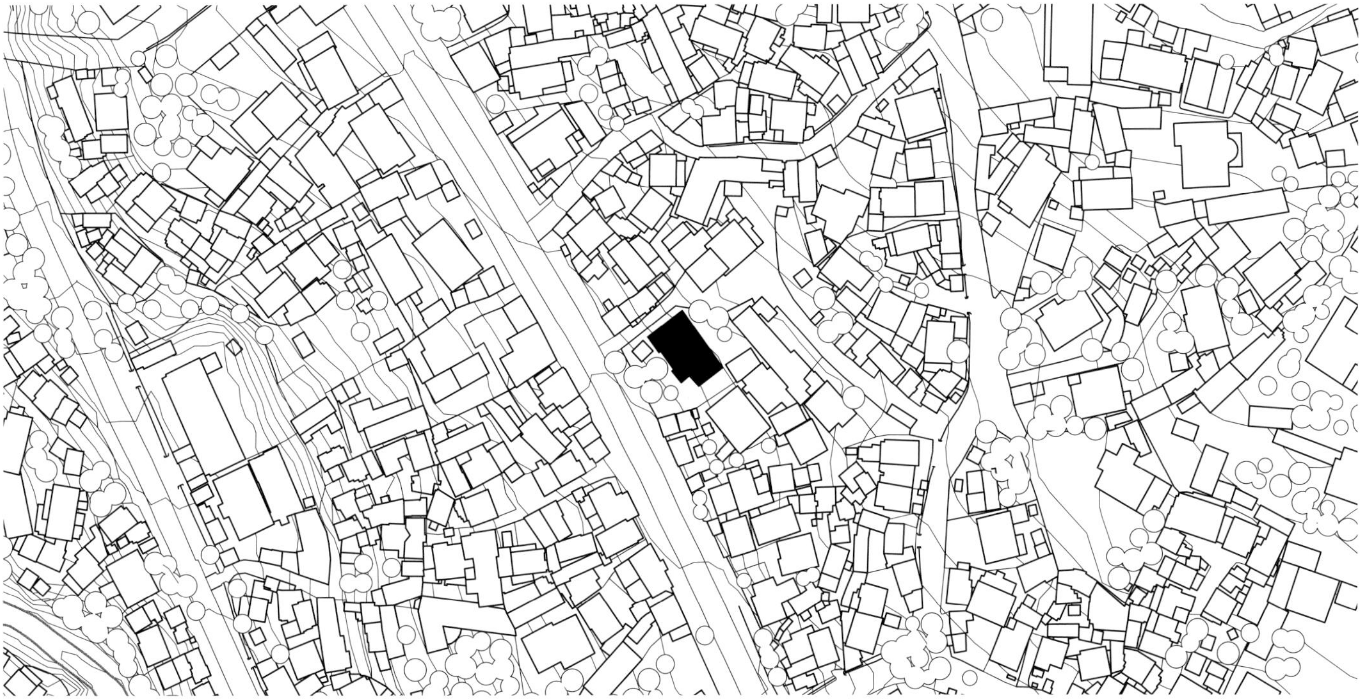

Site plan 1:2000

1 The gtz-database states that the owner was '*Balambaras* Guebre Medhin Gofa', who was Minister of Agriculture under Haile Selassie I. However, this contradicts the information in *Old Tracks*. For this reason, we are not sure to whom the residence belonged. Consequently, our research is merely based on a site visit to the compound.

Elevation south-west

The Case Studies 139

View from the north-west in a photo from the 1980s

Wooden bridge

View from the south

1 Despite many attempts, it was not possible to obtain any photos from after the renovation. Restoration can also lead to the privatisation of heritage.

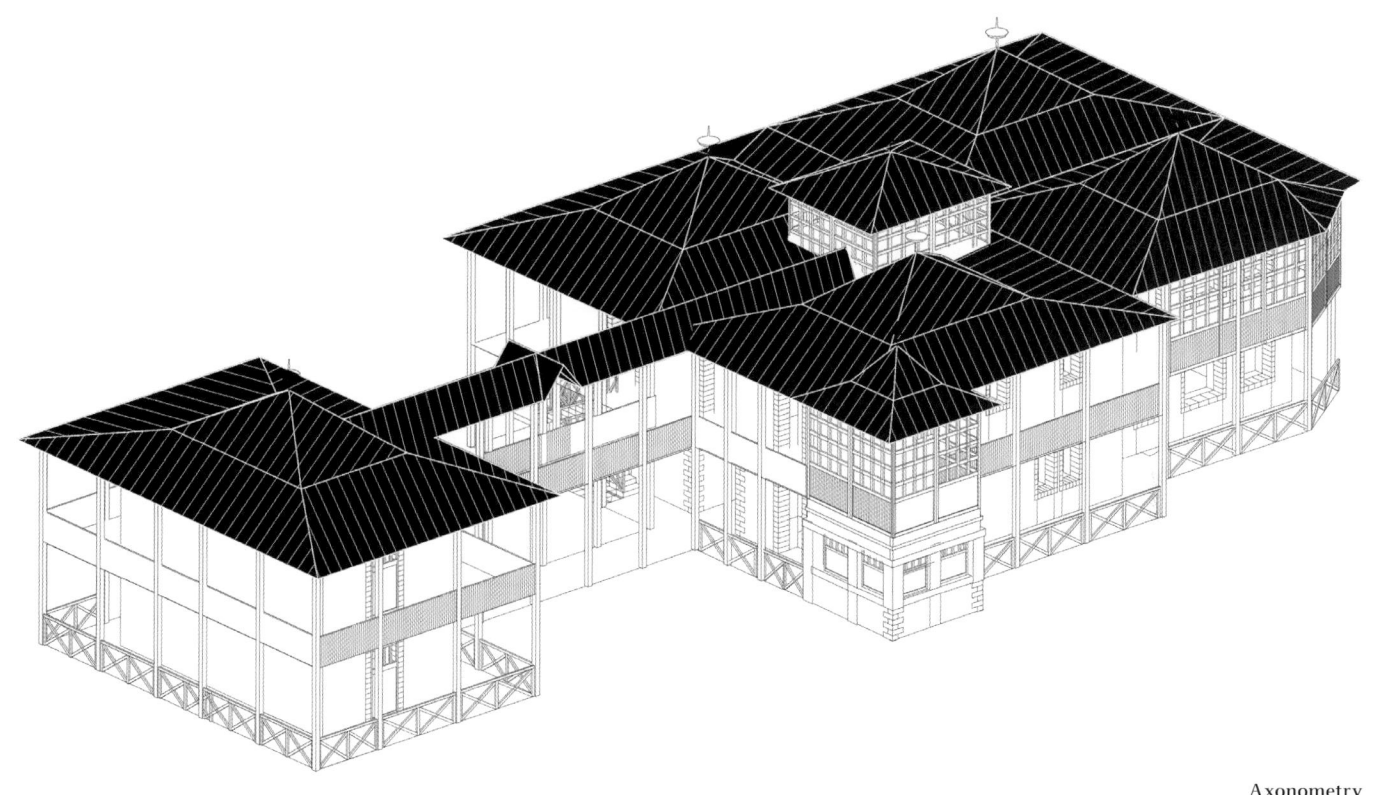

Axonometry

13

Dej. Ayalew Birru Residence[1]

Built around 1910, though some say it was 1920, the *Dej.* Ayalew Birru Residence is situated in the Bole area on a compound measuring approximately 2,400 m². *Dejazmatch* Ayalew Birru was the son of *Ras* Wolde Gabriel and thus a relative of Empress Taitu (Batistoni and Chiari 2004: 180). The property was nationalised in 1975 and about 27 poor families were living there for low rents until recently (Giorghis and Gerard 2019: 264). Between 2013–2015, the building was completely renovated and turned into a guesthouse (Intbau 2021).

The *Dej.* Ayalew Birru Residence is one of the most remarkable structures among the old houses of Addis Ababa due to its expressive, highly decorated roof shape, and its fine composition of different volumes. The building shows a high degree of craftsmanship in many of its details.

The building consists of two volumes, both of which have two storeys. The bigger part in the south, which measures 12 × 16 metres in floor area, is connected via a bridge to a smaller tower-like structure of 6 × 9 metres in floor area. The two volumes and the bridge are lifted on top of a natural

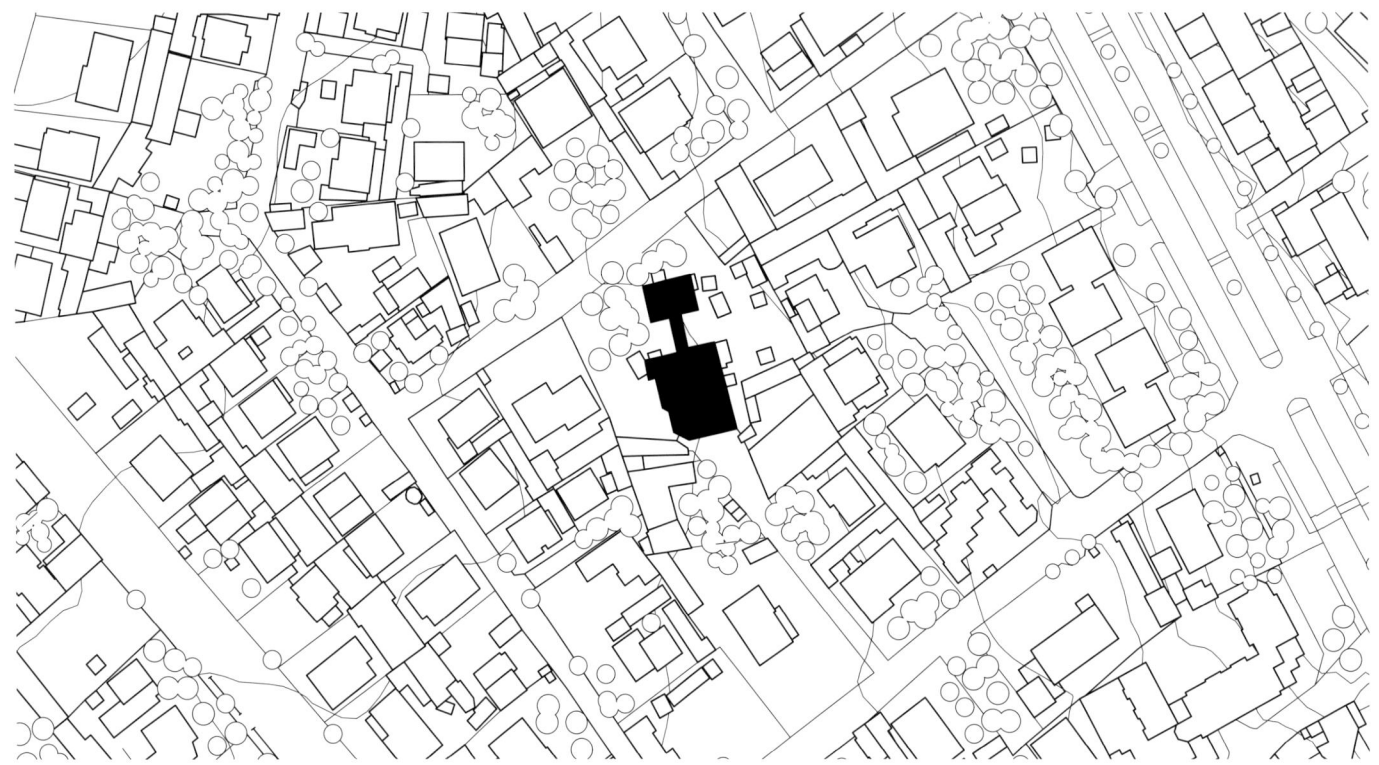

Site plan 1:2000

stone foundation, which in parts rises 1 metre from the natural terrain. Both volumes are enveloped by a perimeter veranda that rests on elegant wooden posts approximately 3.6 metres high. On the upper level, the veranda is partly open and partly closed by wood panels or glazed curtain walls. The balustrade of the veranda and the bridge respectively create a horizontal stripe that binds together the entire composition. The walls of the ground floor are made from natural stone with earth mortar and lime plaster. The cut cornerstones and window frames remain visible. The internal walls as well as the upper storey were realised with a sort of modernised version of a *chikka* wall. As can be seen in photos from the construction site in 2014, it was a regular wooden grid with horizontal and diagonal trusses, with earth and straw filling (Intbau 2021). These walls were plaster with mud and covered with lime mortar as the exterior finish. The highly expressive roof of corrugated metal sheets has continuous eaves that go all around the building at 6 metres above the natural terrain and is articulating a few carefully chosen points by the integration of graceful gables, one of which is placed over the entrance on the southern side while the other marks the middle of the wooden bridge. The line of the eave is amplified by wooden fascias. The roof is crowned by nine finials of metal. The centre of the bigger volume features a light dome that is glazed from four sides with a mosaic of white, yellow, green, and blue squarish glass panels.

The upper level can be reached by two exterior staircases that are integrated into the wooden perimeter veranda. As the veranda measures approximately 1.5 metres in width, the staircases appear quite steep and narrow. From a structural point of view, this is a very efficient solution.

It became apparent during the restoration works that some parts of the building were in a very bad state, while others such as the wooden roof structure could for the most part be kept. The local pine that was used for its construction more than 100 years ago was still strong and resilient.

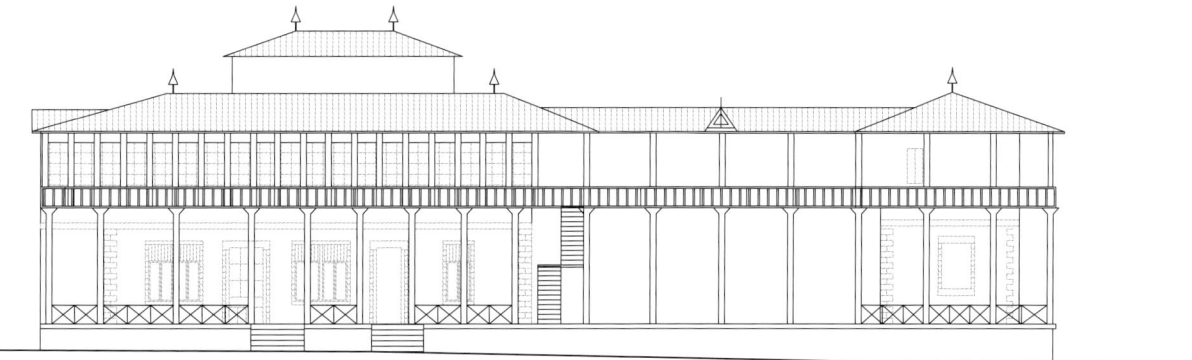

Elevation east

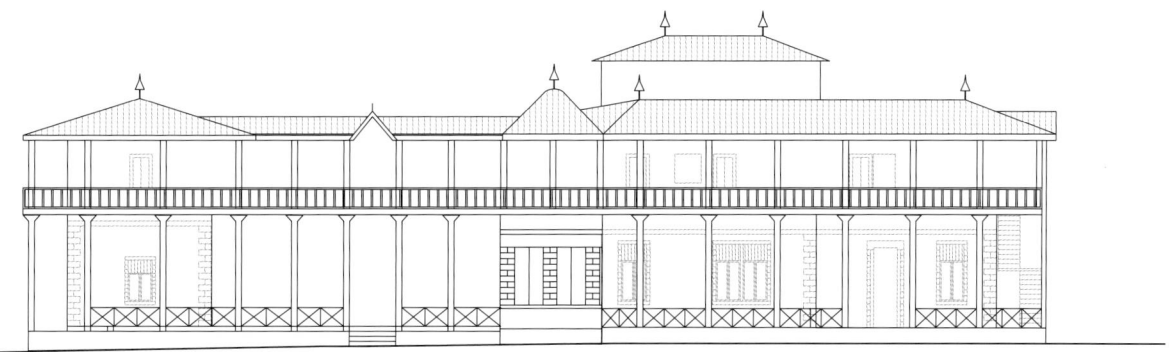

Elevation west

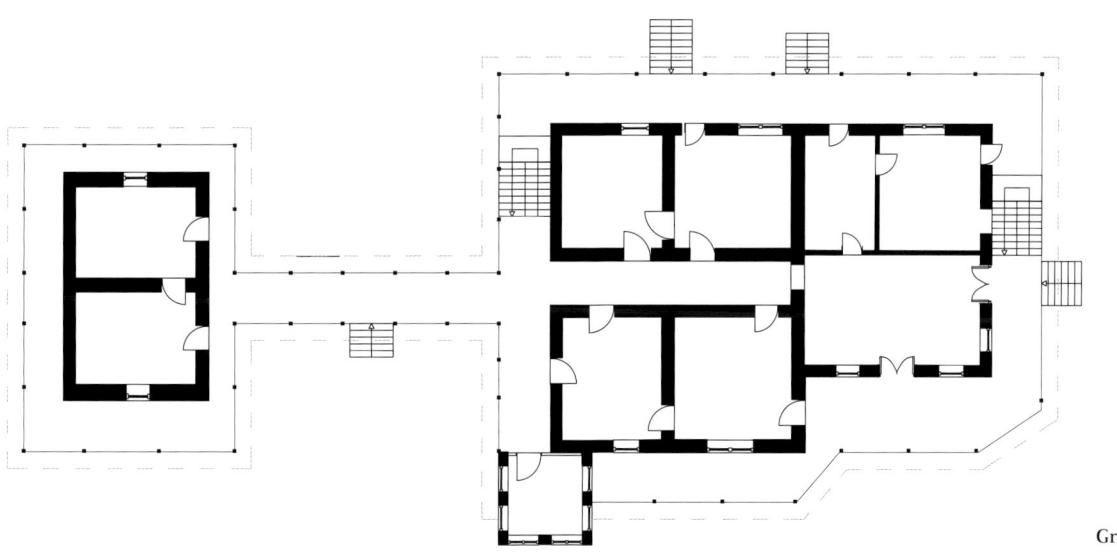

Ground floor

5m

The Case Studies 143

Wooden angel left

Wooden angel right

View from the south-west

144

Destroyed in January 2021!

Satellite image from December 2020   Satellite image from January 2021

Main entrance

Octagonal corner towers

14

Dej. Asfaw Kebede Residence

The Asfaw Kebede Residence was built during the reign of Zewditu. *Dejazmatch* Asfaw Kebede became an influential figure as he was in charge of the supervision of all servants and services under Haile Selassie (Batistoni and Chiari 2004: 124). His son, Seifou Asfaw, recalls in a phone call in 2022 that 'every morning there were hundreds of Addis Ababans coming to the house to ask his father for different kinds of favours', as he was their middleman to the Emperor (phone call on 13 October 2022).

There is very little material available about this building. Only two photographs taken of the front façade for the gtz database in 2006 were available to conduct this research. According to Seifou Asfaw, the house was structured as follows: 'The generously glazed front veranda served as a hallway and was used as a vestibule for guests' (phone call on 21 April 2023). Facing the south-west, it surely also functioned as a 'sunroom', capturing solar heat for the colder season. The octagonal room to the left hosted Asfaw Kebede's office, while the room on the right was the sitting room during the

The Case Studies   145

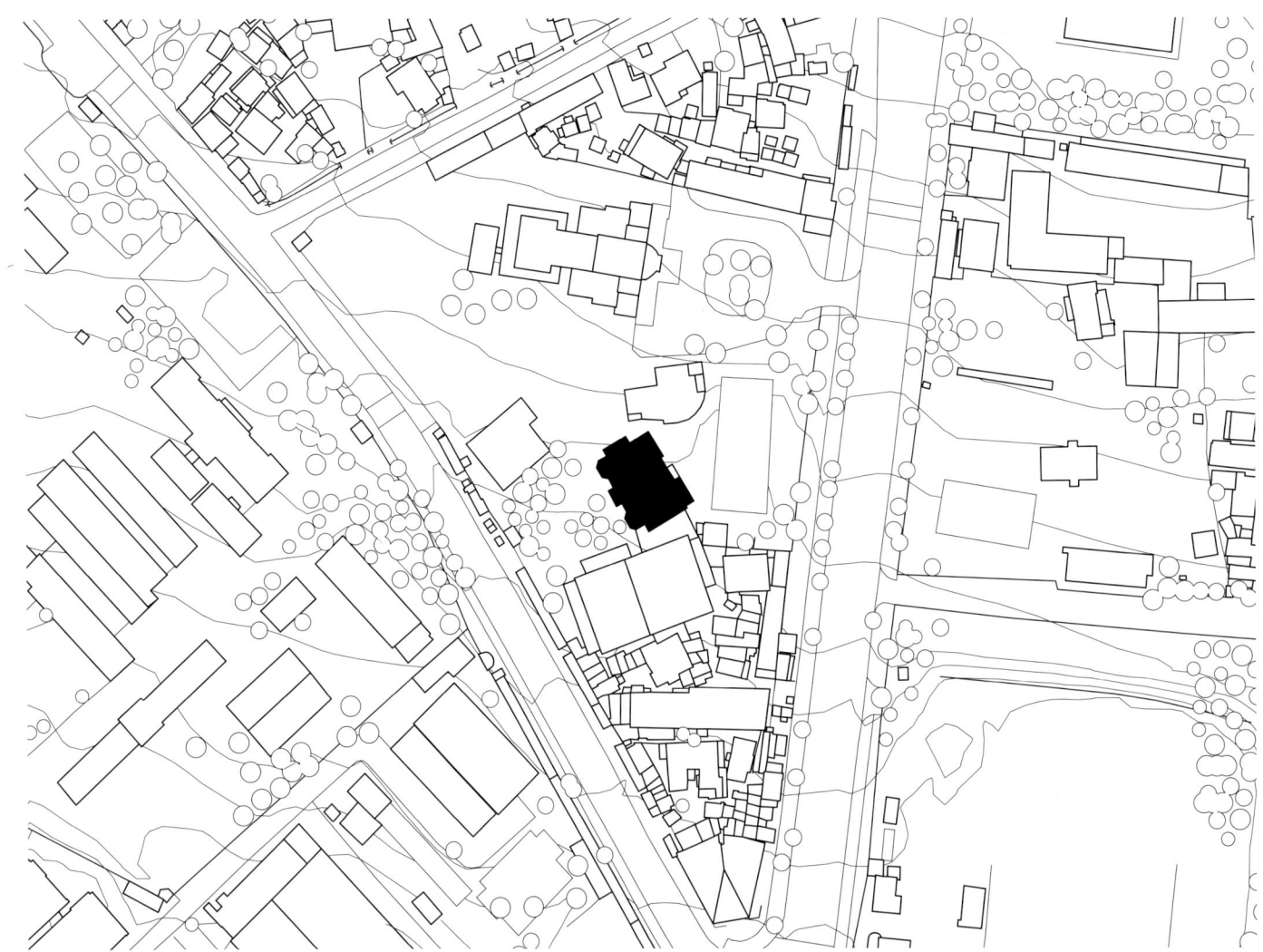

Site plan 1:2000

day and a sleeping room at night. The children's bedrooms were on the rear side. The centre of the house was occupied by a big representative salon, according to Seifou, and the room was furnished with several sets of Louis XIV furniture and expensive Chinese carpets. The big salon got light from windows that faced the garden in the north-east and accessed by another veranda. The upper storey was purely used for storage (phone call on 21 April 2023).

According to Seifou, Haile Selassie invited Addis Ababa aristocrats to the house to present it as an example of modern construction, including modern Turkish-style toilets (phone call on 13 October 2022). During the 1950s, after a period in exile during the war, *Dejazmatch* Asfaw Kebede built a new house for himself on the same compound, and Seifou and his siblings lived in the house by themselves after he returned from his studies in England. The house was nationalised in 1974–1975 and used by the new government as an assembly hall. Its demolition in 2021 provoked an outcry from local professionals, as an outstanding example of Addis Ababa's early architecture was forever lost.

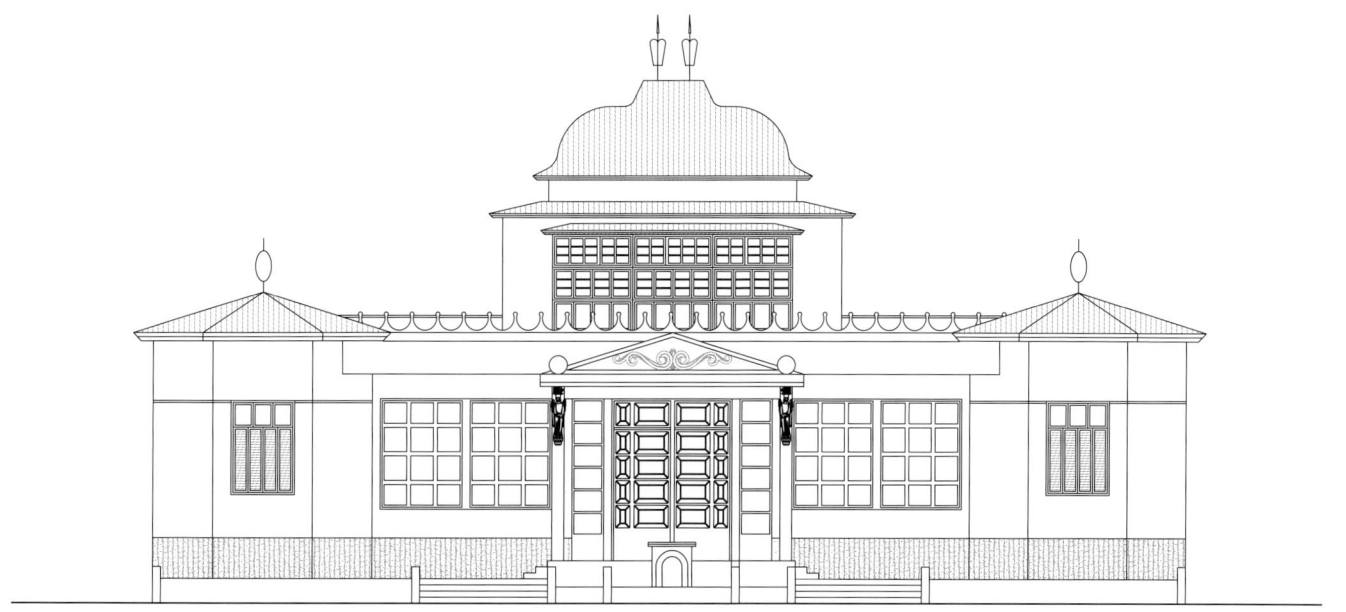

Elevation south-west

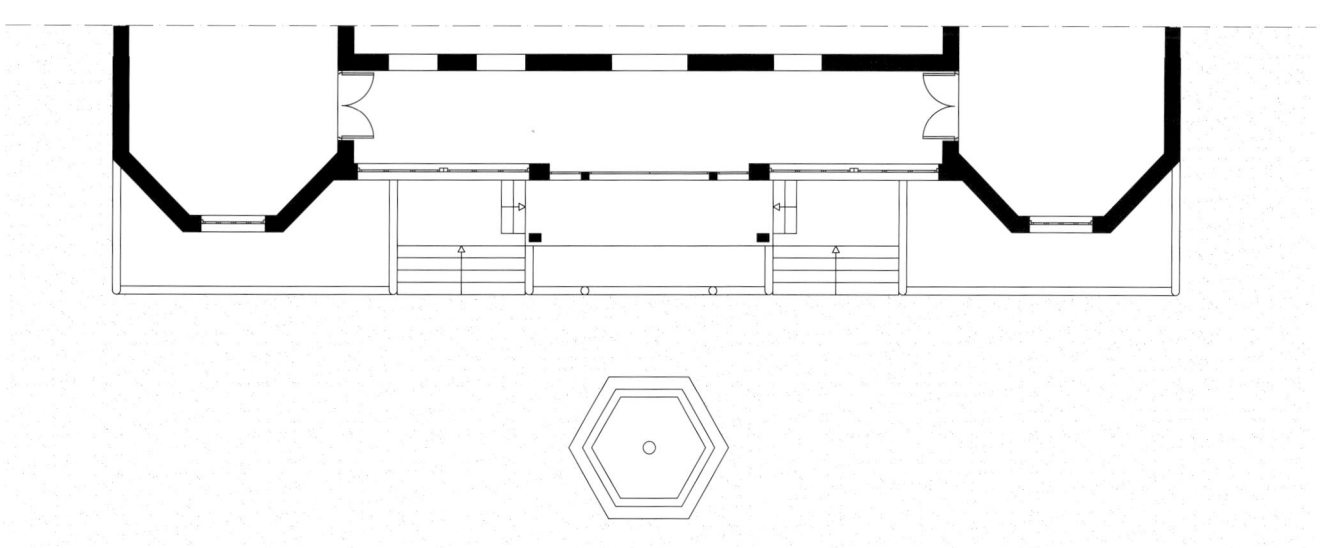

Ground floor (excerpt)

The Case Studies 147

Eastern part of the building seen from the north (photo retouched)

View from the north showing the building length of almost 50 metres

Former main entrance on the south

Octagonal towers

Ras Birru W / Gabriel Residence (Addis Ababa Museum)

The building is located on a hill close to Meskel Square, which is now a site where big public gatherings and festivals take place. During the last century, the building operated as a multi-family residence and later as a restaurant. It was renovated in the 1990s to facilitate its reuse as the Addis Ababa Museum. It used to be the residence of *Ras* Birru Wolde Gabriel, a nobleman raised in the palace of Menelik and the governor of Konta, Welega, Sidamo, and Keffa regions (Fasil and Gerard 2007: 226).

Ras Birru was the father of *Dejazmatch* Ayalew Birru, who was mentioned earlier, and a very powerful figure who enjoyed many favours from the Emperor. Mérab described him as a 'young man in his thirties, his martial figure bears the hallmarks of command and authoritarian absolutism' (Batistoni and Chiari 2004: 181). Simultaneously he was notorious for planning expensive *gibirs*, to which many of the city dwellers were invited (Giorghis and Gerard 2019: 248).

Woodwork of wall openings

Roof finials

Interior use as a museum and exhibition space

Closed veranda space in front of the vestibule

The *Ras* Birru Residence was built in the 1920s (gtz, 2009) about 1.7 kilometres south of and with a line of sight to the *Ghebbi*. It was placed on top of a hill in what was still a vast marshy area at the time. The site was prominent, as the road towards Zuquala, a volcano with a holy crater lake, passed west of it (now Debre Zeit Road).

The building is elevated from the ground thanks to a masonry foundation made out of stone. While the main entrance was originally located on the southern side, the northern façade points towards the imperial compound and is characterised by its many covered verandas of impressive sizes. Seen from the north, it is possible to observe a division into four parts aligned in a row by their different heights and roofs. The building has a total length of almost 50 metres and a depth of 13 metres. The massive core, built from stone and *chikka* and strengthened with wooden beams (Giorghis and Gerard 2019: 248), measures 43 × 8 metres. The string of different verandas, most of which are covered by curtain walls, are placed in front of the core on three sides and interconnected by wooden staircases that add substantially to the

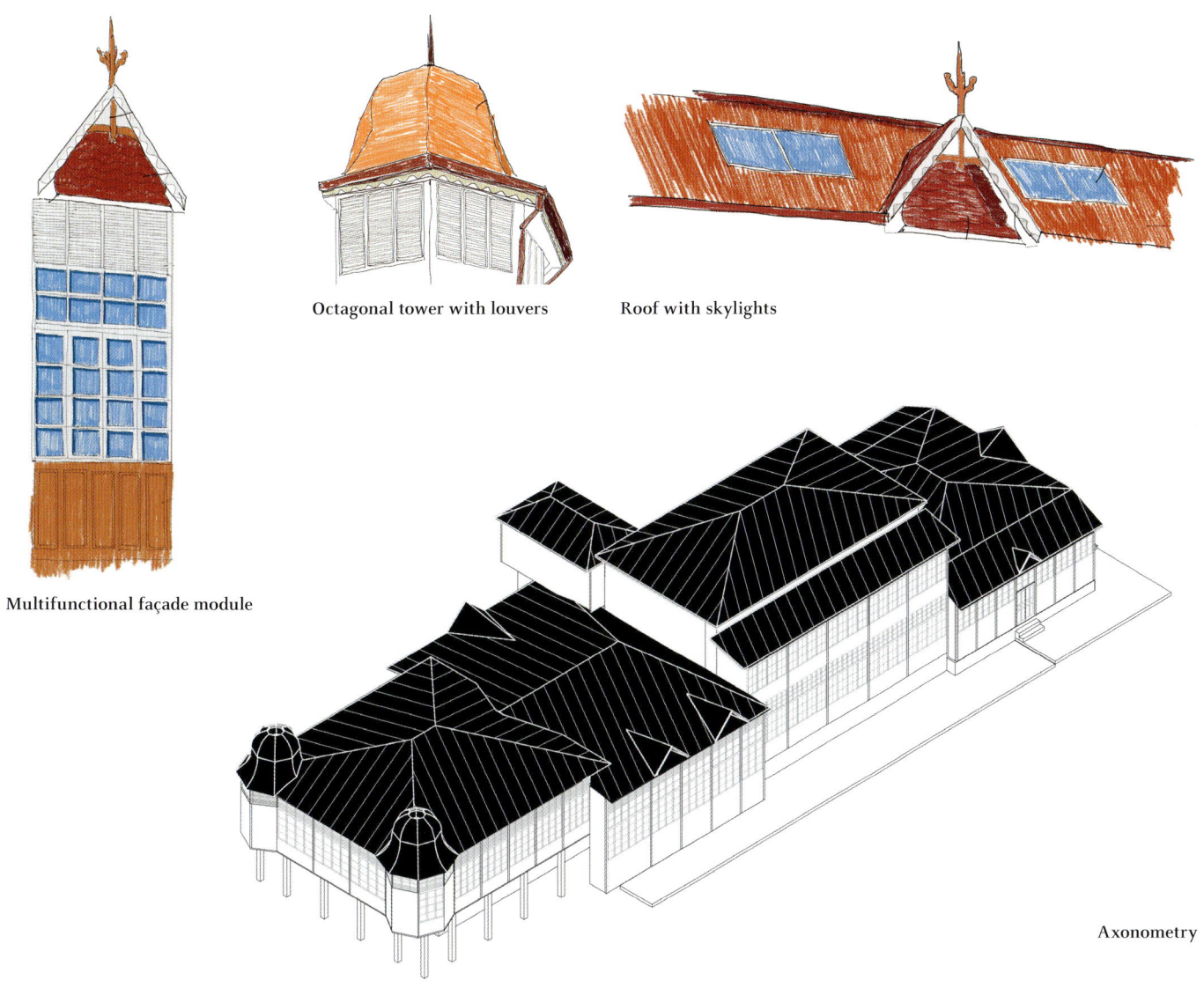

Multifunctional façade module

Octagonal tower with louvers

Roof with skylights

Axonometry

spatial complexity of the building. The depth of the verandas differs from 2.5 to 3.8 metres. The veranda space in front of the vestibule measures about 6 metres in height. While the massive core is pierced by doors and windows, the verandas themselves provide a climatic buffer zone between the inside and the outside. However, placed on the northern side of the building, the verandas did not capture solar gains, but rather protected the residents from rain and wind. Last but not least, the view connected to the imperial compound was important, as the Emperor used to communicate with his followers via semaphore. The curtain wall is constructed in a modular manner with a closed wooden balustrade at the bottom, fixed and movable windows, and fixed wooden louvers at the upper end of the façade.

While the ground floor contained a reception hall, a sitting room, and the vestibule, the upper floor was mainly reserved for the private use of the family. A generous cascade staircase leads to the upper floor, in contrast to a small staircase that leads to the private family quarters in the western part of the upper floor. Each of the rooms is connected to the

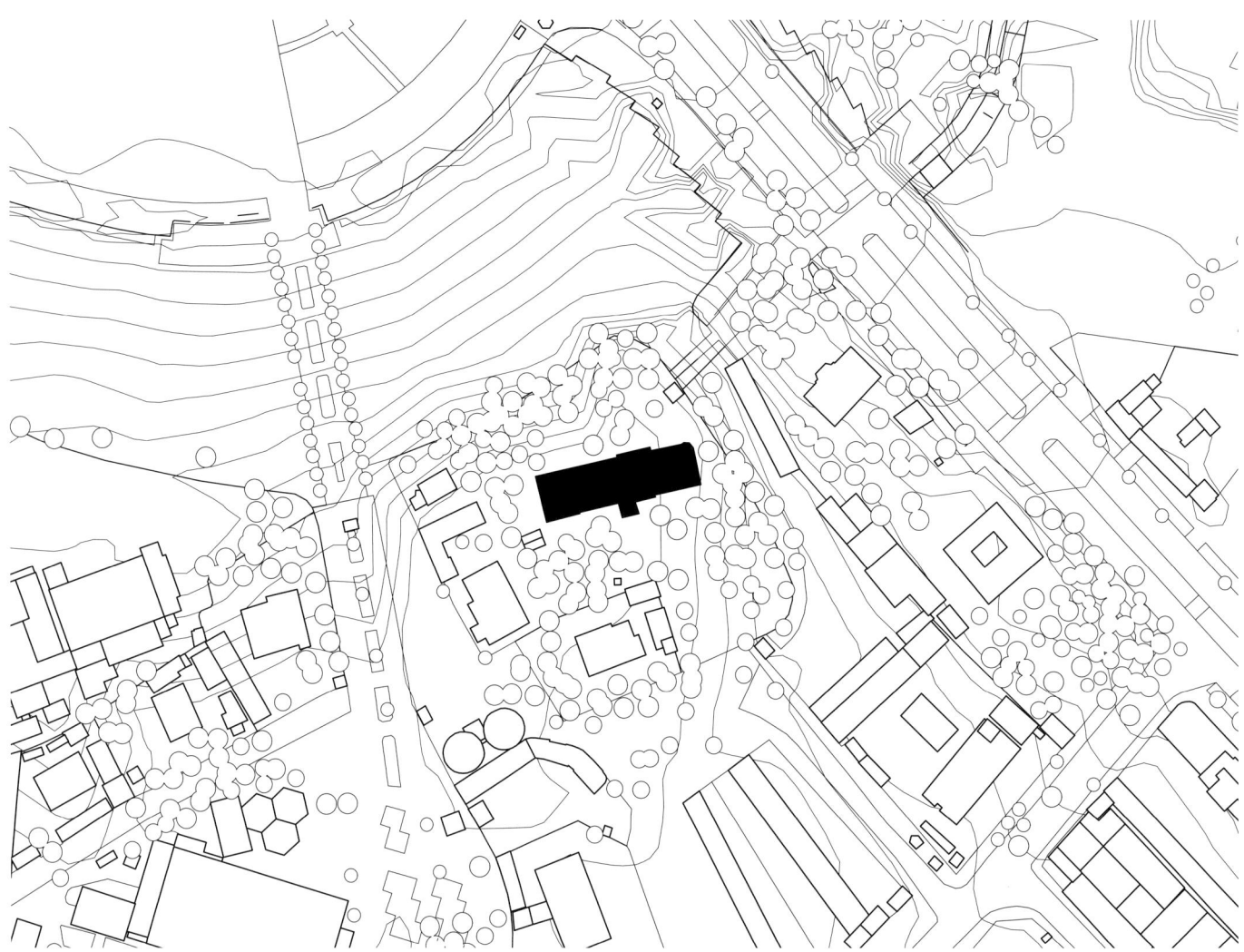

Site plan 1:2000

exterior veranda and also internally by a set of windows and doors. However, on the upper floor towards the east, there is a big space that has a more private character. The master bedroom was supposedly situated here. The two rooms underneath on the ground floor were used as service rooms. A secondary staircase may have been used by the servants. There are two remarkable octagonal towers in this part of the building. Their copula as well as the finials show a strong Indian influence. A third octagonal tower sits on the central part of the roof. Another curious feature is an elevated, detached room on the southern side of the building. It is said to have served as a secret hiding place for *Ras* Birru. The roof is very expressive and formulates a well-proportioned landscape of metal sheets – a prestigious material at the time. There are relatively simple wooden fascias along the eves. The line of the eves is given more refinement by at least six pointed gables, all of which are crowned by sophisticated wooden finials. Together with the toppings of the domes and rooftops, the entire *Ras* Birru Wolde Gabriel residence has at least 16 Indian-style finials.

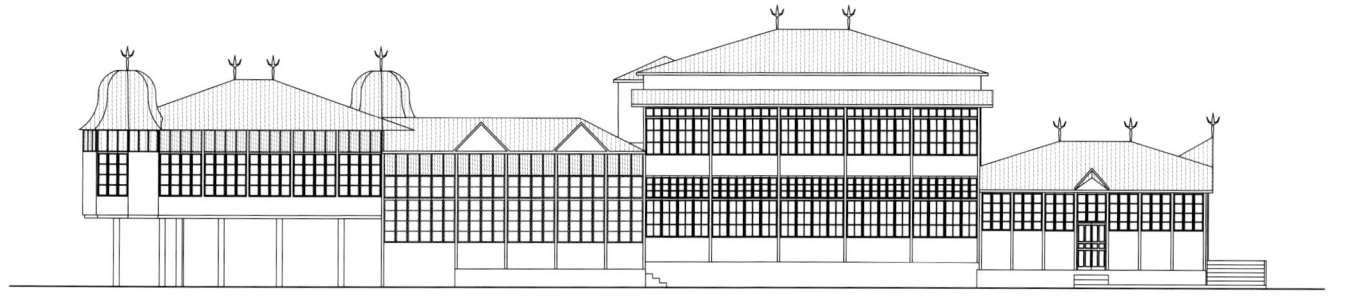

Elevation north

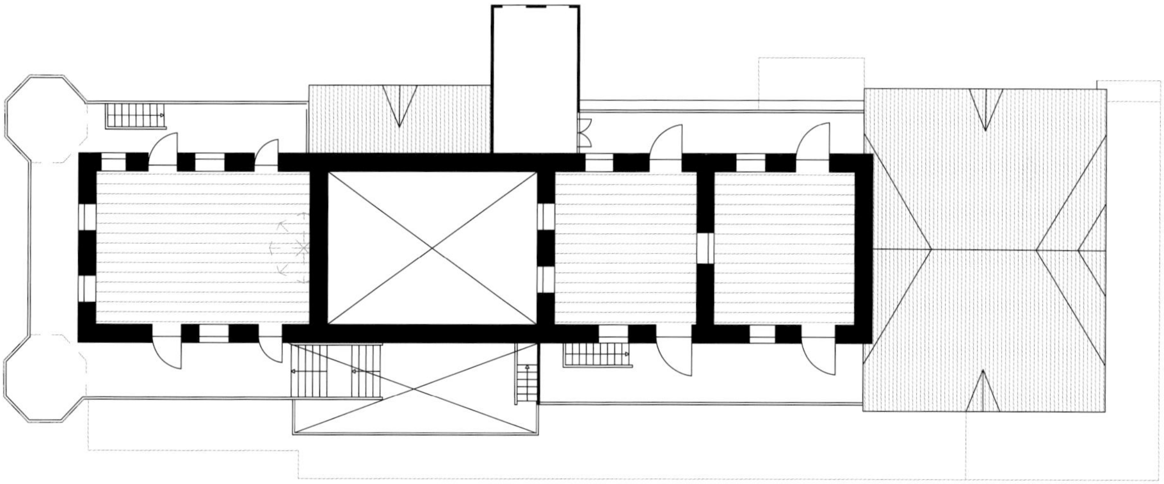

Upper floor

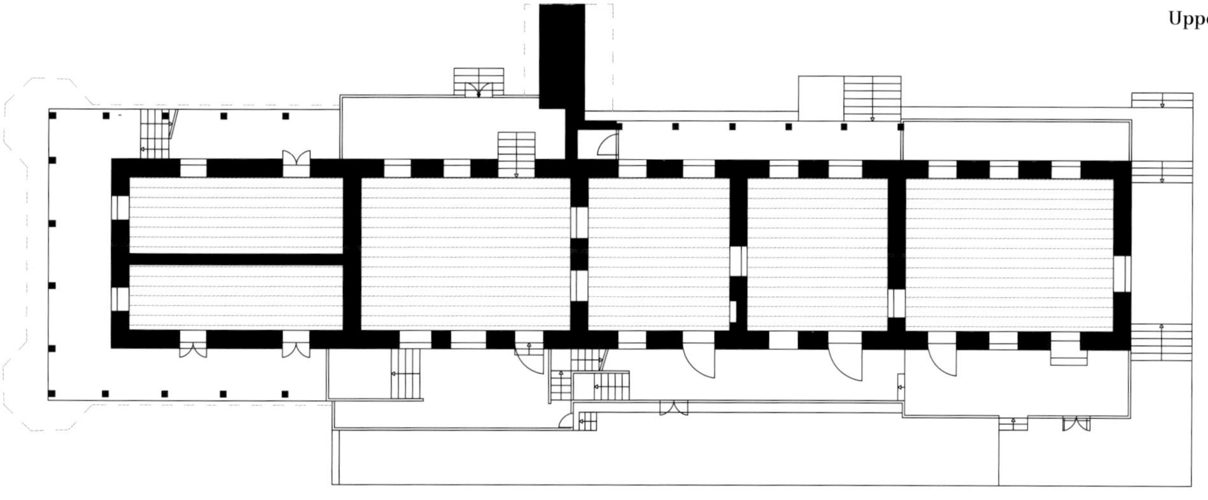

Ground floor

5m

The Case Studies 153

View from the west

Neo-classical façade from the south-west

The inner courtyards create a calm and safe outdoor space

Main entrance

The entrance area is spatially set in scene through elements like arches

Tafari Makonnen School

The Tafari Makonnen School is adjacent to Algeria Street in the north of Sidist Kilo. It was founded by Crown Prince *Ras* Tafari Makonnen, the future Emperor Haile Selassie I, in 1925 in order to promote a new educational system for young Ethiopians. In his inauguration speech for the students, the regent proclaimed enthusiastically: 'This school is an instrument which will operate on our country's behalf through the knowledge which God gives to each of you according to your lot, once you have matured in wisdom and have become vigorous in intelligence. So, I beg of you to help the school which nurtures you, give you the food of knowledge: to see that it does not shrink but expands, that it does not fall but grows in strength' (Link Ethiopia, n.d.). This ambition was in line with Menelik's vision for educating the Ethiopian youth because education was understood to be an indispensable tool for maintaining Ethiopia's independence. The curriculum included French, Arabic, English, mathematics, chemistry and physics, history, geography, gymnastics, and sports, as well as Amharic (Link Ethiopia, n.d.).

 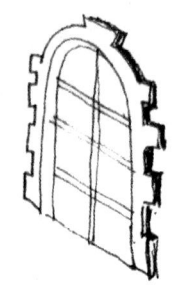  

Foyer with wooden staircase   Arched windows   Indian lantern   Main entrance

Entrance with Tafari Makonnen School sign   Regulae are perfectly framed with two rectangular windows

While the building is said to have cost 300,000 Maria Theresa shillings, according to the crown prince's chronicler, he spent 150,000 ETB of his personal treasury to realise the school. In return, as a memorial to himself, he named it: Tafari Makonnen School (Batistoni and Chiari 2004: 147). It is now called Entoto Polytechnic College.

The building is symmetrical in elevation and floor plan. The building partly sits on a basement floor that compensates for the inclined terrain. The elegant front façade consists of a small two-storey central section with a beautifully curved Indian-style lantern above the roof. The structure is situated between two symmetrical one-storey wings, each with a row of eight rectangular windows followed by three ashlar-shaped arched windows at the ends (Milena and Chiari 2004: 147). All the windows are 90 centimetres above the ground, above a plinth, and on a cornice. The four windows on the upper floor also have ashlar-shaped arches. The façades and decorative elements are built of stone, while the window frames are made of wood and sometimes appear very narrow and long, as is typical of Armenian architecture.

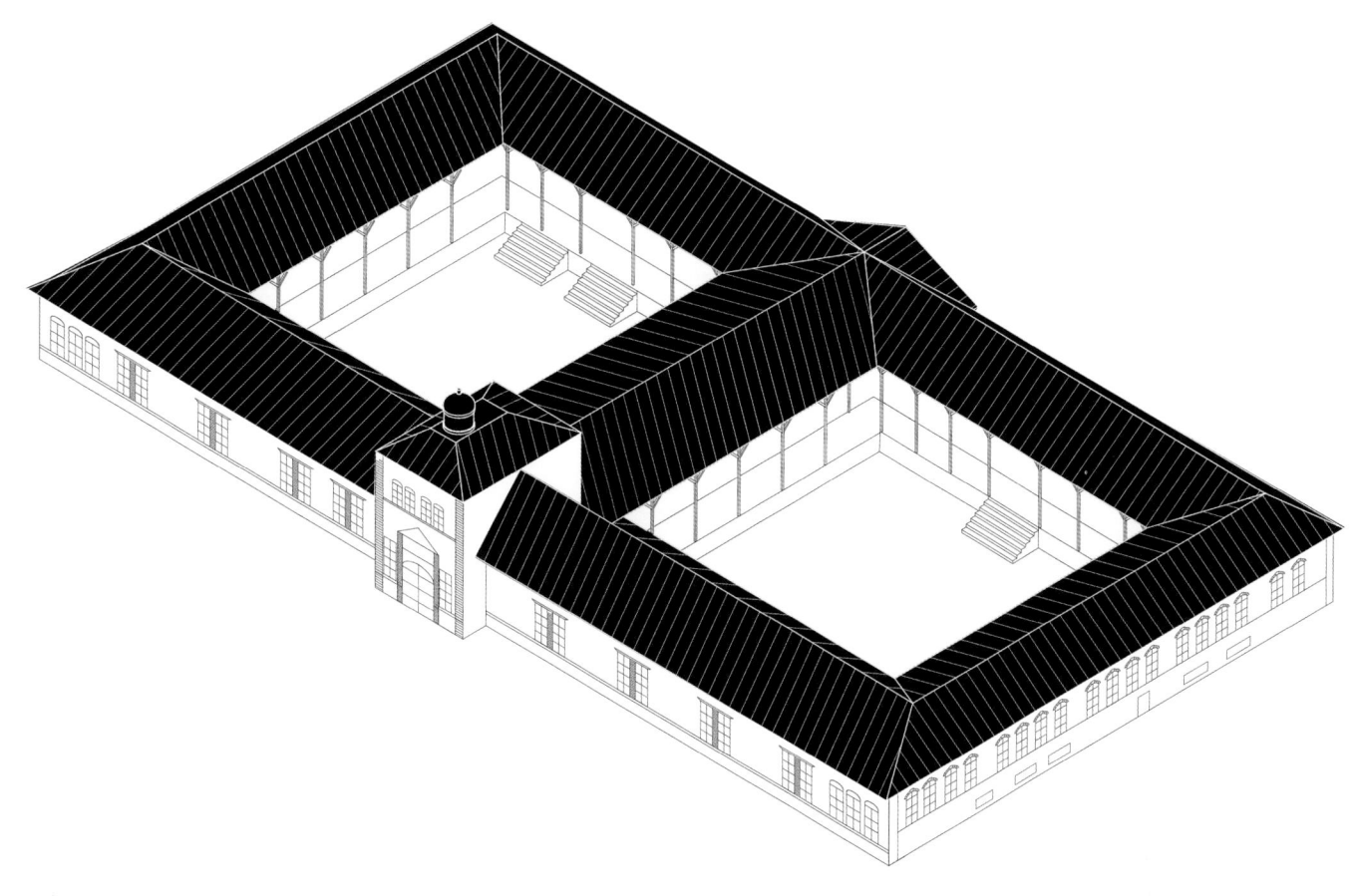

Axonometry

The school complex is built entirely of stone and the walls are ashlar masonry.
The building measures approximately 60 × 30 metres and is symmetrically organised around two main courtyards that give access to the classrooms through a veranda. Classrooms are placed one next to another and verandas are guarded by wooden handrails and a thin wooden structure holding the slanting roofs. The concept of the perimeter veranda that is typical of the Addis Ababa Style has been inverted into a circular access corridor. The wooden doors are wide and the ceilings of the rooms are high, which allows for good natural ventilation. Furthermore, thanks to the double height of the spaces, the numerous windows, and the direct view of each room to the courtyard, the spaces appear very bright, too.
The two green courtyards are divided by a datum block in the middle that is located in the prolongation of the central access, containing a foyer and a central hall. The spatial composition of the foyer space is particularly interesting. The stairs are in fact framed in a wooden structure consisting of arches and pilasters that give the entrance a rather

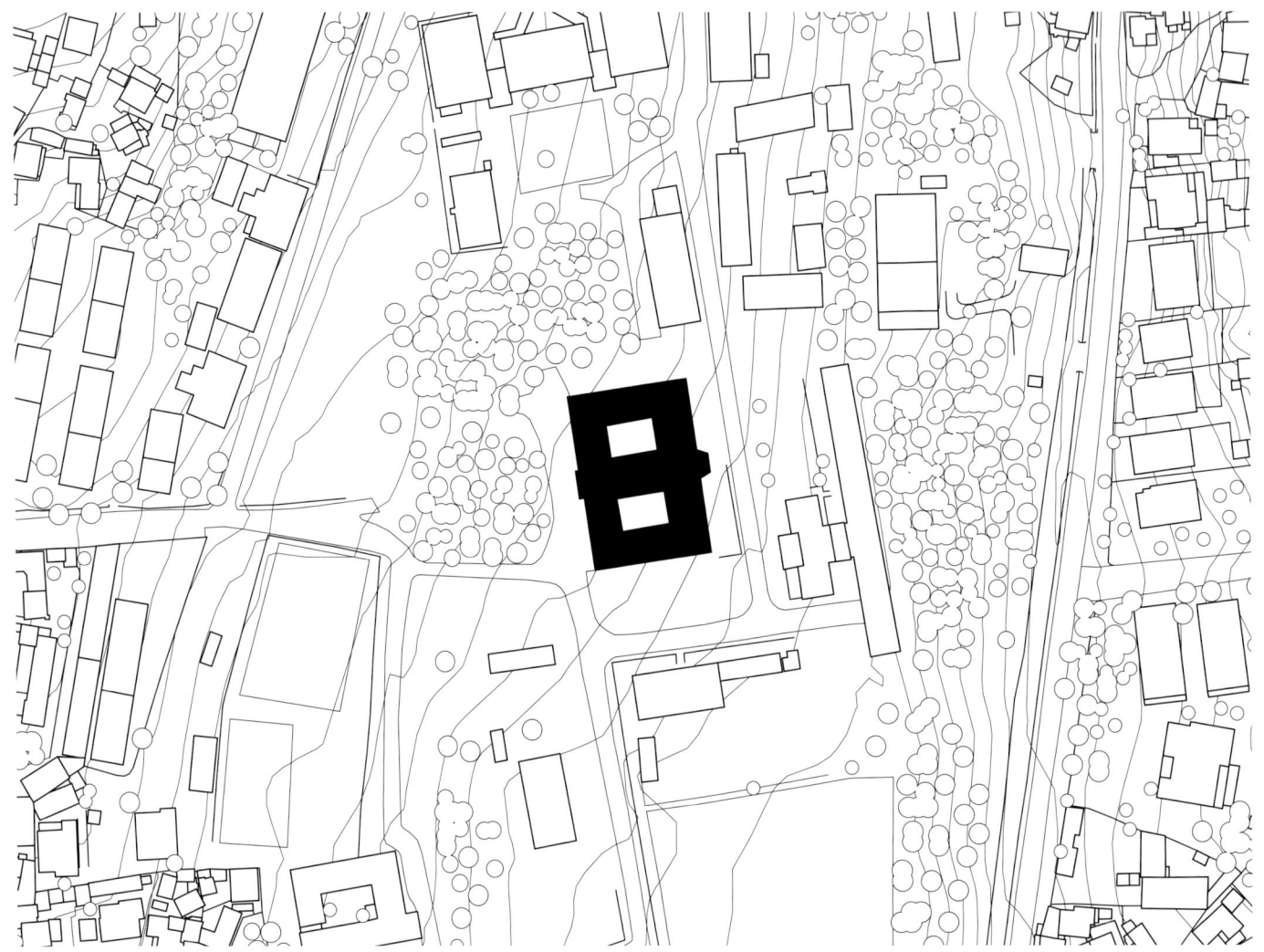

Site plan 1:2000

scenographic aspect. There are two windows in the middle of the stairs that overlook the central hall of the building.
The school is built from cement and chiselled stone (Ignimbrite pyroclastic). With this choice of materials, the Crown Prince wanted to underline his desire to modernise the country. The building generally seems to be strongly influenced by European neo-classical architecture.
In conclusion, Tafari Makonnen School can be considered an innovative institution for a new educational system in Ethiopia. It shows different influences, from European to Indian to Armenian. Local influences seem to have been reduced to a minimum. It offers a first glimpse of the architectural styles that the future Emperor Haile Selassie would favour. As explained by Fasil Giorghis, it was under the reign of Haile Selassie that the Addis Ababa Style started to be seen as outdated (Fasil Giorghis, Talks on Local Building Types: The Addis Ababa House, TU Berlin, 18 May 2021).

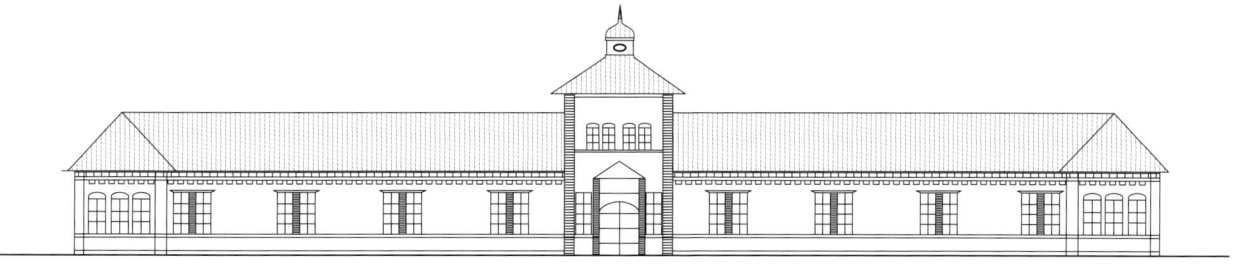

Elevation west

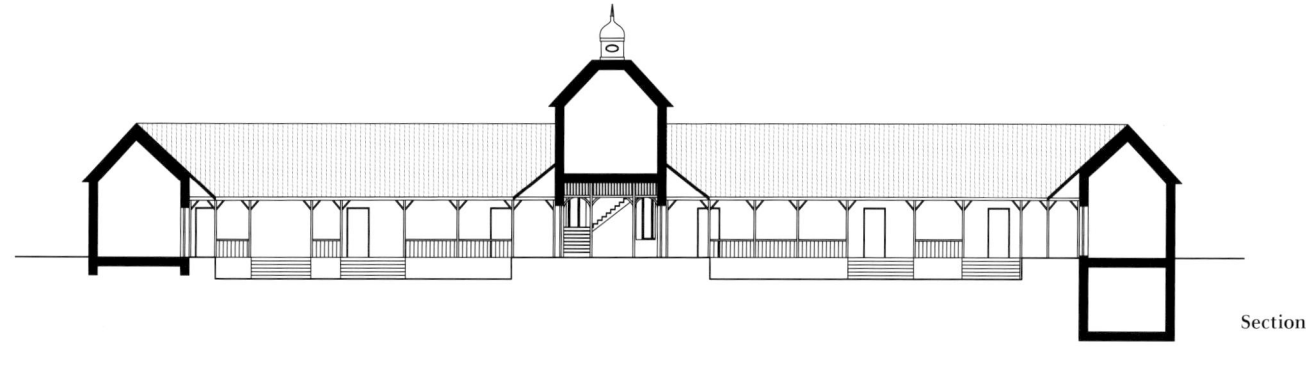

Section

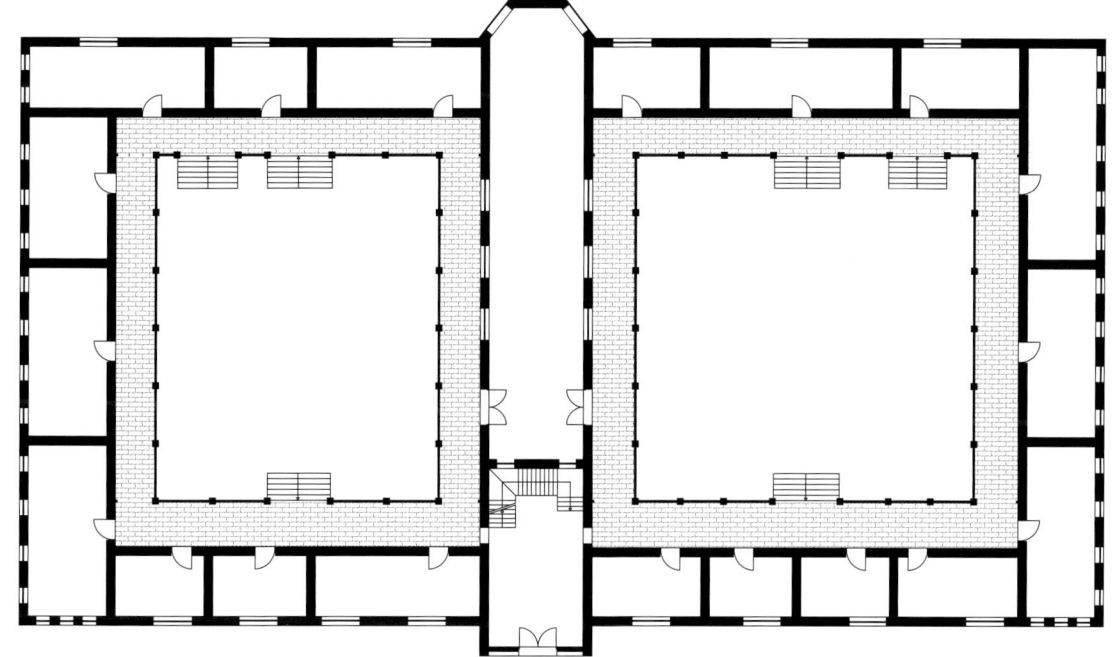

Ground floor

The Case Studies 159

View from the south-west

School façade towards the backyard

Wooden elements building the main façade

Verandas being used for outside circulation

Ground floor indentation creating shade for recreational space

Fit. Atnaf Seged Residence

Fitawrari Atnaf Seged Residence is in the Kasanchis quarter and was probably built during the reign of Zewditu between 1916 and 1930. The building is said to be the design of the Indian Wolli Mohammed, who also designed St. Gabriel Church (Batistoni and Chiari 2004: 168). *Fitawrari* Atnaf Seged served as a commander during the Menelik and Taitu reigns. He was killed in the Battle of Maychew in 1936. After his death, the building was used as a police station. After being nationalised in 1974, it was later turned into an elementary school, which it still is today.

Its original use, however, was as the main residence of *Fitawrari* Atnaf Seged. At the time, the building was perceived as modern, partly because of the use of cement and lime in the construction of the masonry walls (Giorghis and Gerard 2019: 272).

The entire building sits elevated on a stone foundation with a height of approximately 1.2 metres. This foundation formulates a perimeter platform that can be reached only by a single staircase in front of the main entrance to the south. The building has two storeys and a rectangular, almost square-shaped

Inside view of the circular wall

Wooden panels and curtains being used for further shading

Closer look at a window

Closer look inside a classroom in use

plan, which is enveloped by a perimeter veranda on both storeys. The masonry core measures 12 × 15 metres and as the perimeter veranda has a depth of 1.5 metres, the total dimensions of the building are 15 × 18 metres at a height of 9.5 metres from the ground to the eaves.

As the veranda posts are very slender and high, the space created at ground level appears very open and welcoming. The south-facing parts of the upper-level veranda were later covered with a wooden curtain wall, which is typical of the Addis Ababa Style (Giorghis and Gerard 2019: 272).

Two additional volumes are placed harmoniously onto the primary structure: an octagonal tower at the front and a smaller detached rectangular volume at the rear. The latter is made of bricks and contains toilets and a kitchen. Two staircases connect the storeys, bridging the impressive height difference of 4.8 metres. On the east side, there is an open, wooden staircase attached from the outside to the perimeter veranda, which is currently in a terrible state. A second wooden staircase sits in an extra room inside. There is also a natural stone fireplace in the living room on the western side of the building.

Tower extension

Façade element

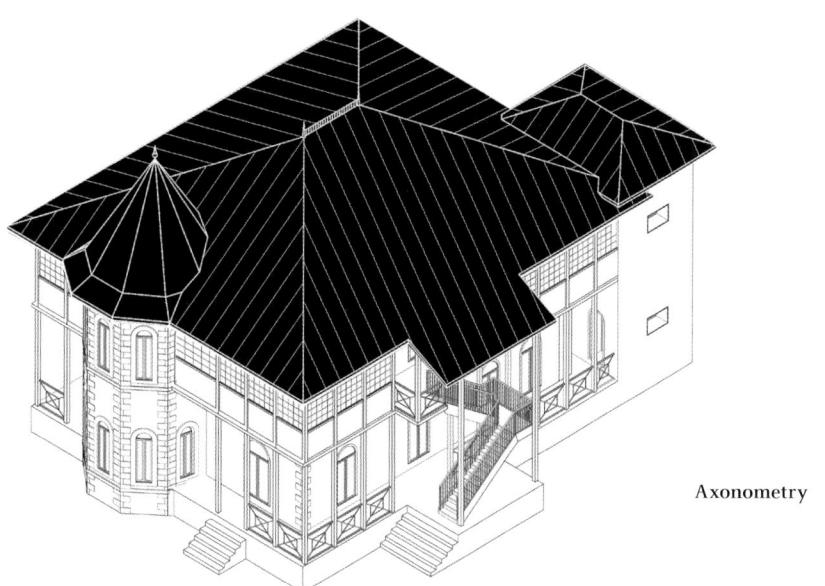
Axonometry

We know a great deal about the construction of the building thanks to a detailed survey from 2019 by Addisu Yisma, EiABC. The slab between the storeys is realised with wooden joists of 15 × 20 centimetres, which were sourced about 500 km from Addis Ababa in the Ginir Bale mountains. Due to the large size of the rooms, there is a wooden support of 20 × 40 centimetres in the middle. As the only available stiff material at the time the foundation was made of stone, with strip foundations under the load-bearing walls of 140 centimetres in width. All the walls are load bearing and 70 centimetres thick and made from stone masonry, which was then plastered with lime and cement.

The roof, which is covered with corrugated iron sheets, has a structure made of timber roof joists and forms two pitched hip roofs. The tower is crowned by a pointed, octagonal pyramidal roof with an Indian-style finial.

The majority of the doors and windows are made of wood and have a characteristic round arch, including the small windows of the beautiful tower-like structure. This feature is known to be an Armenian influence. Wooden shutters are

Site plan 1:2000

placed on the inside of the windows to darken the rooms. The flooring of the interior spaces is wooden parquet, with squarish terrazzo tiles on the lower veranda.

The building shows a range of rather simple ornamentation. Most of the ornamental features also have a structural purpose. Wooden fascias draw the line of the rectangular eaves, which is only interrupted by the octagonal tower. The wooden structure formulating the perimeter envelope of the verandas has nicely carved posts, capitals, and a simple yet beautiful balustrade with wooden crossings. Last but not least, the curtain wall, with its squarish glazing, has been realised with graceful accuracy.

Sadly, some parts of the building are now deteriorating. Nonetheless, local initiatives and architects are proposing ways to restore this historic building and use it in a more appropriate manner.

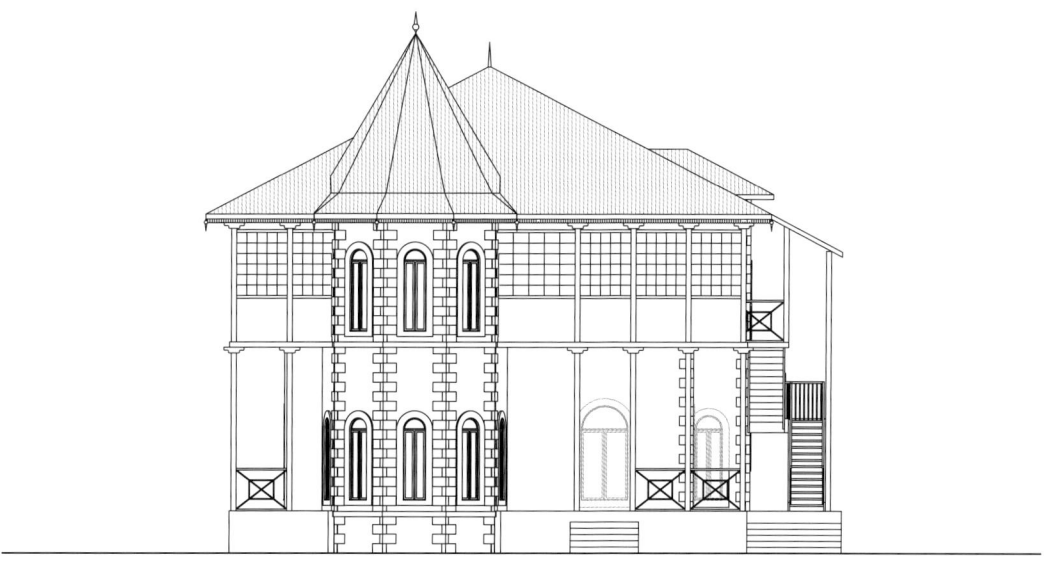

Elevation south

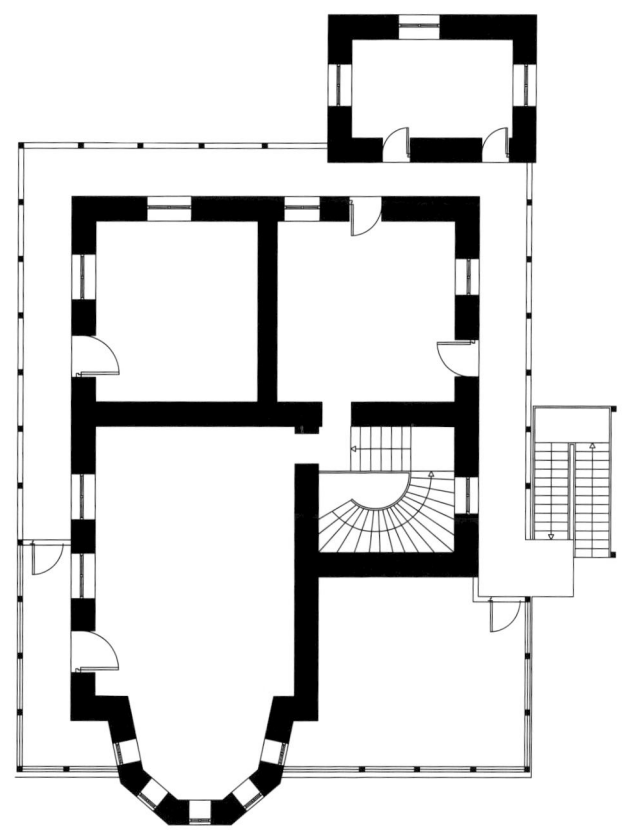

Upper floor

The Case Studies 165

Model by Yonas Tukuabo

3

Genotype
Influence
Analysis

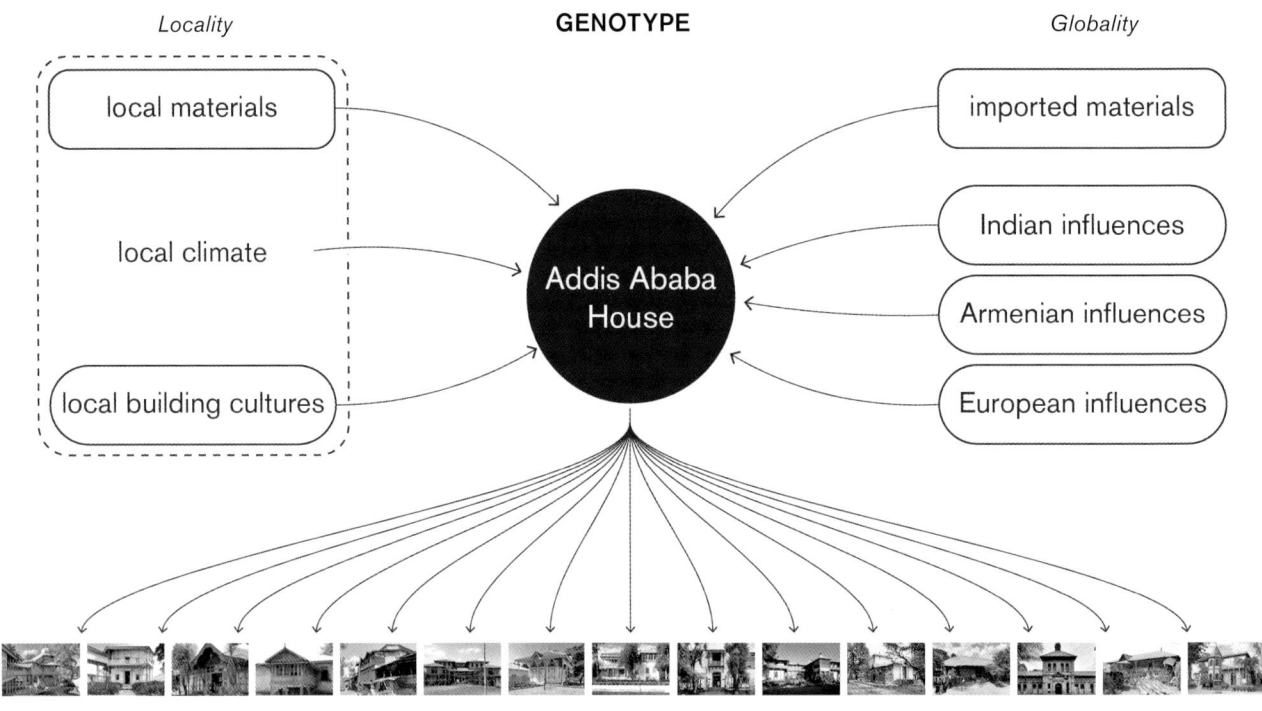

Influence diagram

The Genotype of the Addis Ababa House

As already mentioned in the introduction, this book tries to show the underlying architectural logic of Addis Ababa Style buildings in their embeddedness in local resources, local climate, and craftsmanship – a result of a refined, cosmopolitan approach to architecture that was open to foreign influences while also valuing the indigenous, vernacular construction knowledge of Ethiopia. Architecture has always been a result of its geographical and socio-cultural context. The ambition of builders was always to create the most out of the available resources. Sometimes, scarcity can be a medium for intelligent solutions because the need for thermal comfort, functionality, and beauty has to be realised with locally available means. This especially applies to the young Ethiopian capital between 1886 and 1936, because socio-political developments enabled a flourishing construction sector on the one hand, while on the other, the importation of industrial materials was very limited.

Locality, comprising local climate, local material, and local building cultures, is joined by globality, comprising different foreign building influences as well as a few imported construction materials.

The cosmopolitan setting of the construction sector in the early decades of Addis Ababa is often emphasised in literature. However, it remains unclear what these influences meant in regard to architecture. In *Old Tracks in the New Flower*, Batistoni and Chiari, neither of whom are architects, write: 'Over time, the complex and different aspects of Ethiopian cultures were influenced by those which were Armenian, European, Indian and Indo-Muslim in nature, through a dynamic process that turned out to be much more interesting than simplistic, evolutionary, and often ethnocentric perspectives. [We] (…) aim to show the result of that process is something different from and something more than the sum of the concurring elements' (Batistoni and Chiari 2004: 18). They conclude by describing a 'syncretic complexity' of influences that come together in the architecture.

Hybrid influences (the last available photo of the *Dej.* Asfaw Kebede Residence)

This corresponds with the opinion of the Ethiopian architectural historian Fasil Giorghis, who explained that the way these houses were built was a cosmopolitan endeavour most of the time. A typical construction site may have had a handful of Indian master craftsmen and many local workers, while an Armenian or European engineer or designer was also involved, translating the wishes of an Ethiopian client. This illustrates the 'mutations' that created the specific genetic code of the Addis Ababa House. Fasil Giorghis speaks of a 'hybrid' architecture. As a result, it is not easy to clearly categorise which feature belongs to which influence. This 'syncretic complexity' is illustrated on pages 186–189. It is a more or less random collection of buildings that were discussed in a telephone call with Fasil Giorghis in 2023.

While Ethiopian craft labour was not traditionally seen as very prestigious work, local decision-makers were very open to the introduction of foreign influences. Mérab counted the foreigners in 1909: 334 Greeks, 227 Arabs, 165 Europeans (including other nationals of the British Empire), 149 Indians, 146 Armenians, and 62 other nationalities such as Turks or Russians. This adds up to 1,083 foreigners in total, making up about one per cent of the total population of Addis Ababa at the time (Pankhurst 1967: 80). 'The [Indians] are said to have been the cheapest workers, and according to Mérab, built for half the price of the Greeks or a quarter of that of the Italians' (Pankhurst 1967:95). The Arab influence on the Addis Ababa Style has not been discussed in literature or in oral history to date.

This chapter aims to uncover the 'genotype' of the Addis Ababa House. Even though one cannot completely dismantle every layer in a deterministic way, it is possible to use the different design elements in architecture, be it an ornament, a geometrical form, or a construction technique, as a lens to trace back their potential origins.

Climate Influences

Due to its vast highlands, Ethiopia is also known as the 'Roof of Africa'. At the same time, the Great Rift Valley, which stretches from Lebanon all the way to Mozambique via the Red Sea, cuts right through Ethiopian territory. The resulting extreme geographical modulation of Ethiopia's territory is in strong correlation with its various climate types. This can be well observed in the Köppen climate classification. Indeed, differences in elevation influence on a temperature level as well as on wind distribution and speed, and latitudes have an impact on precipitation.

Ethiopia's geography ranges from equatorial rainforests with high rainfall and humidity in the south and south-west to Afromontane regions on the summits of the Semien and Bale mountains right through to desert regions in the north-east, east, and south-east of the country. Three climatic zones can be distinguished in Ethiopia, with specific differentiations at a local scale.

First, Alpine vegetated zones, also known as Dega, consist of a plateau with cool to mild temperatures and a rainy season from June to September.

Second, the temperate zone (Weyna Dega) and the hot zone (Qola) comprise the arid regions surrounding the plateau at a lower altitude. The rainy season is shorter, from July to August, and temperatures rise up to 28°C. However, the heat intensifies below 1,000 m.

And finally, the Afar region and the eastern Somali region have a desert climate that is hot and dry throughout the year. Altitudes drop to 125 m below sea level. The Afar region is characterised by the Danakil depression and its settlement of Dallol, considered the hottest place in the world. The average temperature there is 35°C.

Addis Ababa, the capital of the country, is located on the plateau. The altitude of its districts ranges from 2,100 m to 2,700 m, resulting in a mild climate. The Köppen climate classification for Addis Ababa is Oceanic Subtropical Highland Climate. The temperature drops at night and heavy rainfall during the rainy season are further characteristics of the local climate of Addis Ababa.

Extreme heat, drought, and flooding are regularly occurring weather threats in Addis Ababa that are becoming more severe due to climate change (Woodwell Centre, 2023).

The following page describes Addis Ababa's climate through four criteria: sunlight, temperature, wind, and rain. All of the case studies analysed in Chapter 2 show interesting architectural adaptations to the local climate, dealing with one or several of these four criteria. Over time, some of the observed responses have become typological characteristics of the architecture of the Addis Ababa House.

The matrix on pages 174–175 shows a collection of climate influences on the Addis Ababa Houses that have been described in the previous chapter.

Subtropical highland climate in the Semien mountains (Dega)

Subtropical highland climate on the plateau (Dega)

Arid lowlands/hot semi-arid climate in the east of Ethiopia (Weyna Dega)

Hot desert climate in Danakil (Qola)

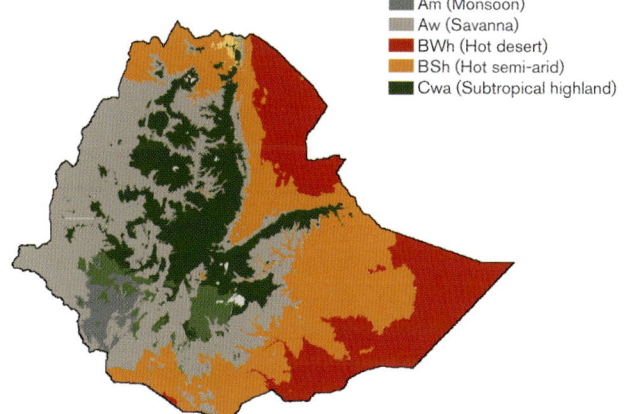
Köppen climate types of Ethiopia

- Am (Monsoon)
- Aw (Savanna)
- BWh (Hot desert)
- BSh (Hot semi-arid)
- Cwa (Subtropical highland)

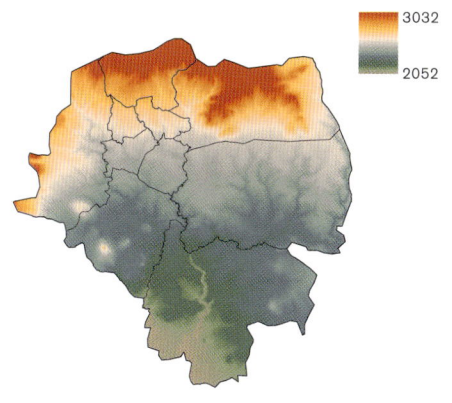
Elevation differences in Addis Ababa in metres above sea level

Influence Analysis

Sunlight

The sun shines on Addis for nine to ten hours a day. Outside of the rainy season, most days are without rain or significant clouds. In summer, sun rays reach an angle of 75°, but only 57° in winter. The Addis Ababa House shows various strategies to protect against these rays, which can easily make inside spaces uncomfortable. While verandas provide a buffer area between inside and out to regulate temperatures, shutters or caps are also specific sun protection systems.

Temperature

Stable throughout the year, the capital's temperature provides a comfortable outside atmosphere during the day. Indeed, average figures revolve around 23/25°C, except at the height of the rainy season in July and August when highs drop to 20°C. However, these temperatures drop at night, with lows around 10°C. Traditional *chikka* walls and other thick masonry are strategies to adapt to this dynamic. Their high inertness makes it possible to maintain a comfortable inside environment.

Rain

In Addis, 60 per cent of annual precipitation falls in only four months. To deal with such heavy rains, roofs are steep and overhanging and materials are as watertight as possible. Today, most buildings use corrugated iron sheets. Moreover, the risk of flooding is high, with an annual probability of 40/50 per cent in the region. Thus, lower materials are minerals, and many residences benefit from a raised ground floor to ensure maintenance and accessibility.

Wind

A chain of hills protects Addis Ababa from north-eastern winds. These are a result of the contrast between the thermal anticyclone of western Asia and Egypt and the equatorial low pressures. However, the wind is also a means of ventilation, important to maintaining a healthy and comfortable interior. Houses in Addis use natural ventilation systems such as atriums, high windows or wooden shutters, ventilation corridors, along with facing openings.

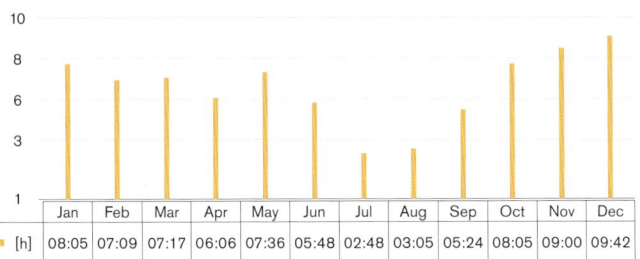

Sunlight hours in Addis Ababa per day

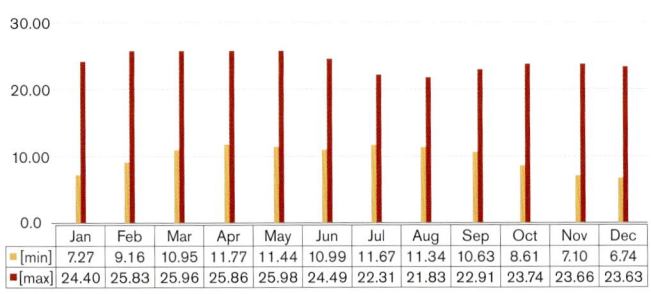

Minimum and maximum temperatures in Addis Ababa per day

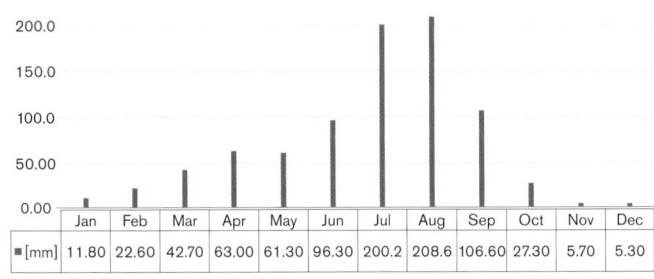

Rainfall percentage in Addis Ababa per month

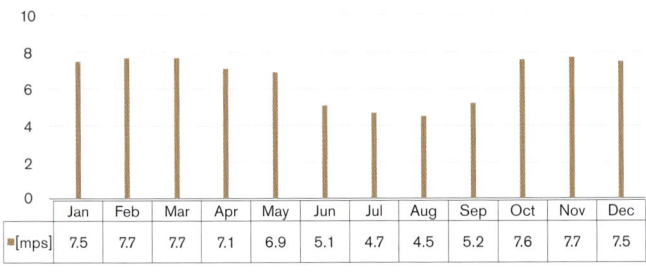

Wind percentage in Addis Ababa per month

Typical weather in Addis Ababa

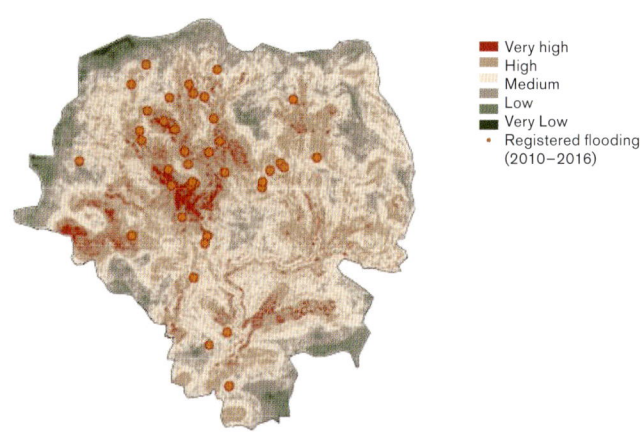

Flood risk possibilities in Addis Ababa (2022, The World Bank, SRTM, Land Cover).

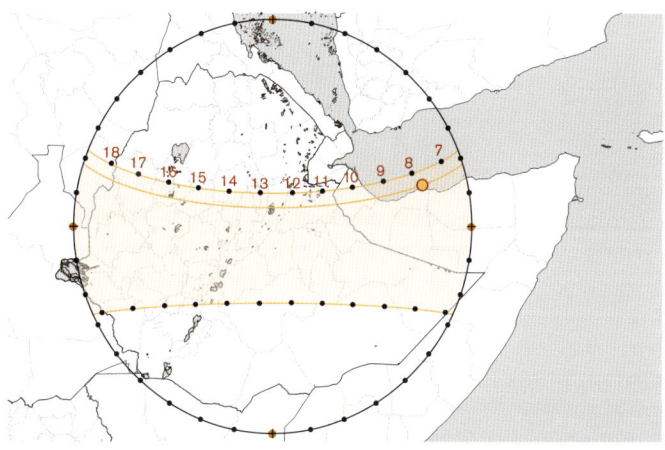

Solar chart of Addis Ababa

Influence Analysis

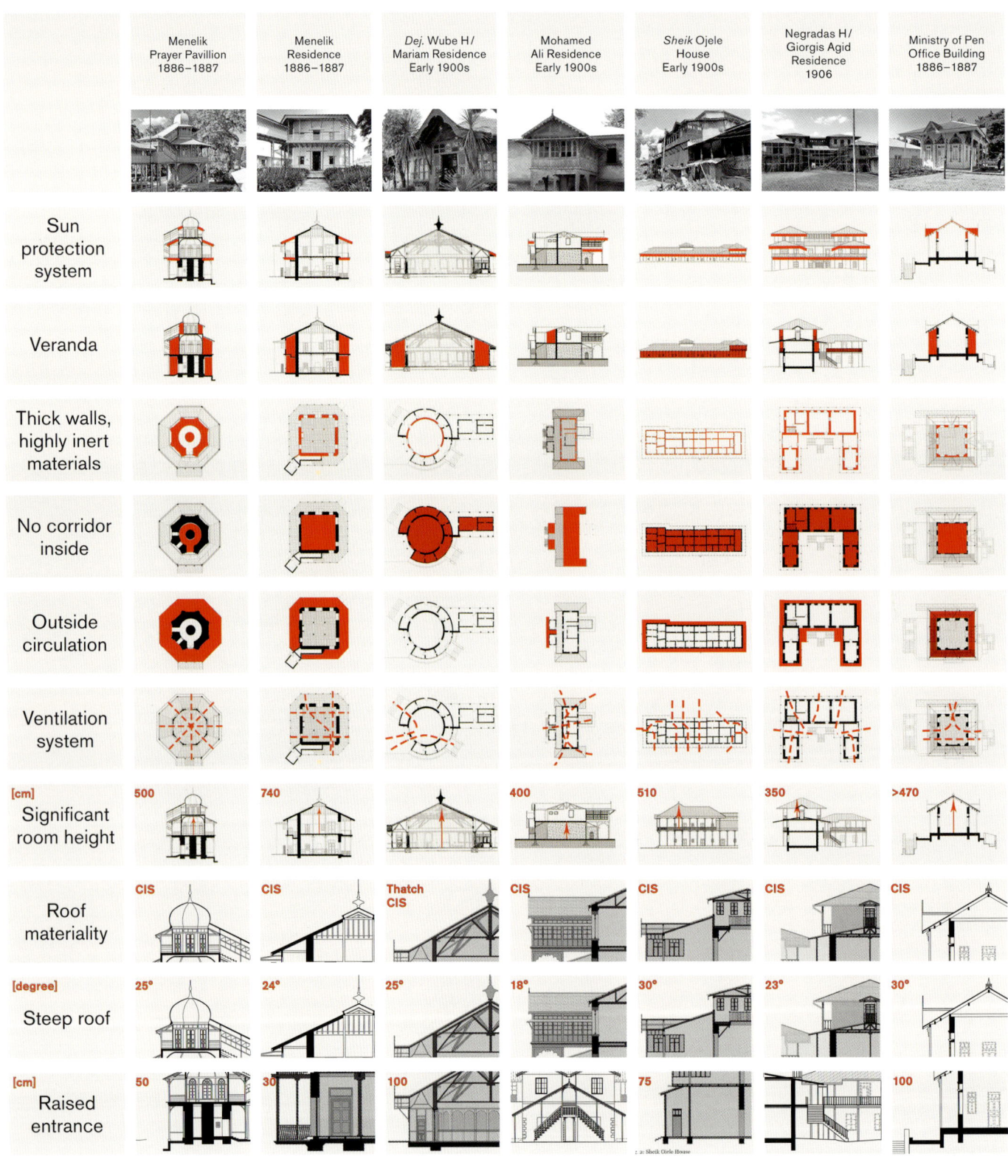

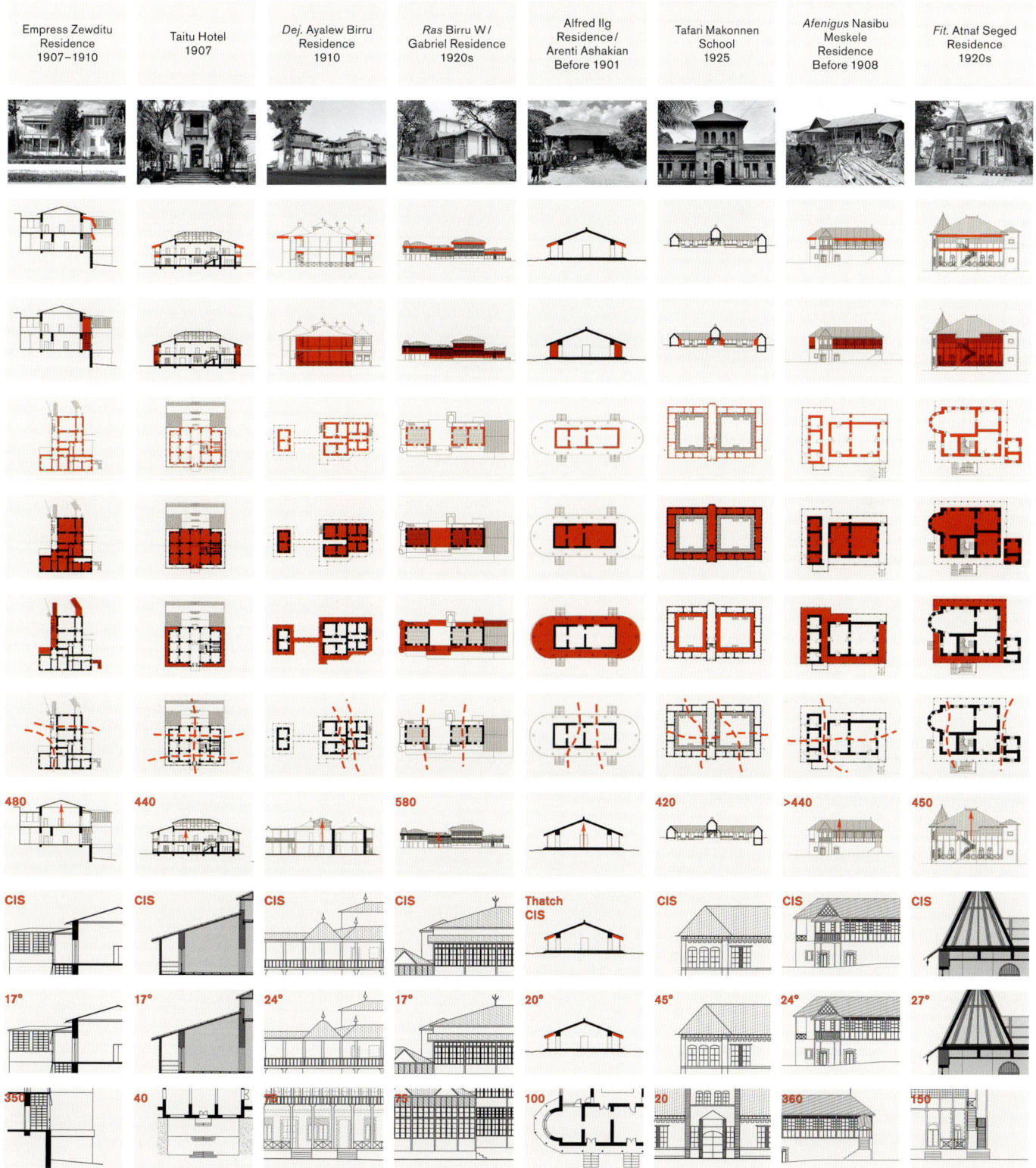

Influence Analysis

Material Influences

Before the foundation of Addis Ababa, by the end of the nineteenth century, construction skills only responded to local and vernacular types. Settlements were mostly nomadic and continuously at war with each other, restraining the architecture from further developing. With the establishment of the settlement in Entoto, Menelik's second capital after Ankober, an interest in developing a more representative and stationary, less ephemeral architecture began to grow. Menelik started to bring to the city different artisans from Gondar, a city known for its craftsmanship (Fasil and Gerard 2007: 178). At this time, specific materials could be found in the local types, such as the thatch used mostly for the construction of roofs and the walls made out of *chikka* (a mixture of fermented straw and topsoil) supported by a wooden framework. Here, there was massive use of wood that came from endemic trees that were not able to grow as quickly in order to compensate the deforestation.

Simultaneously to the foundation of the new capital, Addis Ababa, Menelik welcomed different builders from other parts of the world with the intention of benefiting from their building skills. Indians, Armenians, Europeans, and Arabs were successively integrating with the local culture. Along with their craftsmanship, they also introduced new materials. With the intersection of the local builders and the 'foreign' ones, construction methods were promoted in order to accelerate the architectural development of the city, while the importation of new materials remained quite limited due to the lack of accessibility (Fasil and Gerard 2007: 178). Thus, materials mainly came from different localities that were close to the capital, such as the Menagesha Forest and Ginir Bale. Natural stone and clay could be found on site in Addis Ababa.

The construction of the railway that connected Addis Ababa with the Red Sea and Djibouti was a turning point, as it allowed the development of trade and therefore the introduction of new materials to the local architecture.

In the early days of the foundation of Addis Ababa, specifically in the residences of governors during Menelik's Empire, it is still possible to see use of more local techniques, such as earth plaster and *chikka* walls. However, with the development of the city, the change from typical circular and oval floorplans to rectangular ones, and the establishment of the brick factory in 1907 and the first sawmills, it is clear that new materials and techniques particular of the 'foreigners' builders had been introduced.

With the exception of *Dejazmatch* Wube and Ilg's residences, roofs were made with corrugated iron sheets in all of the analysed case studies. This modern material allowed different shapes and slopes. Partly as found in the vernacular types, foundations were made of stone extracted from the bedrock and used in so-called rubble trench foundations. Wall materials and construction techniques changed depending on location in the building. In many cases, the ground floor always

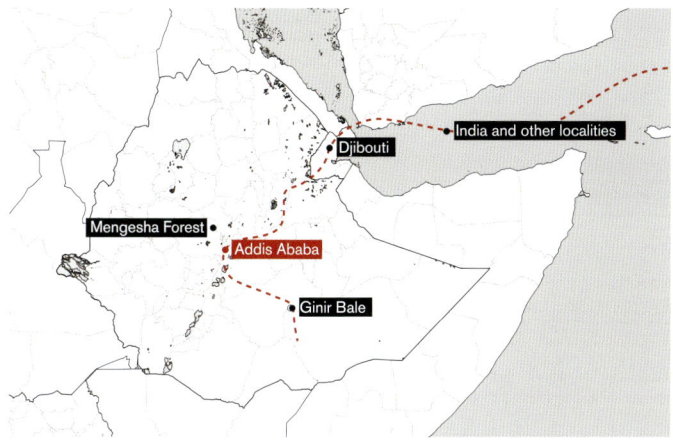

Material origins

Timeline of material influences 1/2

Before

Round oval floorplan. *Chikka* walls and stone foundations, thatched roof.

Menelik's first palace in Entoto.

1886

Establishment of Addis Ababa

Construction of Menelik's first palace. Prayer Pavilion features: stone foundations, wooden verandas, and a thatched roof.

Menelik's palace in Addis Ababa after it was rebuilt due to a fire.

Late 1800s

Bitwoded Haile Giorghis palace. Stone foundations, stone walls for ground and first floor, *chikka* walls for second floor, and wooden verandas.

1897

Arrival of Armenians to the city, opening of Anglo-Ethiopian trading relationships.

Early 1900s

Addis Ababa Restaurant. Round floor plan with adjacent rectangular layout, thatched roof, and introduction of windows panel façades.

1903

Introduction of corrugated iron sheets thanks to the arrival of the railway at Dire Dawa, Ethiopia. Mohamed Ali was the most important importer-exporter of iron sheets.

Mohamed Ali residence, Indian influence, stone walls plastered with mud, and wooden ornamental fascias.

Fitawrari Agunafer Sebberu Residence. Transition from the circular plan to the quadrangular. Construction methods: *chikka* walls and stone foundations.

1905

Increase in the Armenian population in the city.

1907

Establishment of the brick factory.

Materials and building components

Influence Analysis 177

uses stone masonry with *chikka* plaster, with the first floor using wooden panels (usually wattle and daub), protected by a roof and the adjacent veranda.

Due to the choice of materials, it is possible to observe a specific homogeneity between elements when looking at the framing. Although columns and beams vary in shape and dimensions, they are always made of wood. The same applies to the ornamental details and staircases: pediments, handrails, fascias, and roof coronations are always made of wood, with the exception of cast iron in some cases. Here, the use of wood is what allowed the craftsmen to achieve a variety of forms with a high level of details. Other building components like windows present a repetition in dimensions that does not go beyond 50 cm in width or height. Different materials such as wood and glass are used here.

The availability of the materials and imported craftsmanship are what promoted the development of the different typologies. Although some of the styles are more widely practiced than others, all are characterised by an aim to respond to the local climate and surroundings. The sum of all of these features is what makes the Addis Ababa House local on its own.

1908
The first steam roller in the city and the first sawmill appears. One of the first sawmills was built in the Menagesha Forest close to Addis Ababa.

1910s

St. George's Cathedral, rebuilt by an Italian engineer under Greek direction, has an octagonal layout. Use of masonry and bricks.

1915

Balambaras Shaka: wood panel walls, window façade, iron sheets, ornamental details in the roof, stone walls in the first floor.

1916

Coronation of Zewditu

Fitawrari Habte Giorgis House, Minister of War. Use of masonry and bricks. Built by European architects.

1920s

The church was designed by the Greek architect Balanos.

Residence of *Dejazmatch* Asfaw Kebede is built on stone foundations, with a glass window façade and wooden ornamental details.

Fitawrari Atnaf Seged Mengesha Residence, stone masonry walls, cement and lime for plastering, wooden curtain wall.

1930

Coronation of Haile Selassie I

1932

Ras Desta Hospital, the first building that used concrete.

Lagare, built in 1928–1929

1936
Italian invasion

Timeline of material influences 2/2

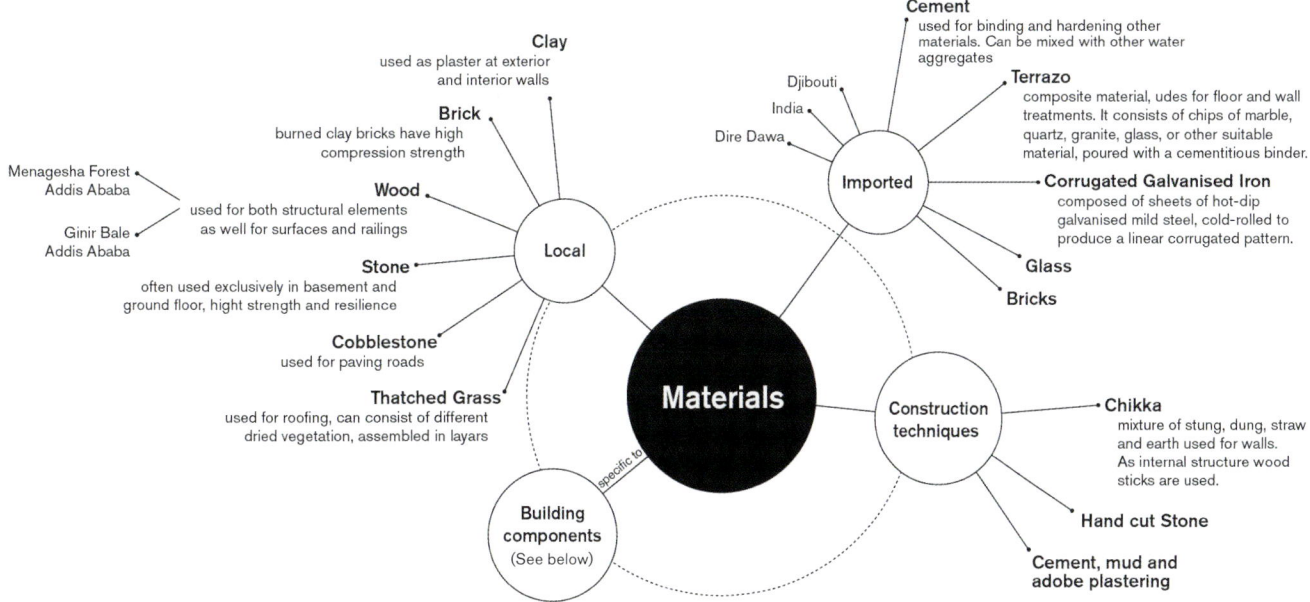

Materials description and uses

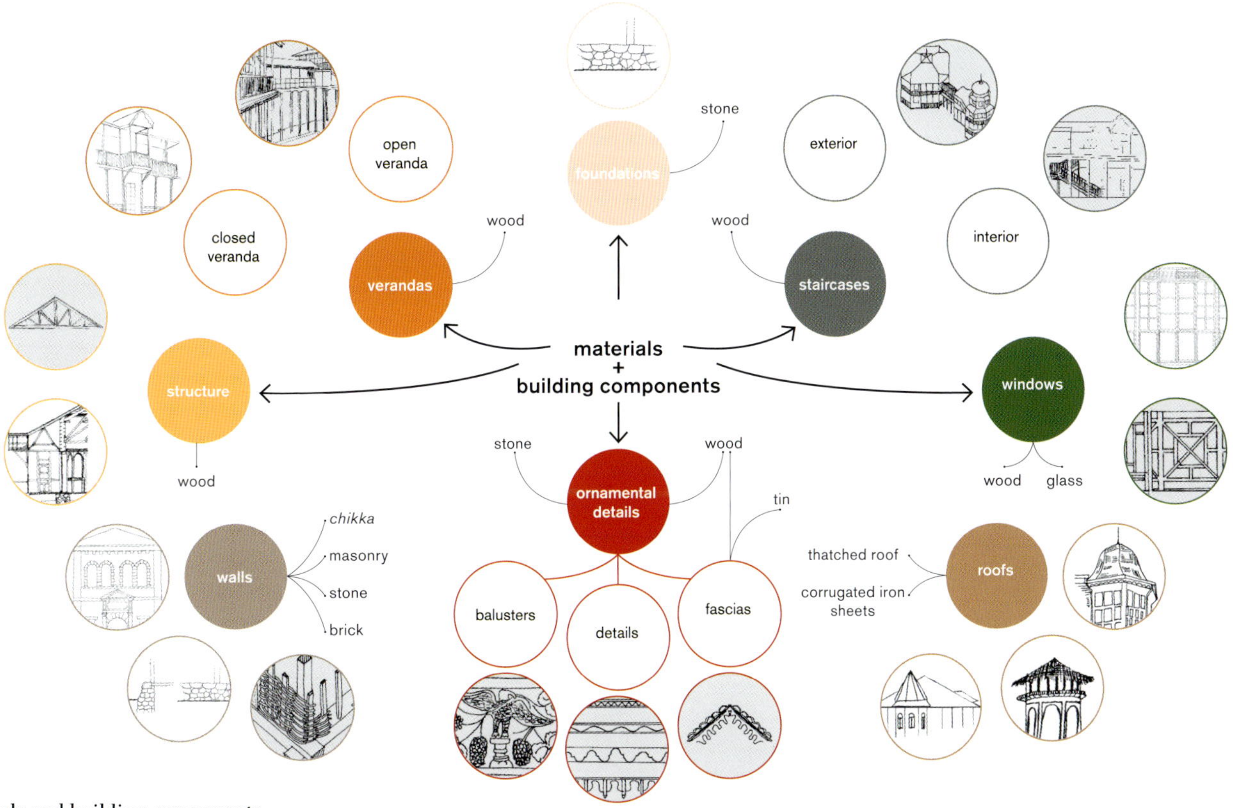

Materials and building components

Influence Analysis

Natural Stone

Natural stone is highly valued for its durability, aesthetic appeal, and low maintenance requirements. It has a compressive strength ranging from 50 to 300 MPa and a density of approximately 2.6 to 2.8 g/cm³. With excellent weather resistance and a lifespan of hundreds of years, it offers a sustainable and long-lasting option for construction.

Brick / Terracotta

Bricks, usually made from burned clay, provide strength and fire resistance to buildings. From around 5000–4000 BCE, mudbricks evolved into fired bricks to increase strength and durability. In the twentieth century, the compressed earth block was developed using high pressure as a cheap and eco-friendly alternative to obtain non-fired bricks with more strength than the simpler air-dried mudbricks.

Chikka

Chikka can be seen as the Ethiopian wattle and daub construction method. It combines a wooden framework with mud and straw infill. It offers a lightweight solution with a thermal conductivity of approximately 0.3 to 0.6 W/m·K, providing good insulation properties. Wattle and daub structures can have a compressive strength ranging from 0.2 to 1.0 MPa, depending on the materials used and the construction techniques.

Timber

Timber is a renewable material with an excellent strength-to-weight ratio and thermal insulation properties. Its compressive strength ranges from 20 to 60 MPa, with a density of about 0.4 to 0.9 g/cm³. Timber also has a low thermal conductivity of approximately 0.1 to 0.15 W/m·K, making it an energy-efficient choice for construction.

Menelik Prayer Pavilion

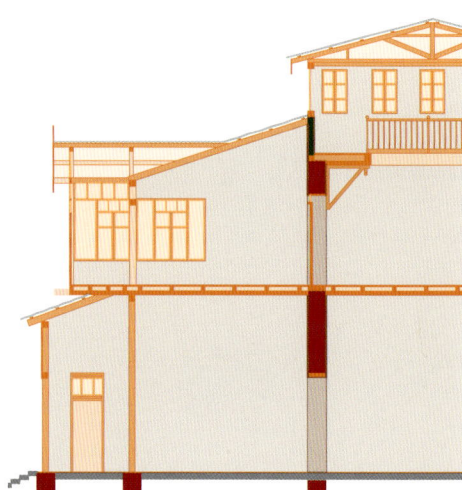

Sheik Ojele House

Fit. Atnaf Seged Residence

Taitu Hotel

Adobe / Clay

Adobe construction utilises sun-dried mud bricks with a typical compressive strength of 0.7 to 2.5 MPa and a density of around 1.6 to 1.9 g/cm³. The thermal conductivity of adobe is approximately 0.7 to 1.5 W/m·K, contributing to its excellent thermal performance. In dry climates, adobe structures are extremely durable and account for some of the oldest existing buildings in the world.

Glass

Glass offers transparency, allowing abundant natural light into buildings. Its thermal conductivity typically ranges from 0.8 to 1.2 W/m·K, and its density is approximately 2.5 to 2.8 g/cm³. With advancements in energy-efficient glazing, glass contributes to sustainable construction by reducing heat transfer and improving thermal insulation in buildings.

Cast Iron / Tin

Cast iron provides strength, fire resistance, and intricate detailing to architectural elements. It has a compressive strength ranging from 200 to 400 MPa and a density of about 6.9 to 7.8 g/cm³. Cast iron's durability and corrosion resistance make it suitable for structural applications, with a lifespan exceeding 100 years in many cases.

Corrugated Iron Sheet

Corrugated iron sheets are lightweight, weather-resistant, and cost-effective for roofing and cladding. They typically have a tensile strength ranging from 250 to 550 MPa and a density of approximately 7.8 g/cm³. Corrugated iron sheets offer good durability, easy installation, and can have a lifespan of 20 to 50 years, depending on maintenance and environmental factors.

Dej. Ayalew Birru Residence

Menelik Residence

Mohamed Ali Residence

Dej. Wube Haile Mariam Residence

Influence Analysis

Local Influences

To analyse the influences that local building cultures had on the architecture of the Addis Ababa Style, one has to understand the historical context in which it evolved. Unlike most African capitals, the foundation of Addis Ababa was an indigenous initiative, following indigenous rules of space-making and organisation (Giorghis, Zoom talk, 18 May 2021). The Emperor invited regional rulers from all parts of the country and gave them land to settle, including their respective followers. This is documented in the so-called 'Taitu Plan'. These settlements, which in their spatial layout resembled military camps, were called *Sefer*, a concentric arrangement with the important person (the dignitary, high official, or high-ranking military officer) in the centre. As a result of this, Addis Ababa grew quite organically, with hills and rivers between the *sefers*.

Fasil Giorghis writes: 'Towards the end of the nineteenth century, the level of construction was rather low in Ethiopia because capitals had been for centuries impermanent settlements of tents and semi-permanent residences like Ankober. It is obvious that in these conditions, architecture could not develop. The continuous wars amongst regional rulers and the low esteem given to artisans' work further affected the development of architecture and construction know-how' (Giorghis and Gerard 2019: 198).

Most buildings in Addis Ababa at the time were still built in the traditional way: round walls of *chikka* (a local version of a wattle and daub construction) with a wooden roof structure covered with thatch. However, in the times of Entoto, the architecture of palaces was different from ordinary vernacular buildings, as the level of decoration and sophistication in construction was substantially higher – otherwise only found in the architecture of churches. In that case, walls were made of natural stone with earth mortar, and the construction of ceilings was given greater attention (see p. 186).

The architecture of Addis Ababa was characterised by different transformations – or better 'transitions' – in order to refer to the notion of continuity, which always links back to the vernacular knowledge. The oval shape was typical of the Northern Shewa region, the area around Derbe Brahan or Ankober. The round shapes correlate with Ethiopian eating culture and its respective furniture. The rectangular shape was not endemic to the region and signifies an attempt at modernisation. The perimeter veranda can be found in vernacular types of Ethiopia. Open verandas offered a shaded outside space that protected from sun and rain. These were eventually closed using light wooden constructions and glazed in order to widen the private rooms and create a corridor that connects different rooms. At the same time, they created a thermal buffer zone.

The matrix on pages 148–149 shows six design principles that link the architecture of the Addis Ababa Style with local building cultures including construction and use of space. Most of the clients of Addis Ababa Houses were Ethiopians, most of whom had never been abroad.

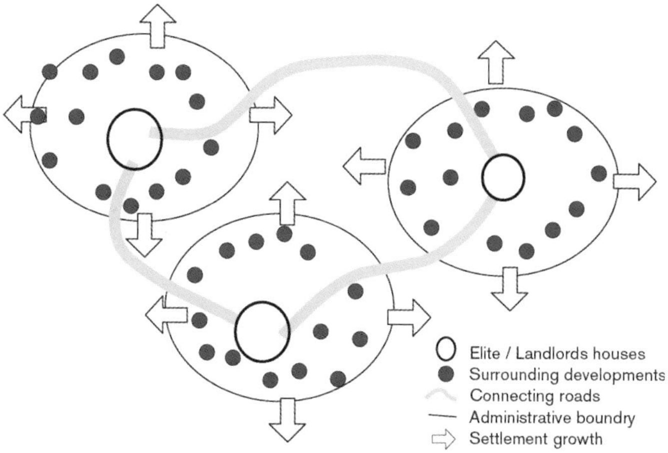

Structure of a traditional built-up environment (G. Alem)

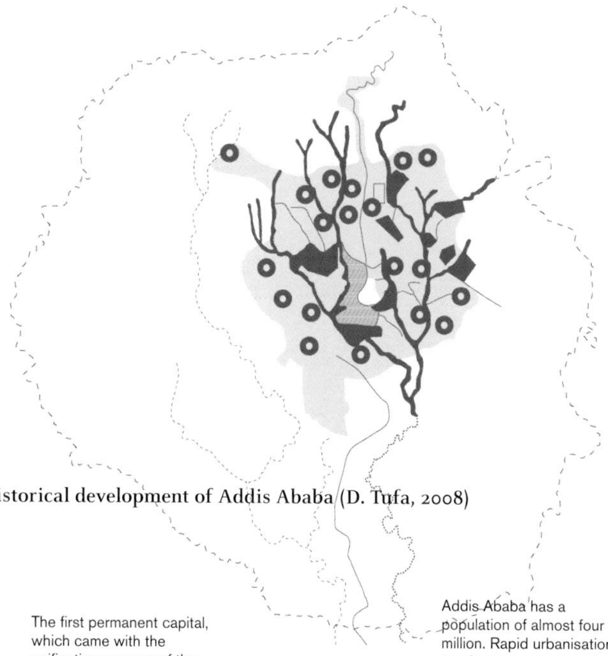

○ Elite / Landlords houses
● Surrounding developments
〜 Connecting roads
— Administrative boundry
⇨ Settlement growth

Historical development of Addis Ababa (D. Tufa, 2008)

Timeline

1270 — Establishment of the Ethiopian Empire (Abyssinia)

1635–1855 Gondar — Gondar in today's Amhara region is the long-time capital of Ethiopia. Skills in urban architecture are cultivated.

1823 Ankober — Menelik's first, temporary capital resembles a military camp. Afred Ilg already works for Menelik.

1880 Entoto — Menelik's second capital. lies on the Entoto Mountains. Indian craftsmen build St. Raguel Church.

1886 Addis Ababa — The first permanent capital, which came with the unification process of the Ethiopian Empire.

1936 — Italian invasion under Mussolini. The occupation ends in 1941.

study cases building period

today — Addis Ababa has a population of almost four million. Rapid urbanisation continues.

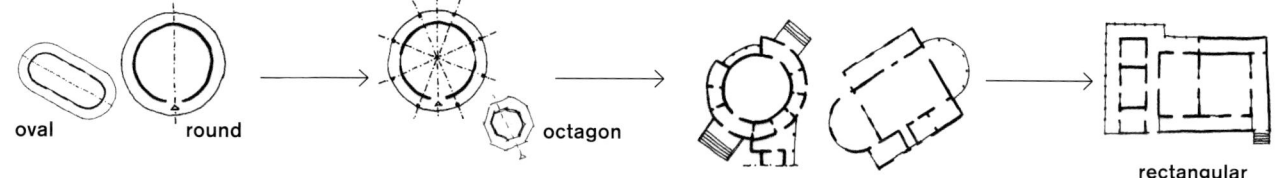

oval · round → octagon → → rectangular

Vernacular Types
- one multipurpose room
- one exterior porch
- few openings

This vernacular form englobes indigenous social behaviour such as eating culture (round table for eating Ingera).

Veranda (open / covered)
- exterior veranda
- more openings
- new concentric geometries

More comfort is achieved by minor modifications in construction and successive use of timber and stone.

Extensions
- compartmentation
- exterior veranda turns into indoor space
- many openings

The initial simplicity is lost. Social behaviour changes and one single room is no longer enough for living in the house.

Addis Ababa House
- more complex forms
- rectangular overall shapes
- extra rooms, surrounding verandas

The spatial requirements increasingly reflect an urban society. Buildings become more and more complex.

Typological transitions during case study period

Influence Analysis

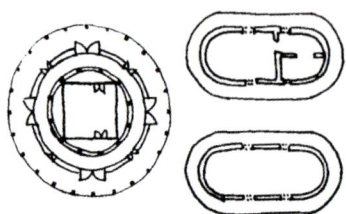

Stand-alone Building

Most of the buildings are designed as solitary, facing multiple directions. This goes back to the traditional Ethiopian way of organising space within a compound. The houses of the aristocrats stood in the centre of the *sefer*, organically surrounded by the *tukuls* of their servants. Placement was chosen with consideration of the natural features of the site, such as topography or view.

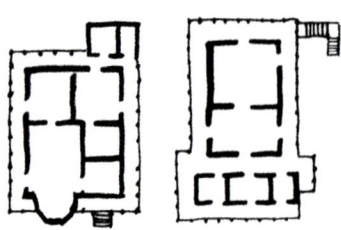

Perimeter Circulation

The perimeter circulation corresponds to the traditional Ethiopian building type, which usually consisted of a single room and had a circular or oval shape. Internal corridors did not exist in the traditional types. The roof overhang of the traditional building type created a functional perimeter zone around the building, which transitioned to perimeter circulation in the Addis Ababa House.

External Staircases

The few examples among the traditional building types that have multiple storeys have an exterior staircase protected by a generous roof overhang. Menelik's Entoto Palace is one example. The structural advantage is that the exterior staircase leaves the building's structural system untouched and does not take up additional living space geometries. Gradually, open porches were transformed into buffer rooms with glazed curtain walls.

	Menelik Prayer Pavilion 1886–1887	Menelik Residence 1886–1887	*Dej.* Wube H/ Mariam Residence Early 1900	Mohamed Ali Residence Early 1900s	*Sheik* Ojele House Early 1900s	Negradas H/ Giorghis Agid Residence 1906	Ministry of Pen Office Building 1886–1887
Stand-alone building							
Perimeter circulation							
External staircases			no upper floor				no upper floor
Bridges							
Linkage of outside-inside							
Chikka walls							

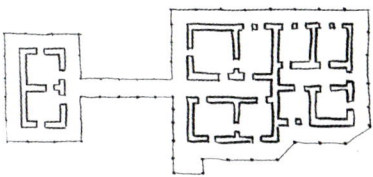  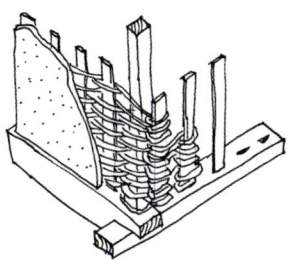

Bridges

In some Addis Ababa Houses, it is possible to observe a bridge connection between two buildings. This elaborate composition results from a traditionally obligatory separation of profane and religious functions.

Linkage of Outside-Inside

The climate in the Ethiopian highlands allows many activities of daily life to take place outdoors; this is a culturally ingrained feature of Ethiopian life. Consequently, traditional Ethiopian building types are not hermetically constructed. Doorways remain open, and spaces adjacent to the house can be seen as an unbuilt extension of the building. These perimeter spaces reinforce social connectivity.

Chikka Walls

Chikka is the local version of wattle and daub, a traditional building technique based on mud and wood. *Chikka* is the most common and cost-effective construction method and is found in many houses in Addis Ababa. Its additional advantage is its thermal capacity and humidity regulation. On the other hand, *chikka* requires regular maintenance, and a roof overhang or other protective measures are mandatory.

Empress Zewditu Residence 1907–1910	Taitu Hotel 1907	*Dej.* Ayalew Birru Residence 1910	*Ras* Birru W/ Gabriel Residence 1920s	Alfred Ilg Residence/ Arenti Ashakian Before 1901	Tafari Makonnen School 1925	*Afenigus* Nasibu Meskele Residence Before 1908	*Fit.* Atnaf Seged Residence 1920s

			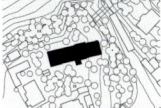		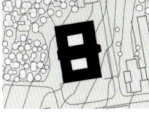		
	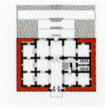	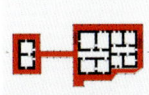	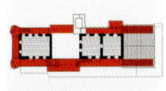	 (no upper floor)	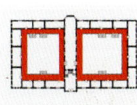	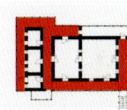	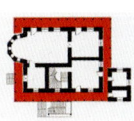
	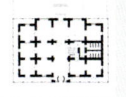 ca. until 1936	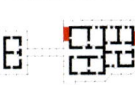	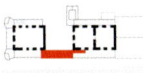		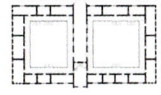	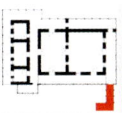	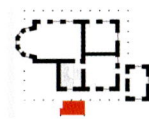
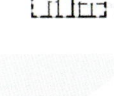	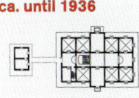	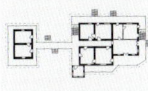			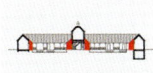		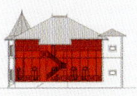
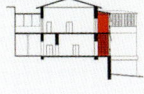							
		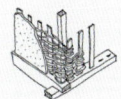	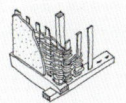				

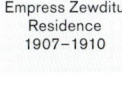

Local influence matrix (diagonal = feature not present)

Influence Analysis

The Addis Ababa Houses 'Syncretic Complexity'[1]

A traditional roof construction as a local influence, seen here in the house of the European engineer Alfred Ilg. He applied the same construction method for Menelik's first palace in Entoto.

Chikka is an indigenous construction method that was applied in many early Addis Ababa Houses. The building stock that is more than one hundred years old proves that *chikka* is durable for a long period of time when properly maintained. The photo shows the production of *chikka* in 2022.

Designed by the Armenian architect Minas Kerbekian in the early 1920s, the roof shape of this house clearly shows Armenian influences. The gable can be interpreted as an Indian influence. However, the Armenians likely adopted it to indicate the entrance.

The *Sheik* Ojele Residence is a good example of a combination of local and Indian influences.

1   Based on a conversation with Fasil
    Giorghis, February 2023.

The local wattle and daub construction is known as a *chikka* wall. While it was traditionally used to build round or oval *tukuls*, the method was adopted for the rectangular shape of the Addis Ababa Houses. The photo shows an unmaintained *chikka* wall with its different components, which are all cheap and locally available.

Crude masonry was a typical local construction method that did not require many skills. The earth plaster used proves to be quite durable. Applied in most Addis Ababa Houses, this construction method can be seen as a local influence.

This type of gable is marked by both Indian and Armenian influences.

Many buildings in the Armenian quarter are mixed form: Indian craftsmen were heavily involved in the construction of these buildings. While we see pyramidal roofs as an Armenian feature, the use of *chikka* is an Ethiopian influence.

Influence Analysis   187

The Addis Ababa Houses 'Syncretic Complexity'[1]

The round shape of residences is not found in India or Armenia, but it is typical of Ethiopian dwellings. The photo shows the *Dej.* Wube Residence.

The traditional Ethiopian church floor plan (onion-shaped) is combined with the vertical staggering of floors found in Armenian Orthodox churches, so that light enters the central part of the building. The octagonal plan is also an Armenian or Greek influence. The façade itself features European pediments and classical ornamentation.

Ras Nadew Aba Wolo's first residence showed many local influences, like the round-shaped rooms and *chikka* walls.

Ras Nadew Aba Wolo was one of the first delegates to be sent to Europe by Menelik and his second residence has strongly European influences.

1 Based on a conversation with Fasil Giorghis 02/2023.

Asfaw Kebede Residence: The roof decoration and the curved shape of the roof show strong Indian influences. On the other hand, the glazing and octagonal room additions can be attributed to Armenian influence.

The glazing (curtain wall) is found in buildings that are predominantly Indian- and Armenian-influenced.

Kervokoff Store: Strongly Armenian but belongs to the second phase when heavier materials were used. Greek craftsmen were presumably involved in the construction.

The clear story is an Armenian influence. However, it is said to have been built by Indians and Pakistanis. The *Dej.* Letyibelu Gebre Residence is now a *Tej-bet*.

Indian Influences

The history of the Indian presence in Ethiopia dates back centuries. It is known that Indian craftsmen designed and built the first castle in Gondar, then Ethiopia's capital, in the late sixteenth century (Pankhurst 1995: 11). The Muslim city of Harar was another place with a strong Indian commercial presence. The outstanding architecture of what is now the Arthur Rimbaud Museum, which is said to have belonged to Jewaji Ibrahimji (Harre 2015a: 10), is an illustrative witness of Indian-influenced architecture before Menelik's rule. However, the Indian influence increased significantly with the reign of Menelik II. This fact is strongly linked with an Indian who traded ivory and gold. Hajji Khawas Khan, who was from Peshawar (now in Pakistan), is said to have worked for Menelik since the 1870s when the capital was still in Ankober. After moving to Entoto, he was commissioned to design and supervise the construction of a new church: St. Raguel, a four-storey, octagonal construction that was unique in the context of Ethiopia at the time. Hajji Khawas Khan and a team of maybe half a dozen of Indian craftsmen also designed and built Menelik's new palace close to the sources of the Filwoha thermal springs where Addis Ababa was founded. Destroyed after a fire, this palace had to be rebuilt just one year later. This group of Indians would later also build a palace for Menelik in Addis Alem, which was turned into a church after the Emperor's decision not to move the capital there, and eventually a mayor palace in Holeta. Several historical events led to the increase in the Indian population in the coming decades. In the years after Menelik conquered Harar in 1887, some Indian merchants who ran successful businesses there moved over to the capital, Addis Ababa. Among those was Mohamed Ali, a trader from the region of Gujarat. He was the main importer of corrugated iron sheets and served as a representative for the Indian community (Giorghis 2007: 254). The Battle of Adwa was followed by an Anglo-Ethiopian Agreement in 1897. This facilitated a further influx of Indian craftsmen to Ethiopia. As a result, the Indian community reached 149 in 1909. This made Indians the third largest foreign community in Ethiopia's young capital. These numbers were documented by Dr. Mérab, a contemporary Georgian resident.

The Indian craftsmen excelled in carpentry as well as cut stone masonry. They were also the first to use corrugated iron sheets for roofing. The Indians that came from Harar introduced the typology of the residence-store – multi-storey buildings that combined commercial activities on the ground floor with residences on the upper levels. The residence stores were typical in the trading ports of the Indian Ocean in places like Bombay, Zanzibar, and Madagascar (Harre and Gashaw 2018: 62).

At the beginning of the twentieth century, Indian craftsmen could build much cheaper than Greeks or Italians. Additionally, their pavilion-like buildings became fashionable for the

Historical architecture from Gujarat, India

Historical architecture from Gujarat, India

An early example of a residence-store from an Indian merchant. It is now the Arthur Rimbaud Cultural Centre in Harar.

1640	Indians play a role in construction work at settlements in the Lake Tana area, including the famous Gondar castles.
1870 Hajji Khawas Khan from Peshawar (now in Pakistan) works for Menelik in Ankober.	**After 1850** In the second half of the nineteenth century, traders from Gujarat, India, were among the first foreigners to settle in the Muslim city of Harar, strengthening Ethiopia's links with the Indian Ocean trade.
1881 Menelik transfers his camp to Entoto, a mountain north of present-day Addis Ababa.	**1883**
1886/1887 Establishment of Addis Ababa. Haji Khawas and a number of his compatriots were immediately put to construction work in the town.	 St. Raquel Church on Entoto Mountain, designed by Hajji Khawas: a structure of unusual shape and design, it was octagonal and had a first-floor surrounding balustrade, a very large squat octagonal pagoda, and four storeys. A fine structure according to local Indian tradition.
Early 1890s  Menelik Palace in Addis Ababa  St. Gabriel Church: situated within the palace compound with an octagonal shape. It was the work of Indian craftsmen, who cut and polished the stones out of which it was fashioned.	**1896 – Battle of Adwa** A great deal of construction in the capital in the following decades. As a result, Addis Ababa begins to suffer from an acute dearth of wood.
1900s  Grazmach Tase Asegid, designed by Indian Woli Mohammed  Mohamed Ali House  Sheik Ojele House  Dej. Wube Residence	**1897** The capital's population at the time included 'half a dozen' Indians, headed by Hajji Khawas Khan.  The Anglo-Ethiopian Treaty and the opening of diplomatic relations between the two countries facilitated the arrival of an increasing numbers of Indian merchants and craftsmen. **1900** New capital Addis Alem planned: Hajji Khawas's new Palace for Menelik is there and is later turned into a church.

Timeline of Indian influences 1/2 (gtz 2009 / Pankhurst 1995)

1902

Hajji Khawas Khan and many of the Indians were transferred to work on an entirely new palace in Holota.

Hajji Khawas and his companions, who had by then constructed a huge rectangular stone structure designed for a royal palace, were then given the task of adapting their construction into a building for religious use.
The Indian roof builders working under the direction of Hajji Khawas, and one in particular, Woli Mohammed, whom he had brought from India, called a strike. Woli Mohammed and his son Mawla remained in Ethiopia until their deaths. One neighbourhood in Addis Ababa is still called the Woli Mohammed *Sefer*.

1905

Hajji Khawas Khan dies.

1909

Indian-style stone buildings with wooden balconies were situated in various parts of the town.

Afenigus Nasibu Residence

St. Gabrial Church is the oldest church built from stone by Hajji Khawas and it shows strong Indian influences. The balustrades resemble the ones from the Enqulal Bet.

1910s

1920s

Muse Christo Magliaris / Negadiras Residence

Fitawrari Atnaf Seged Residence

Residence of Indian architect Woli Mohammed

Dej. Yilma Mekonnen Residence

Dej. Asfaw Kebede Residence

Dej. Ayalew Birru Residence

Tiezas (Azaye) Terefe W / Gebriel.

1930s

Kuraz Printing Press / Mega Enterprise

1936 – Italian invasion

Timeline of Indian influences 2/2 (gtz 2009 / Pankhurst 1995)

Main door of the Aderash with decorated spandrels (roughly a triangular space, usually found in pairs, between the top of an arch and a rectangular frame)

The Red Fort in New Delhi, India

residences of nobles, high officials, and businessmen. Here, a central reception room surrounded by smaller rooms replaced the stores.

Older members of the Indian community recall the following features as typical of the Indian influence: double thickness of external walls in comparison with the indigenous walls, building heights of more than 3.5 metres, two-tier roofs with windows between the tiers serving ventilation (typical of the Gujarat region), open or closed verandas supported by wood-carved posts, main entrances sheltered by double doors, roof finials, eaves with ornamental fascias, and watchtower-like structures – also typical to the Gujarat region (Batistoni and Chiari 2004: 22). This list belongs to oral history and is surely neither completely accurate nor complete. The element of the finial is also typical of different vernacular building traditions in Ethiopia. It is possible to say that the Indians contributed to the evolution of this element.

From the literature review and comparison with traditional Indian architecture as well as in discussions with experts, we have identified six main features that can be linked with the Indian influences on the Addis Ababa Style. These are described on the following page.

A residence-store is an Indian typology. Mohamed Ali came from the Indian region of Gujarat.

Corner towers are an Indian influence, here in the *Ras* Birru Residence

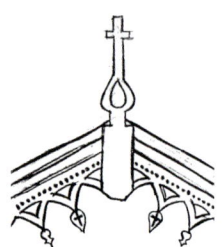

Roof Finials

Roof finials are a decorative element at the top of the roof. They were suggested by Indian craftsmen and were very attractive to Ethiopians because similar elements were common in the local culture, whether for traditional houses or churches. In India, these finials feature a symbol or the owner's name.

Curved Roofs or Domes

The curved roof or dome is a typical Indian feature. One finds this form in the traditional architecture of the subcontinent, for example, in the Red Fort in New Delhi. Its construction required exquisite carpentry skills provided only by Indians. The curved shape is, in a sense, the counterpart of the pyramidal roof, which has an Armenian influence.

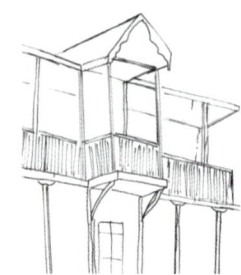

Verandas with Pointed Gables

The wooden porches are a dominant feature of the Addis Ababa House and may have several origins. However, it was the Indian craftsmen who excelled in producing these building elements with a high level of technical and artistic skill. Sometimes these porches are combined with pointed gables and have quite complex geometries. Open porches were gradually transformed into buffer rooms with glazed curtain walls.

	Menelik Prayer Pavilion 1886–1887	Menelik Residence 1886–1887	*Dej.* Wube H/ Mariam Residence Early 1900	Alfred Ilg Residence/ Arenti Ashakian Before 1901	Mohamed Ali Residence Early 1900s	*Sheik* Ojele House Early 1900s	Negradas H/ Giorghis Agid Residence 1906
Roof finials							
Curved roofs or domes							
Verandas with pointed gables							
Ornamental fascias							
Arabesque ornamentation							
Residence-store							

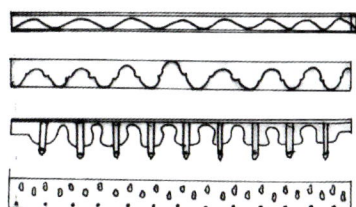

Ornamental Fascias

Indian carpenters brought with them a rich vocabulary in decorating eves. Fascias give the roof a soft, almost textile appearance. At the same time, they protect the roof structure from rain. As a rule, they were made of wood, but in some cases, such as the Ministry of Defence, they were made of tin.

Arabesque Ornamentation

In many Addis Ababa Houses, the Indian influence can be seen in the ornamental details found in spandrels, on the doors, or on wooden surfaces. Arabesque ornamentation is associated with the Islamic world and generally consists of 'surface decorations based on rhythmic linear patterns of scrolling and interlacing foliage, tendrils'.

Residence-store

The typology of the residence-store was introduced by Indians merchants, such as Mohamed Ali. It consists of shops, workshop or storage on the ground floor, and a residence on the upper floor. This multi-storey building type was frequently used in the Indian Ocean port towns. An early example of a residence-store owned by Indian merchants is the present-day Rimbeau House in the city of Harar.

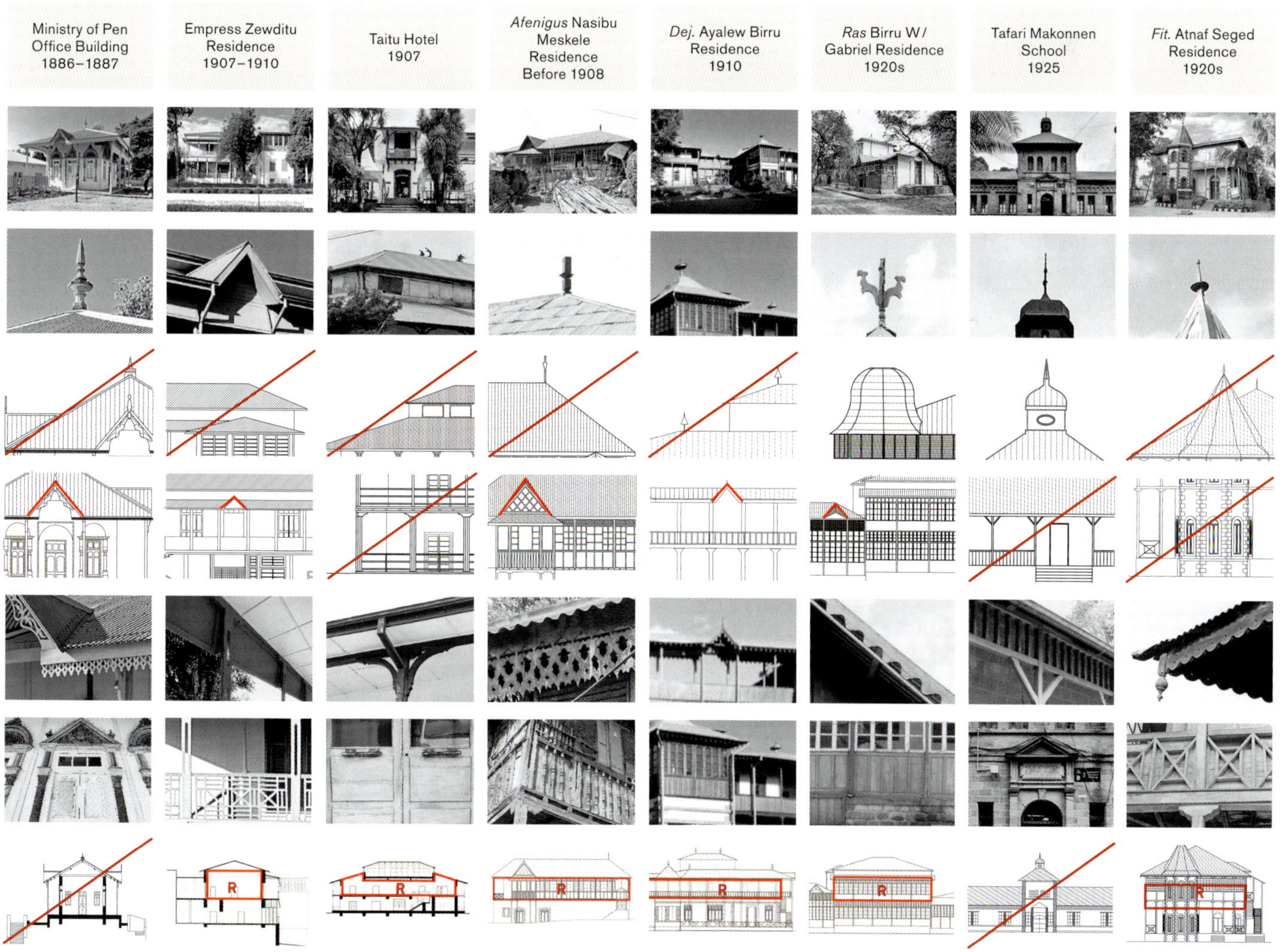

Indian influence matrix (diagonal = feature not present)

Influence Analysis 195

Armenian Influences

Armenians have traded with Ethiopia as far back as the first century CE (Wikipedia, 2022). The link between the two countries was facilitated by their Orthodox Christian faith. The number of Armenians who came to Ethiopia increased significantly after 1895 as a result of the genocide in the Ottoman Empire. The map from 1909 shows the Armenian Quarter as 'Quartiere Armeno'. In that year, the community numbered 146 people (Pankhurst 1967: 80), but it reached its zenith in the 1960s when it numbered 1,200. Despite their small numbers, Armenians had a crucial role in modernising Ethiopia, working as tailors, doctors, businesspeople, composers, and goldsmiths in the imperial court (BBC News, 2020).

Fasil Giorghis states that in comparison with the Indian community, fewer Armenians are involved in the construction sector itself. However, they wanted houses that gave them the same qualities they found back home in their country. Consequently, they influenced the architecture of the Addis Ababa House in a more indirect way. One of the most renowned Armenians was Krikor Jovian, who realised innovative bridges that were entirely made out of stone without using cement. After his death in Addis, Minas Kerbekian became his successor. Other Armenian constructors or carpenters included Haroutin Avakian, Hapet Oughourlian, and Serkis Terzian (Batistoni and Chiari 2004: 20). The latter was initially an arms trader, who imported the first steamroller to Ethiopia for the construction of new roads (Pankhurst 1967: 58).

It is possible to distinguish two phases of the Armenian-influenced architecture in Addis Ababa. During the first, houses were built in a lighter way, and the use of *chikka* and wood was common, as one can still see in the Armenian Quarter where Indian craftsmen were involved in construction. Taitu Hotel, which was designed by the most influential Armenian engineer, Minas Kerbekian, and the residence of Elias Bessmelian are examples of the first phase of Armenian-influenced architecture. Two-tier roofs and clear stories are typical architectural features as well as skydomes, realised in different shapes and sizes, that bring light into the building's volume. Presumably, there is a connection to the traditional architecture of Armenian churches in the careful arrangement of space and light.

Cut stone buildings and a heavier geometry with round arches characterise the second phase of Armenian-influenced architecture. Octagonal masonry and pyramidal roofs were a reminiscence of the architecture of Armenian Orthodox churches. The use of dressed stone became fashionable for the wealthier part of the Armenian community. In this context, the store of Matig Kervokoff in Arada, housing the largest Armenian trading firm, must be mentioned.

As the Armenian community was tied to the imperial history of the country, it strongly declined in numbers after the coup of the socialist *Derg* in 1974.

Taitu Hotel was designed by Kerbekian and is a good example of the Armenian Influence. The hotel had a clear story before the Italians closed it to make an 'officer's club' on the second floor.

The Elias House in Arada shows strong Armenian influences. It has been well restored by the original family who still owns the house.

Saint George Armenian Apostolic Church, built in 1928 and inaugurated in 1935

Timeline of Armenian influences

1st century CE
Trading relations between Ethiopia and Armenia.

Early 16th century
One of the first recorded diplomatic missions to Europe from Ethiopia was led by Matthew the Armenian to appeal for aid against Islamic incursions into Ethiopia.

1870
The first time Armenians came in groups to Addis Ababa due to the Ottoman Empire genocide. Many more come in around 1905.

1915

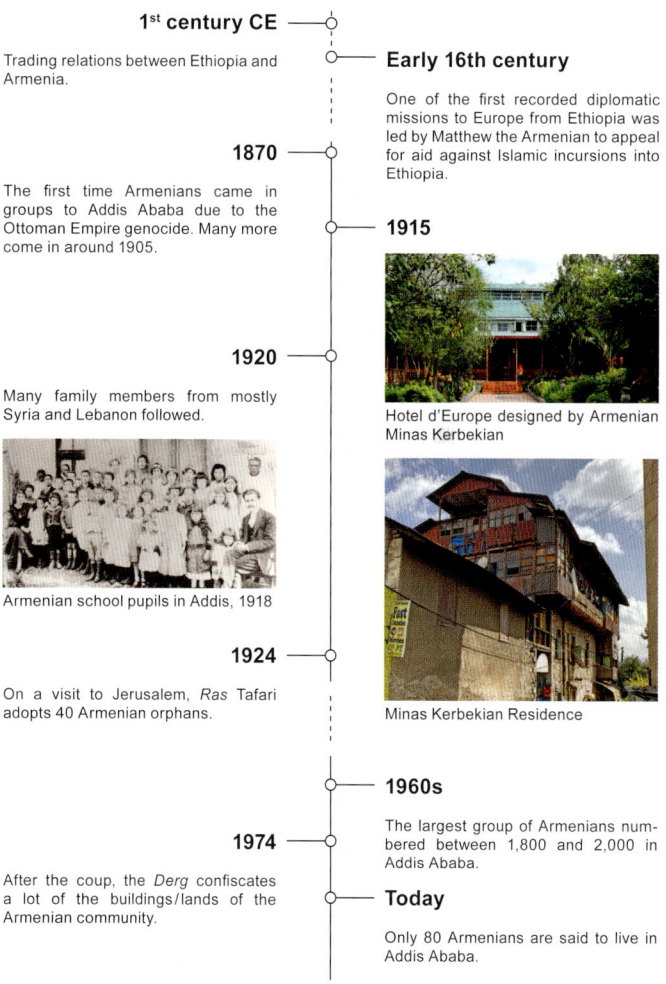

Hotel d'Europe designed by Armenian Minas Kerbekian

1920
Many family members from mostly Syria and Lebanon followed.

Armenian school pupils in Addis, 1918

Minas Kerbekian Residence

1924
On a visit to Jerusalem, *Ras* Tafari adopts 40 Armenian orphans.

1960s
The largest group of Armenians numbered between 1,800 and 2,000 in Addis Ababa.

1974
After the coup, the *Derg* confiscates a lot of the buildings/lands of the Armenian community.

Today
Only 80 Armenians are said to live in Addis Ababa.

Influence Analysis   197

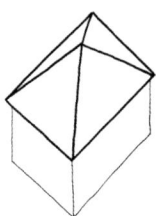

Pyramidal Roofs

Pyramidal roofs are said to be an Armenian feature. The lines of a pitched roof converge in a single point, emphasising the verticality of a part of a building. In residential buildings, it adds an eclectic touch to the building. This roof form is also found in traditional Armenian Orthodox churches.

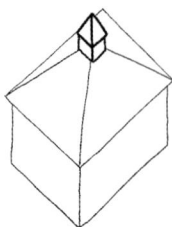

Central Skydomes

Central skylight domes come in many different sizes and shapes. They are located in a central position on the roof and usually have the function of directing light to the centre of the building. In some cases, they become large enough to accommodate an entire room.

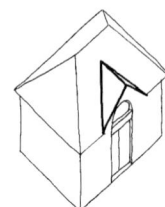

Pointed Gables Used for Entrances

Pointed gables are found in many different forms and contribute greatly to the physiognomy of many buildings. This feature has both Armenian and Indian influences, so it can be easily confused. However, Armenians typically used it to accentuate the entrance of a building.

Selection of Case Studies with Armenian Influence	Enteque Hotel 1907	Matig Kervorkoff Residence Elias Hotel 1910	Muse Yakob – Aqop Bagdasarian's 1st Residence 1910s	Finetine Hotel Hotel d'Euope 1915	Muse Minas Kerbekian Residence 1915	Merha Tibeb Printing Press 1920
Pyramidal roofs				✓		✓
Central skydomes		✓				
Pointed gables used for entrances						
Two-tier roofs	✓	✓	✓	✓	✓	✓
Clear stories	✓	✓			✓	✓
Heavy geometries		✓	✓			✓

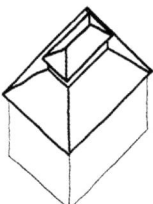

Two-tier Roofs

A two-tier roof allows for a crown of windows to be placed in the upper portion of the roof. This allows for efficient lighting and ventilation of interior spaces. It is usually built on a rectangular plan, but octagonal two-tier roofs are also found in some variants. This feature corresponds strongly with the clear story.

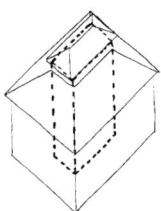

Clear Stories

A clear floor is a double-height space that projects from the roof so that windows can be added above to provide light and ventilation to the space. Deeper building volumes can be created in this manner. Typically, this feature results in a concentric arrangement in plan and has been used not only in residential buildings but also in Ethiopian churches (e.g., St. Giorghis Church).

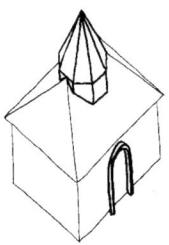

Heavy Geometries

As Armenians in Addis became wealthier, they also built more massively. Cut stones and round arches dominate the second phase of Armenian-influenced architecture. This is also related to specific geometries such as the octagonal or round plan of buildings or parts of buildings. In contrast to the first phase, these buildings appear much more rigid and less playful.

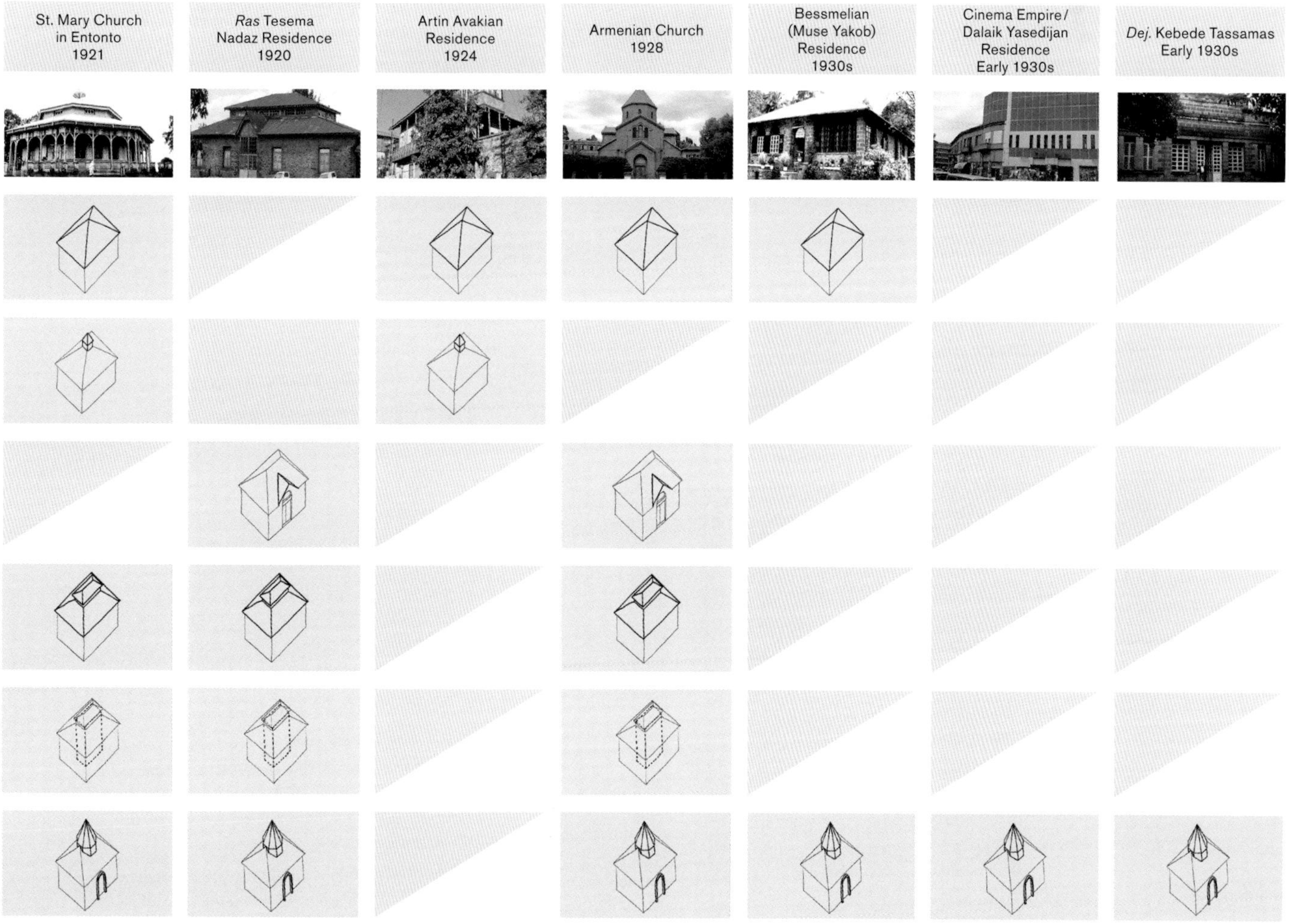

Armenian influence matrix (diagonal = feature not present)

Influence Analysis

European Influences

'In contrast to other African nations that were coming under colonial rule and thereby acquiring the imprint of single metropolitan power, the foreign influences in Ethiopia were far more varied and international in character' (Pankhurst 1967: 29). The reason is Menelik's victory against the Italian colonial powers in the Battle of Adwa in 1896, which was a true turning point in Ethiopia's political as well as cultural history. European nations started to admire the African nation and sent diplomats to the young Ethiopian capital. European embassies were constructed, often with ambitious designs and in European styles. Doric and Ionic columns, capitals, and pediments are repeated features. However, European influences did not stop at architectural elements. They can also be seen in the composition of the volumes, referring to a symmetry found both in the plan and in the elevation.

In fact, the first, larger group of Italians came to Addis as prisoners of war in 1896 and they were primarily used for the construction of roads. However, some of the Italian prisoners made careers in the construction sector, such as Sebastiano Castagna, who designed the Bank of Abyssinia that opened in 1907. He also designed St. Giorghis Church, which was built between 1905 and 1911 (Batistoni and Chiari 2004: 23).

It is reported that the years after the Battle of Adwa saw a considerable amount of construction – Mérab even called Addis Ababa a 'boom city'. During that period, the large Reception Hall was also constructed at the *Ghebbi*, which shows strong European influences. Menelik's chronicler, Guèbrè Sellassié, enthusiastically wrote about the '16 clusters of electric light, which dazzled people as with the rays of the sun, and gutters from which during the rains the water poured out like a torrent' (Pankhurst 1967: 50). Europeans also introduced modernist building materials in Addis Ababa. The private Ras Desta Hospital, which was designed by the Italian architect Alessandro Molli Boffa and opened in 1932, was among the first Addis buildings made of armed concrete (Batistoni and Chiari 2004: 24). The Leghare Train Station was built in 1928–1929 using a design by the French architect Paul Barrias and is one of the first examples of the structural use of steel.

Other Europeans that worked in the construction sector in Addis included the French architect Péne, the German architects Haertel and Kametz, and the Swiss Ilg (Batistoni and Chiari 2004: 24). The latter is maybe the most outstanding engineer. He had already worked for Menelik since the 1870s during the Ankober period.

As the numbers of foreigners in 1909 shows, the Greeks were a big community back then. Many of them migrated to Addis Ababa in 1904 after their contract at the Franco-Ethiopian railway expired. Some Greek residences were built in Arada in neo-classical European styles as in the case of Paulos Kordas' and Karakachiani's residences.

Coronation Hall in the *Ghebbi* in 2022

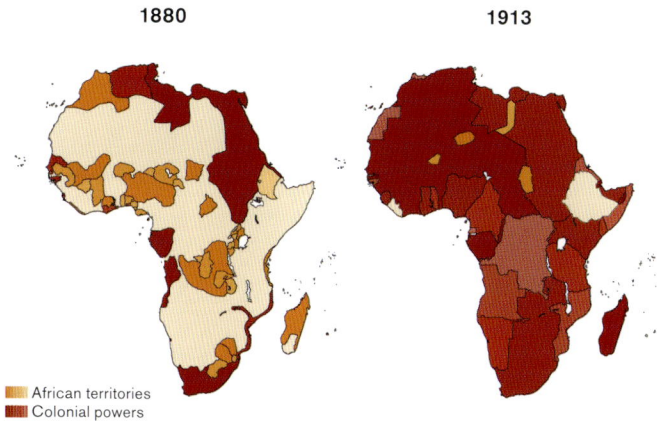
Ethiopia in the era of the Scramble for Africa

African territories
Colonial powers

Coronation Hall in the *Ghebbi* in 2022

Coronation Hall in the *Ghebbi* in 2022

1886

First home of Menelik II in Entoto, designed by Swiss Alfred Ilg

1907

The first brick factory leads to one of the first brick buildings.

Bank of Abyssinia, designed by Italian war prisoner Sebastiano Castagna

1909

Early public buildings: European-influenced buildings where often heavy looking and intended to be grand, with trachytic stone.

Menelik II School

1880

Europeans moved to Addis Ababa due to strong trade relationships.

After 1896

Italian members of the defeated army became assigned members and were involved in construction, carpentry, and mechanical labour. The graphic shows the First Italian Invasion.

Early 1900s

Increase in the Greek population located in the Piassa area: Buildings characterised by the neo-classical style

Residence of the Greek dentist Karakachiani

Timeline of European influences 1/2

Influence Analysis

1910

St. George Cathedral, designed by an Italian engineer under Greek direction.

1917

Arrival of the Franco-Ethiopian railway in Addis Ababa, which facilitates the import of new construction materials.

1910s

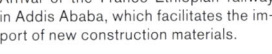

Former residence of Lij Iyasu, Emperor of Ethiopia 1913–1916.

1928–1929

Leghare: The station was built approximately ten years after the arrival of the railways.

1931

Construction of the new Ethiopian Parliament building.
New building techniques were applied by Italian architects. With characteristics like plain, smooth, and undecorated surfaces, straight lines dominating, circular lines achieved by smooth plaster and paint rather than natural materials.

1935

Lul Mekonnen Palace (son of Haile Selassie), designed by German architect Kametz.

1935–1937

The Second Italo-Abyssinian War ends with the Italian occupation of Ethiopia and the foundation of Italian East Africa.

After 1936

Italian Fascist influence and a master plan by Ignazio Giudi and Cesare Valle. The modernist urban planning included the plan to segregate society following racist ideology.

Today

Addis Ababa is still facing a lot of change today. A fast environment and the urge to grow and develop underline the urban architecture and its surroundings. Concrete blocks and high-rises dominate the urban structure between heritage buildings, and foreign investments have a hand in the style it is changing to. The image shows Addis Ababa today.

Timeline of European influences 2/2

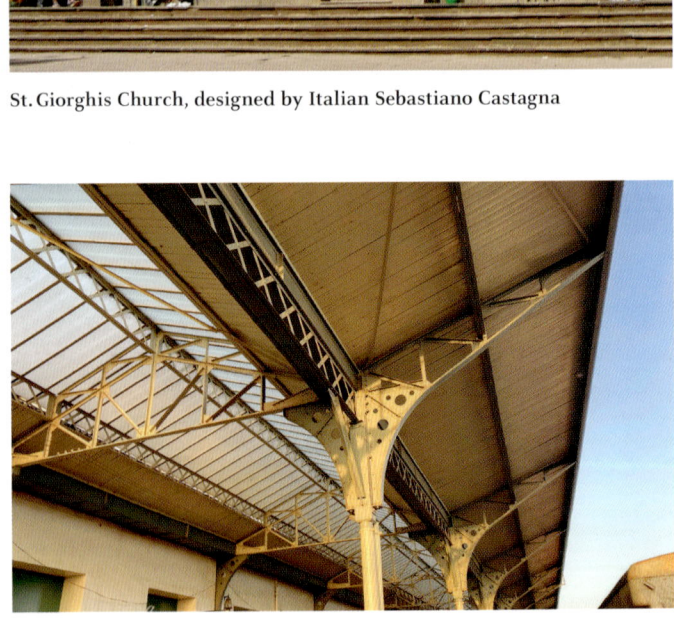

St. Giorghis Church, designed by Italian Sebastiano Castagna

Leghare ('La Gare'), designed by French architect Paul Barrias

Axial Symmetry in Façade and Plan

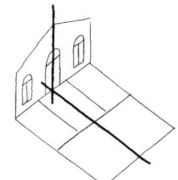

European-influenced buildings have a clear main façade with evenly proportioned windows. The central entrance is often emphasised by a portico. The axially symmetrical design continues inside the building. This creates balance and emphasises the concept of simplicity.

Pediments

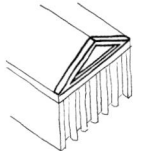

Pediments appear in various forms and are triangular gables that form the end of the roof slope above a portico or window. They were used in Ancient Greece and experienced a revival in the Italian Renaissance. They are often used in combination with columns or pilasters.

Flat Sloped Roof

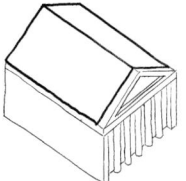

Most European-inspired buildings have a flat pitched roof with a frieze emphasising the ornate balustrade or pediment above. Since the Italian Renaissance, there has been a tendency to make the roof invisible to create a more abstract, geometric harmony in the façade.

Modernist Materials, Steel and Concrete

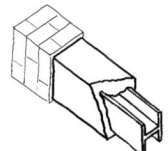

Creating a European look was expensive. Therefore, heavy and durable materials such as precisely cut natural stone (e.g., trachyte) played an important role. With the reign of Haile Selassie, modernist materials such as concrete and steel gradually entered Addis' early architecture.

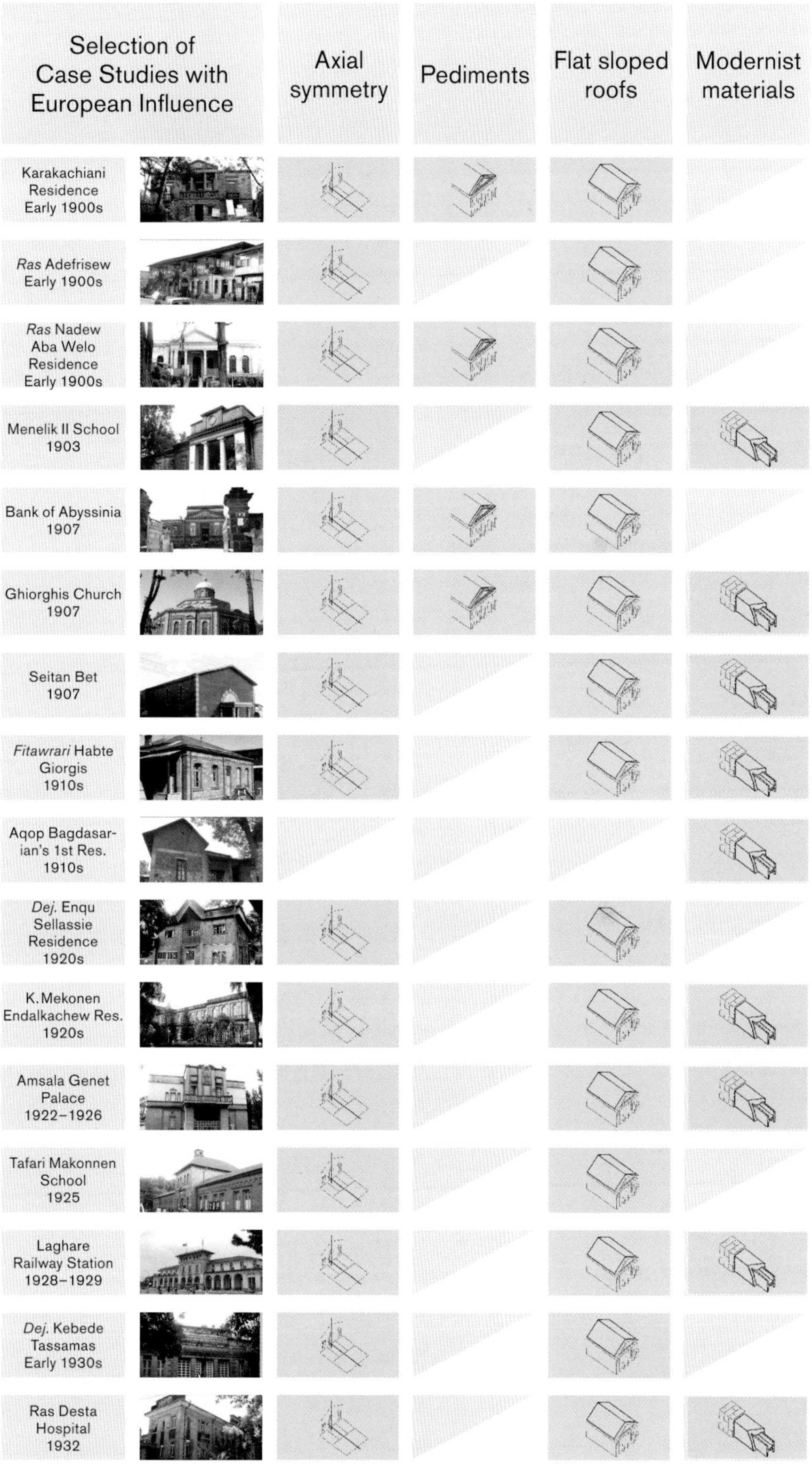

Selection of Case Studies with European Influence	Axial symmetry	Pediments	Flat sloped roofs	Modernist materials
Karakachiani Residence Early 1900s	✓	✓	✓	
Ras Adefrisew Early 1900s	✓		✓	
Ras Nadew Aba Welo Residence Early 1900s	✓	✓	✓	
Menelik II School 1903	✓		✓	✓
Bank of Abyssinia 1907	✓		✓	
Ghiorghis Church 1907	✓	✓	✓	
Seitan Bet 1907	✓		✓	✓
Fitawrari Habte Giorgis 1910s	✓		✓	✓
Aqop Bagdasarian's 1st Res. 1910s				✓
Dej. Enqu Sellassie Residence 1920s	✓		✓	
K. Mekonen Endalkachew Res. 1920s	✓		✓	✓
Amsala Genet Palace 1922–1926	✓		✓	✓
Tafari Makonnen School 1925	✓		✓	✓
Laghare Railway Station 1928–1929	✓		✓	✓
Dej. Kebede Tassamas Early 1930s	✓		✓	
Ras Desta Hospital 1932				✓

European influence matrix (diagonal = feature not present)

Model by Md Esfaqur Rahman
& Lea Hirschmann

4

Genes

Architectural Alphabet

Architectural Alphabet

The Architectural Alphabet is a collection of architectural design principles that lie underneath the analysed heritage buildings. These architectural principles have a purpose that exists 'beyond time and cultural context'.

We propose a code to categorise these principles in terms of (a) where in the building the principle is situated: 'scale', (b) what function or reasoning it follows: 'purpose', and (c) how important it is to characterise the specific architecture of the Addis Ababa House: 'significance'.

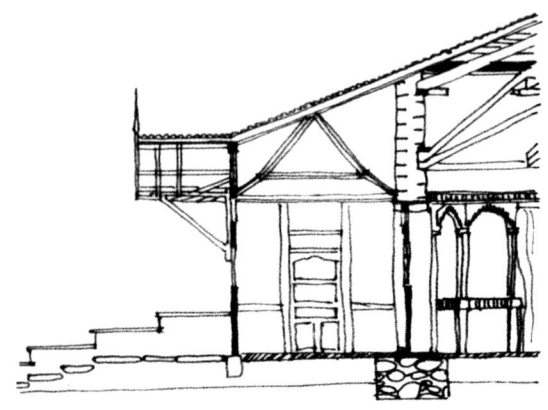

CU4
Through verandas, buildings open up towards the public realm, while maintaining sufficient privacy for residents.

SCALE
M – Material
T – Construction technique
C – Building component
A – Entire architecture

PURPOSE
E – Efficient use of resources
T – Constructive sense
P – Production sense
R – Room climate
U – Utilisation
D – Artistic / decorative

SIGNIFICANCE
4 – Very high
3 – High
2 – Middle
1 – Low

Example:

TT2
Fascias mark the edges of roofs.
They protect the roof construction
from damaging driving rain.

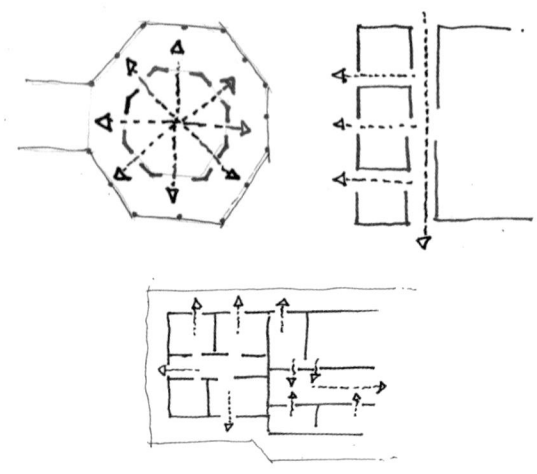

AR4
Placing doors and windows on opposite walls of rooms helps to ventilate the inside.

An Alphabet is without a hierarchy. Letters can be put together in many ways to create words and meaning. Reflecting on the purpose of the design principles beyond time and context opens the door for contemporary adaptation.

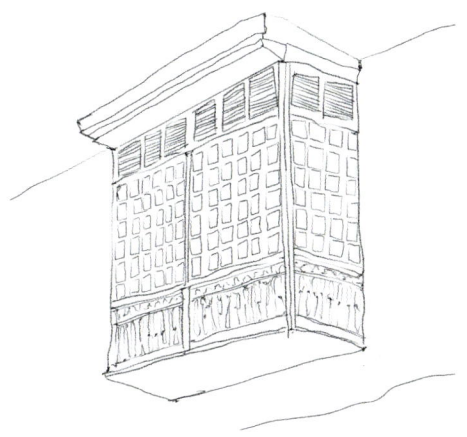

CP2
Assembling standardised small-shaped components to create bigger architectural elements facilitates cheaper production, more efficient use of raw materials, and easy handling on site.

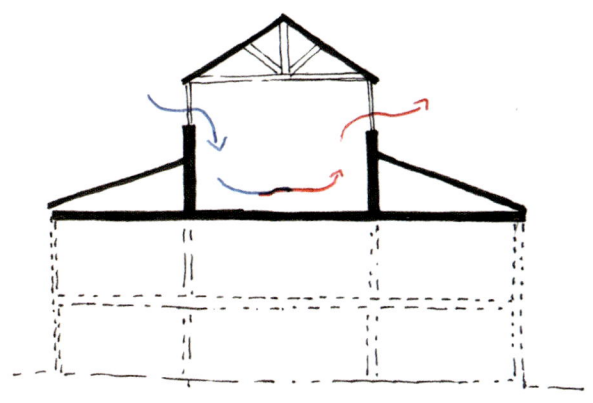

AR3
The double height of atriums in the centre of buildings helps to prevent rooms from overheating. The warm or used air flows vertically, thus, fresh air can flow after.

CD1
Wooden reliefs in doors express the social status and wealth of the owner.

CU4
Verandas and exterior staircases allow outside circulation of the building.

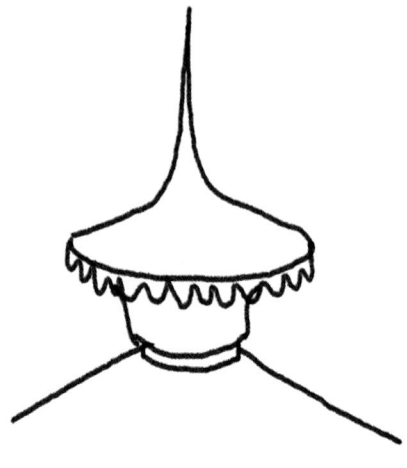

TT2
Finials are placed on rooftops where the different structural parts of the roof come together. They protect the joints from water leaking in. Similar to fascias, they are designed in a decorative manner.

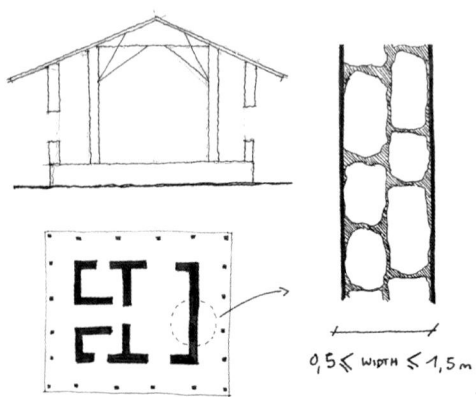

TT3
Along with small openings, thick walls provide dark and cool rooms that are less attractive to insects.

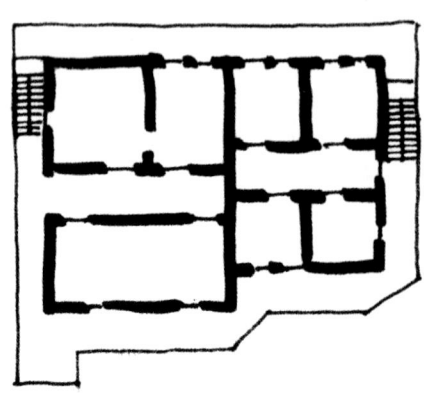

CT3
The placement of exterior staircases allows the building structure to remain untouched. An interruption of the structural system can be avoided.

TT2
Segmental and round arches are used to derive forces around openings in load-bearing walls.

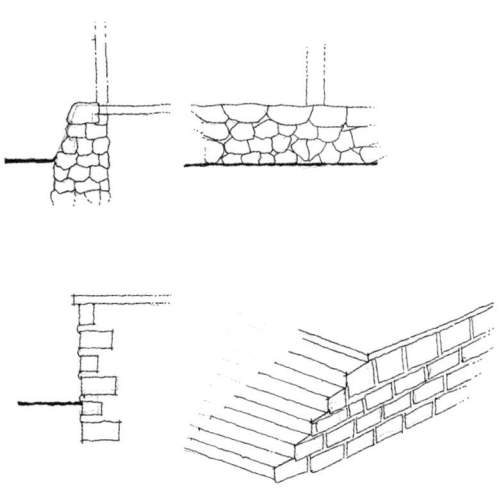

AT3
Raised ground floors protect the construction from flooding.

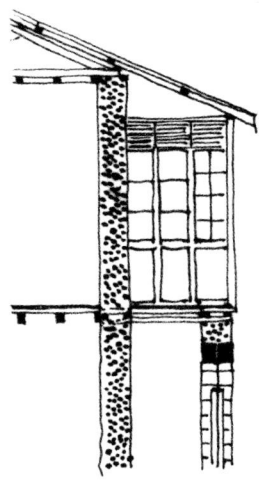

CR4
Closed verandas create a thermal in-between space connecting the indoor with the outdoor.

MD3
Local materials show a great variety of expressions. They maintain the interconnectedness of architectural form and constructive sense.

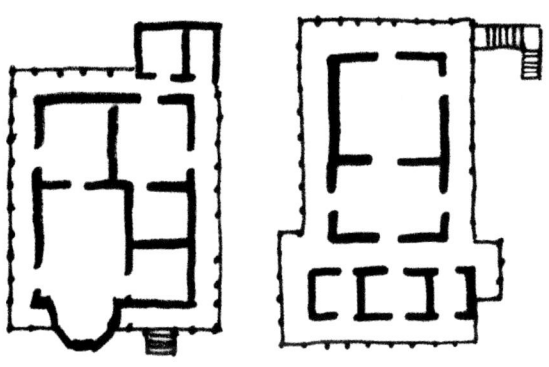

AE3
Perimeter verandas make corridors unnecessary.

TT2
Fascias mark the edges of roofs. They protect the roof construction from damaging driving rain.

MT3
Balconies use wood as a material because it is lightweight. The carpentry is often done in an ornamental fashion.

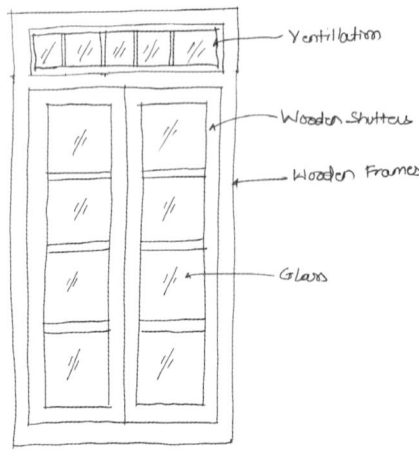

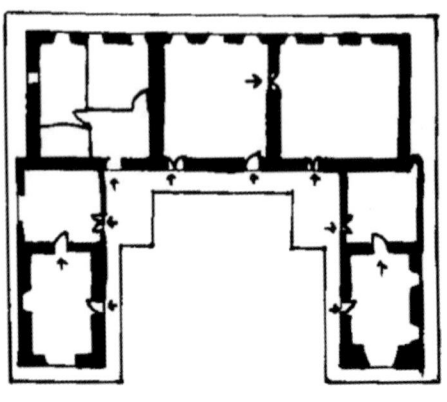

MT2
Windows are mostly made by using wood as a material for the frames, squarish glass panels make natural lighting possible, and wooden shutters protect from the sunlight.

AE4
Rooms are arranged in a row and interconnected with internal doors and sometimes windows. This provides a flexible and efficient use of spaces.

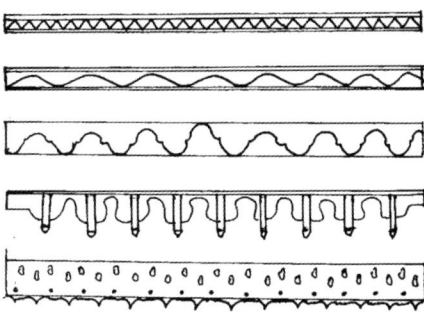

TT3
Fascias with different patterns are located along the eaves. In addition to their decorative purpose, they keep rainwater off the walls.

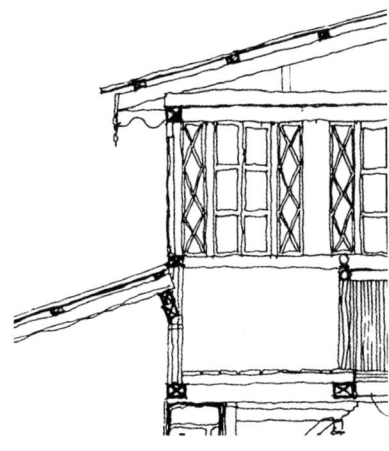

TT4
Large roof overhangs provide shade and protect the walls from rain.

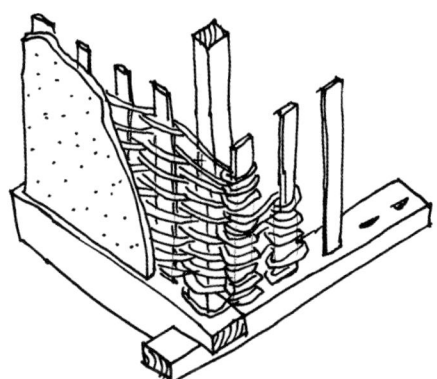

TT2
Chikka is a mixture of fermented straw and topsoil and can be used for wattle-and-daub construction. It is by far the cheapest way to build a wall and it has good thermal properties.

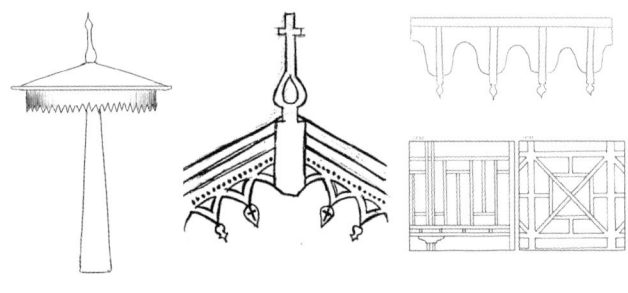

MD3
As wood is a quite soft material that is easy to process, building parts made of wood are often elaborated in a very decorative manner.

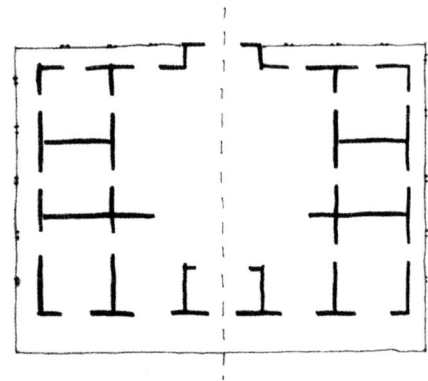

AU4
Symmetrical floor plans with squarish rooms offer flexible use. Secondary spaces are avoided as a 'waste of space'. A hierarchy is achieved by the room size and their relationship to the centre of the house.

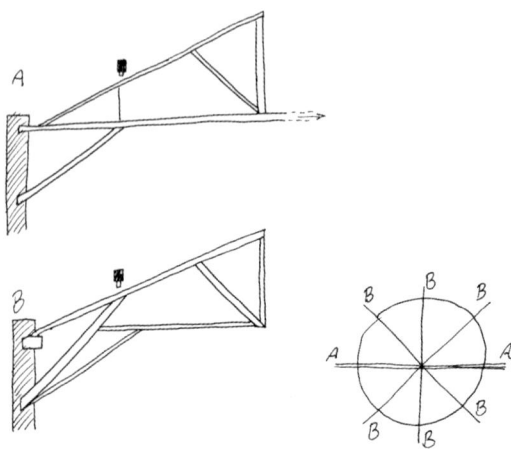

TE3
Timber trusses have great tensile strength while also being lightweight. They can span over more than ten metres.

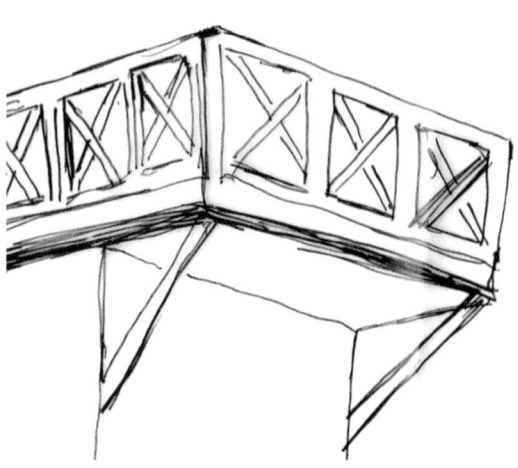

TP3
Balustrades are often made of wood and are square shaped. A cross in the middle gives them rigidity. They are simple to produce and are used as railings on exterior stairs, porches, and verandas.

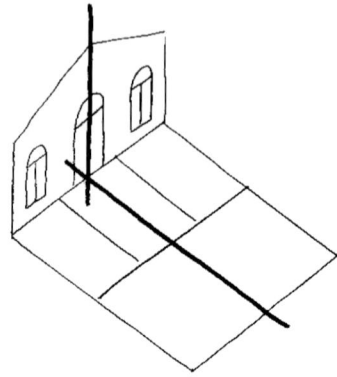

AD1
Symmetrical façades give the buildings a more representative expression.

CD2
The application of rather small façade grids allows the integration of openings, such as doors or windows, without disturbing the homogeneity of the façade.

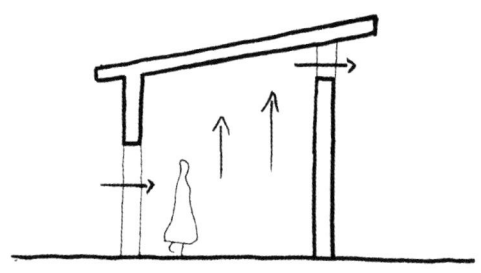

AR3
Room heights of 3.2 metres or more allow the warm air to stream upwards and escape the building through high openings. Fresh air is then sucked into the building through lower openings.

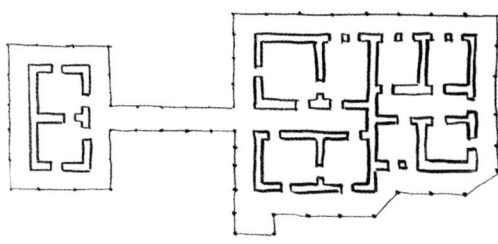

CE3
Bridges between buildings enable a safe and comfortable transition. Bridges can spare the construction of a second staircase.

CE4
Highly functional façade modules are efficiently prefabricated, saving material, time, and money. Assembled together, they resemble a wooden curtain wall.

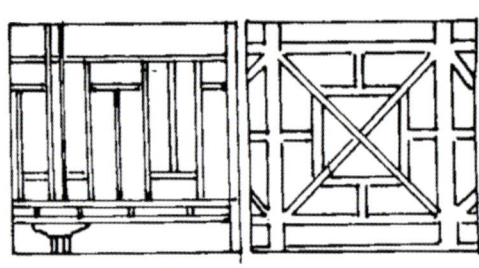

CU3
Railings have different geometrical patterns that are inspired by different cultures. They provide safety for verandas.

MR2
Thatch as the traditional material for roofing is locally available and biodegradable. It absorbs sound and provides a thermal buffer.

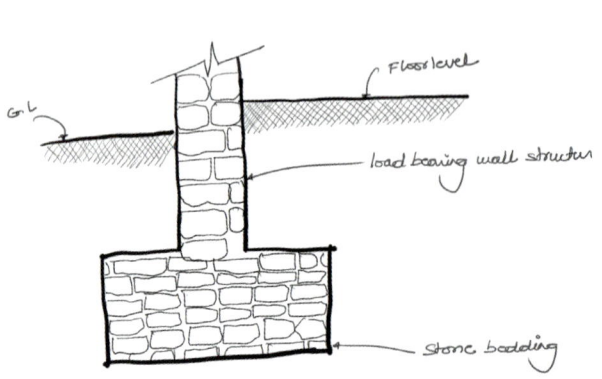

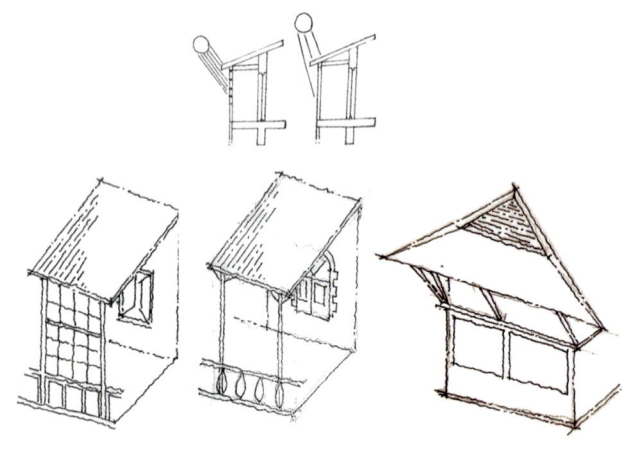

MT2
Of all the local materials, stone is the most rigid and thus, used for durable foundations.

CR3
Verandas offer a private outside area, while protecting residents from sun and rain. Different forms of eaves also fulfil this function.

AU2
Watchtowers are located on the top floor of buildings, providing views in all directions.

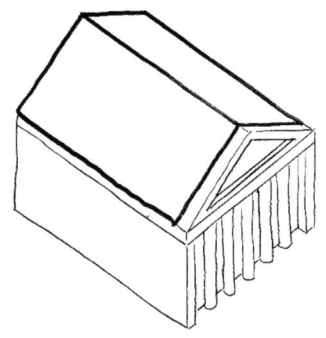

CE3
The inclination of roofs (typically 15–30°) makes the most efficient use of structural material while ensuring rainwater is quickly washed away.

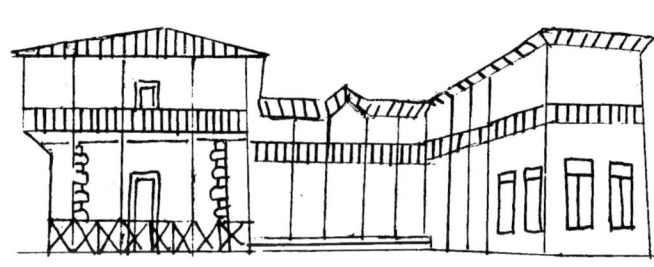

MP3
By limiting to a few construction materials, it is possible to create a harmonious overall architecture. The combination of wood and metal sheets allows a lightweight construction that is easy to erect.

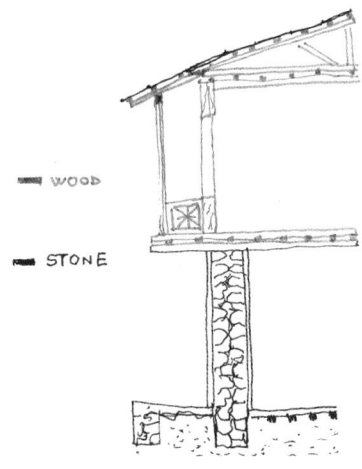

TP3
Applying heavy construction materials on the bottom and lighter materials on the upper storeys makes it possible for different trades (crafts) to work sequentially.

Architectural Alphabet

TE3
Fixed wooden louvers are located under and protected by the eaves. They provide ventilation. Placed above windows, they remove the need for lintels.

AU3
Jharokhas or bay windows protrude from the front façade of buildings on an upper level. They provide a prominent room for observing the outside or communicating with people on the street.

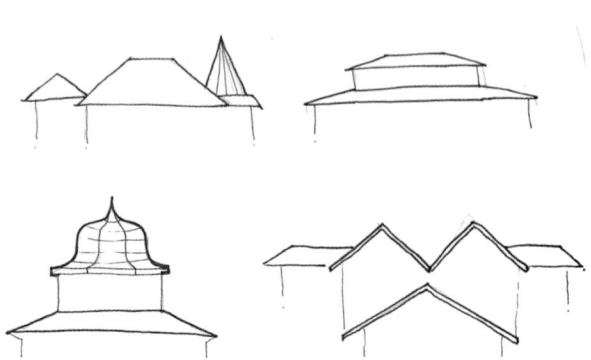

MD4
Corrugated iron sheets as a skin on top of a wooden structure allow a high variety of roof shapes that strongly add to the expressive character of buildings.

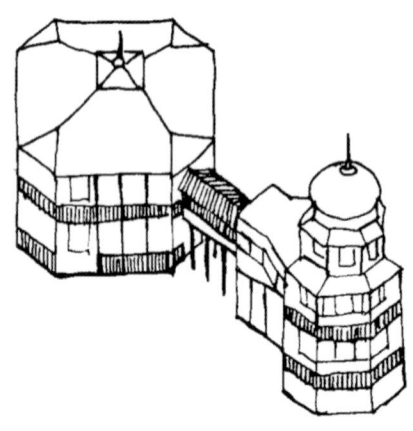

AU2
Bridges allow the special separation of functions in a building, such as profane and religious.

CD2
Arabesque ornaments with different geometrical patterns add to the aesthetic value of the building. Valuing a building adds to its durability.

AU4
Spaces underneath verandas are arcades. They create a semi-public zone at the intersection of street and residence, providing space for a variety of activities such as commercial or recreational.

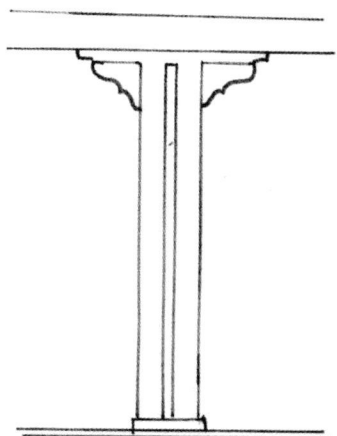

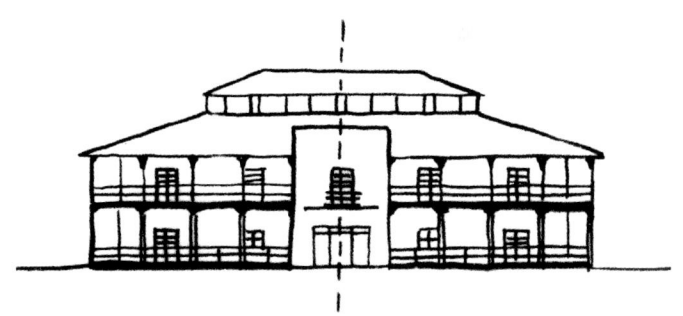

TE3
The square shape of wooden columns makes the best use of the tree's diameter. Double columns carry twice as much load.

CP3
Two-tier roofs allow the placement of windows at the upper end of the walls, allowing light to come into the depths of buildings.

Architectural Alphabet   217

Model by Salma Khobalatte

5

Appendix

Heritage at Risk

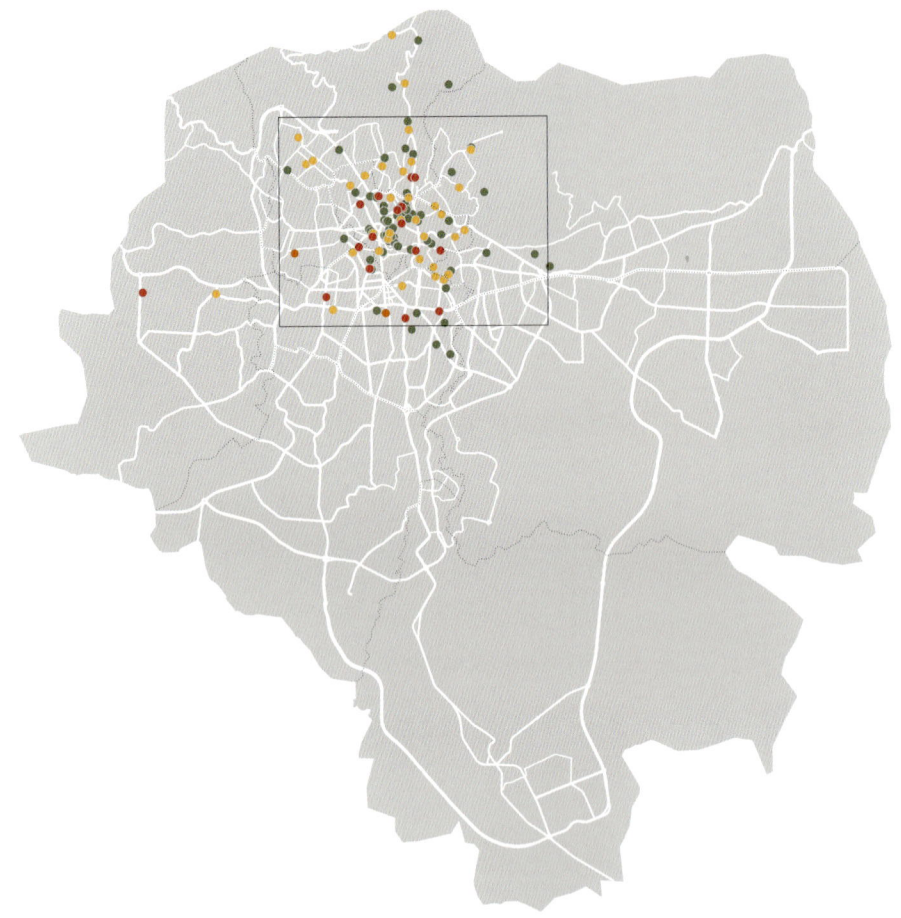

Mapped urban heritage

Enhanced Mapping: The Addis Ababa Urban Heritage Database

The NGO Addis Woubet has collaborated with GTZ, the German organisation for international cooperation (now GIZ), since 2006. What started as personal initiatives successively developed into a systematic approach to collecting information about heritage buildings in Addis Ababa. The list had a focus on the pre-modernist architecture – not exclusively but predominantly. Some 173 heritage buildings and monuments were identified and mapped.

This database was at the very start of our research in spring 2021, as we transferred it into an interactive Google map accessible to everyone and easy to use. Simply scan the QR code on the right. When you are in Addis, you can also navigate through the old neighbourhoods using the app.

The first thing that catches your eye is the distribution of buildings in a wide territory, which contrasts drastically with historical city growth in the European context, for example (also see p. 183). By consulting older satellite images – the oldest available are from November 2002 – it was possible to observe how heritage buildings were being affected by urban development. Starting there, we categorised the different

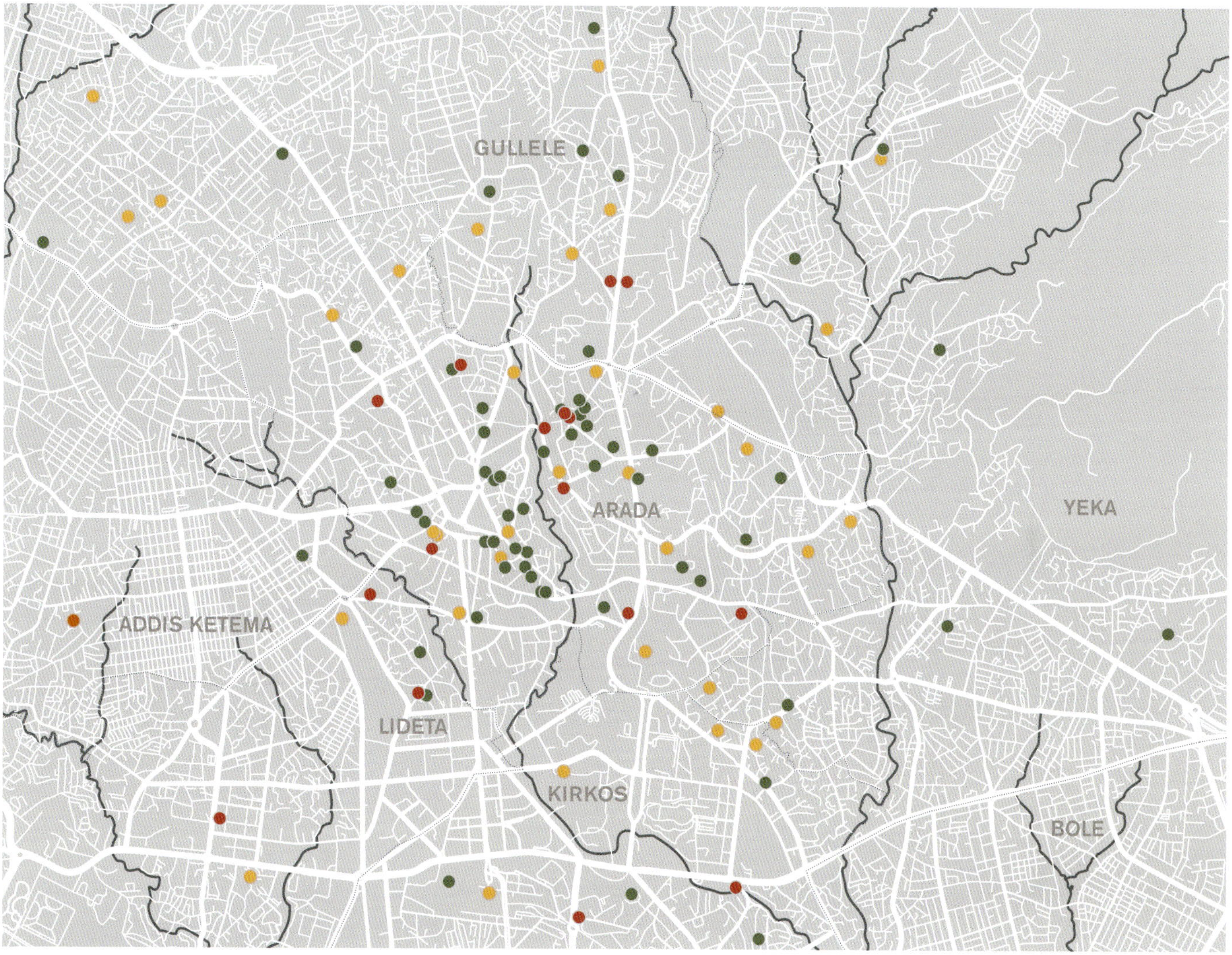

Mapped urban heritage, zoomed in

grades of vulnerability of heritage and used a colour code to visualise it. The appendix shows 80 exemplary heritage buildings from the 'Urban Heritage Database' through a period of approximately 20 years, mapped in four satellite images for each building. New buildings and the demolition of buildings were mapped. Overall, this provides a relatively precise picture of the urban dynamics that have been established around urban heritage since the beginning of the century.

Scan the QR code with your smartphone to access the interactive Google map.

Heritage at Risk 221

The People Behind the Database

Maryam Senna Asfa Wossen

Michael Maiwald

Omnia Aboukorah-Voigt

Monika Wiebusch

Two years after her return from exile, Princess Maryam Senna co-founded the NGO Addis Woubet in 2005 with Nahu Girma. The NGO's aim was to raise awareness of the need to preserve, restore, and maintain urban heritage. Addis Woubet raised funds for the preservation of endangered heritage buildings, gave grants to heritage studies, and promoted the installation of a legal framework for heritage protection that was published in May 2006. Alongside the work on the database, she organised a big exhibition at the National Museum.

Between 2003 and 2011, Michael Maiwald worked in the Addis Ababa City Administration as a CIM expert. His admiration for the old houses of Addis Ababa resulted in him meeting Princess Maryam Senna. In cooperation with her and as a member of Addis Woubet, he enhanced the heritage database with photos by Dr. Philipp Schauer (then Permanent Representative of the German Ambassador in Addis Ababa). In his function as a CIM expert, Michael cooperated with gtz.

Dr. Omnia Aboukorah-Voigt was an advisor to the Addis Ababa City Government and gtz between 2006 and 2010 on how urban heritage conservation could become an example of urban governance. She provided recommendations on how enhancing, renovating, and developing heritage can be a tool for a more inclusive and sustainable readjustment of urban spaces. She participated in the elaboration of mapping urban heritage and their state of conservation that was included in the database.

Monika Wiebusch was gtz project manager with the Addis Ababa Mayor and City Administration from 2007 to 2009. Concerning the rehabilitation of traditional houses, she cooperated with CIM expert Michael Maiwald, Princess Maryam Senna as member of the Addis Woubet Initiative, and with Dr. Omnia Aboukorah-Voigt as consultant. In June 2009, she integrated the heritage database into the gtz 'Urban Heritage Agenda for Addis Ababa' documentation.

Example:

Ghiorgis Armanis Residence
Early 1900s

11/2002

06/2009

Explanatory Key

The list, starting on page 224, contains a representative selection of 80 out of 173 heritage buildings from the database. The list is organised in chronological order.

To understand how heritage is at risk in Addis Ababa, take note of the following:

❶ building name and year of construction as found in the database

❷ picture from the database

❸ Google Earth satellite image

❹ number in the database

❺ building's current status

❻ symbols indicating different characteristics of spatial transformation in the urban context

❼ descriptive text, excerpt from the database

Timeline

Google Earth satellite images were used in order to document the urban transformation that affects heritage buildings in Addis Ababa. The oldest usable images date back to November 2002, which allowed an analysis over a period of 231 months (approx. 19 years). The images were captured between 79 and 69 months (six years) apart. The dates were chosen based on the quality of the available satellite images: November 2002, June 2009, May 2015, and February 2021.

Urban Transformation

White indicates the heritage building.

Yellow indicates the structures that were demolished during the following six-year period.

Red indicates the newly built structures with reference to November 2002 when the timeline starts.

Status

Status was defined using a literature review, internet research, and with the help of Fasil Giorghis.
- Restored
- Preserved
- Altered
- Dilapidated
- Demolished

Transformation in the Context

Type of transformation
- Building
- Infrastructure
- Landscape

Pace of transformation
- <u>Constant</u>: the transformation has developed throughout the years
- <u>Instant</u>: the transformation has happened suddenly

Spatial development
- <u>Territorial</u>: the transformation happened on a large scale
- <u>Punctual</u>: the transformation happened on a small scale

---

05/2015

02/2021

Ghiorgis Armanis Residence
No.:185
❹ ❺ ❻

The former residence of the Greek merchant Ghiorgis Armanis. The building dates back to the first decades of the twentieth century. Unusual on account of the contrast between the hexagonal plan of the ground floor and the circular plan of the upper floor.
❼

Menelik Palace / *Ghebbi*
1889

11/2002

06/2009

Menelik II Entoto Palace
1892

11/2002

06/2009

***Dej.* Birru Haile Mariam Residence**
End of the nineteenth century

11/2002

06/2009

Yeshimmabeth / Ayele Abuye Residence
End of the nineteenth century

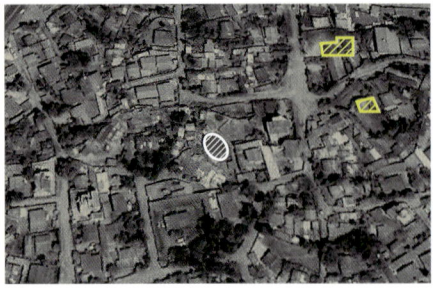
11/2002

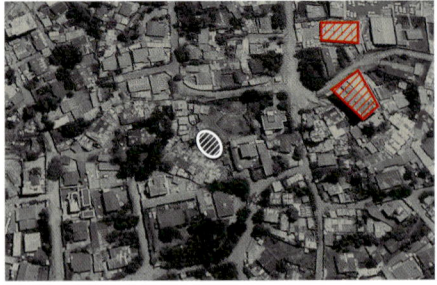
06/2009

05/2015

02/2021

Menelik Palace / *Ghebbi*
No.: 55

A town within the town, the *Ghebbi* is home to dwellings, offices, streets, workshops, stores, and a mint. The Elfign was the imperial residence, sided by the Prayer Pavilion. First built in 1889 (photo 1930s). Security area, no public access.

05/2015

02/2021

Menelik II Entoto Palace
No.: 127

Menelik's first palace. It is evident that the buildings were built in several phases following the changing needs of the royal household. The first building was built under the direction of the Swiss advisor Alfred Ilg. After the fire, in 1890–1892 Menelik decided to build the existing one as a larger and more magnificent palace surrounded by 50 houses.

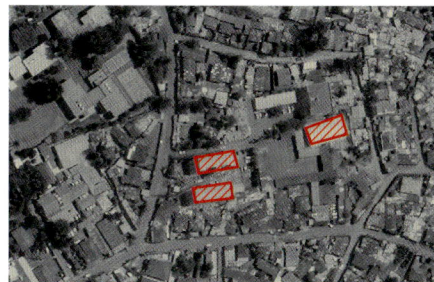
05/2015

02/2021

Dej. Birru Haile Mariam Residence
No.: 152

Former residence of *Dejazmatch* Birru Haile Mariam, cousin of Emperor Selassie. Built at the end of the nineteenth century, it is the biggest building in the area and it is also located higher than the others.

05/2015

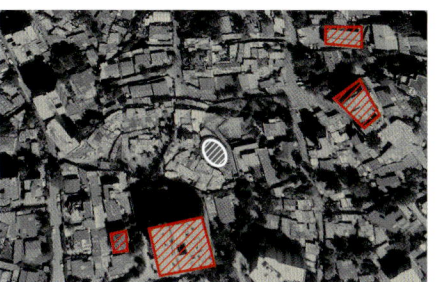
02/2021

Yeshimmabeth / Ayele Abuye Residence
No.: 186

Former residence of Woizero Yeshimmabeth, sister of *Fitawrari* Bekeke Ayele. Probably built at the end of the nineteenth century.
It is one of the most interesting oval buildings. The building has two floors and outside stairs. There is a small emphasis on the roof and the first floor is higher than the ground floor. The stone walls are half a metre thick.

Heritage at Risk   225

Mohamed Ali Old Store Building
Approx. 1900

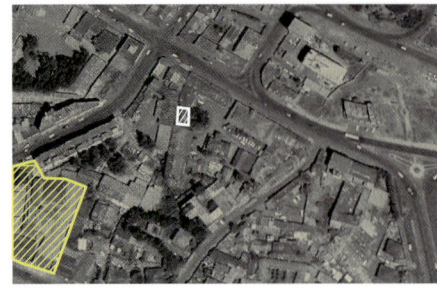

11/2002

06/2009

Grazmach Tase Asegid
1900

11/2002

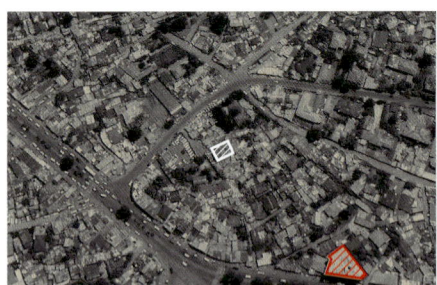

06/2009

Fitawrari **Wube Abawollo Residence**
1901

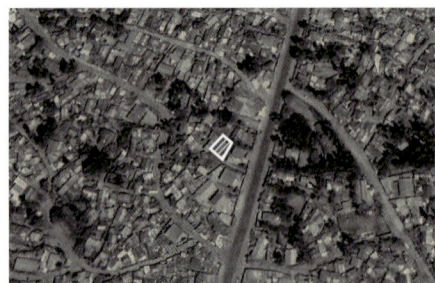

11/2002

06/2009

AA Restaurant / *Dej.* Wube Haile Mariam
End of nineteenth or early twentieth century

11/2002

06/2009

05/2015

02/2021

Mohamed Ali Old Store Building
No.: 30

Mohamed Ali's first 'modern' general store opened at the beginning of the twentieth century. Interesting wooden decorations, a mixture of Indian elements with Armenian influence. The two-storey house has a nice veranda and exterior staircase. The inauguration occurred in the presence of Emp. Menelik II around 1904.

05/2015

02/2021

Grazmach Tase Asegid
No.: 73

Former residence of Grazmach Tashe Ashebir, a technician working for Menelik. Designed by the Indian architect Woli Mohammad. Built around 1900. Indian-influenced architecture.

05/2015

02/2021

Fitawrari Wube Abawollo Residence
No.: 160

Former residence of *Fitawrari* Wube Abawollo, nephew of *Ras* Bitwaddad Tessema. The house was built on the order of Lij Iysu in 1901. Designed by three Indian constructors. Noted fighter against Italian occupation, died in battle 1936 in Maychew.

05/2015

02/2021

AA Restaurant / *Dej.* Wube Haile Mariam
No.: 18

Former residence of *Dejazmatch* Wube Haile Mariam, a nobleman of Menelik's court. Built at the end of the nineteenth or early twentieth century. Indian-influenced architecture.

Heritage at Risk 227

Mohamed Ali – Residence
Early 1900s – collapsed in May 2023!

11/2002

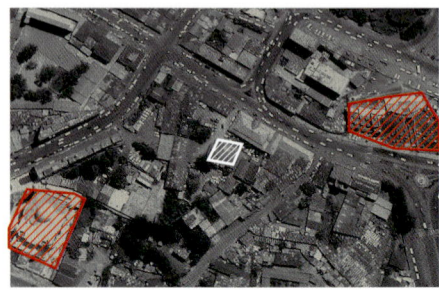

06/2009

Karakachiani Residence
Early 1900s

11/2002

06/2009

Ymtubezznas Residence
Early 1900s

11/2002

06/2009

Badgelling Hotel
Early 1900s

11/2002

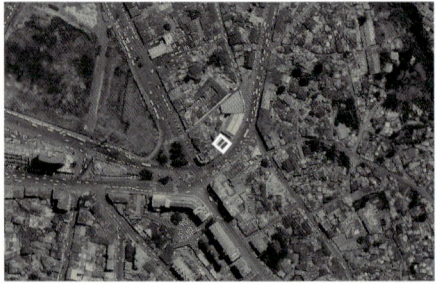

06/2009

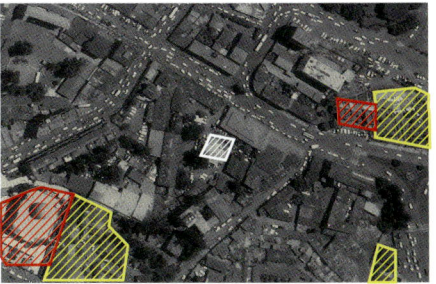
05/2015

02/2021

Mohamed Ali – Residence
No.: 30

The compound belonged to the renowned Indian firm G.M.Mohammedally, a powerful trading company during Menelik's reign. The complex consists of four buildings, including stores, offices, warehouses etc. Built at the beginning of the twentieth century. One of the richly decorated side buildings today hosts a first instance courthouse.

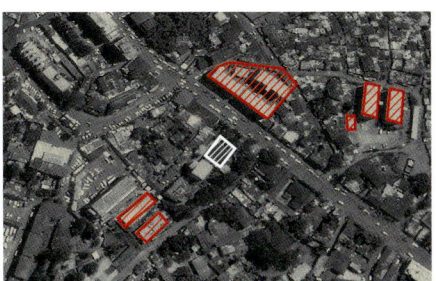
05/2015

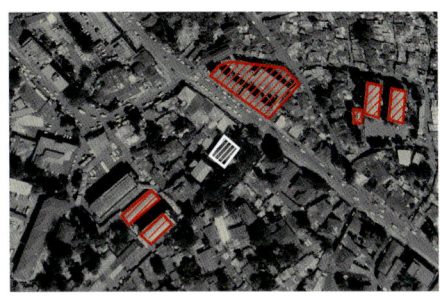
02/2021

Karakachiani Residence
No.: 45

Former residence of Empress Zewditu's Greek dentist, Karakachiani. Built at the beginning of the twentieth century. Neo-classical architecture.

05/2015

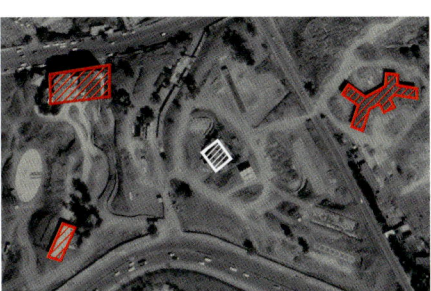
02/2021

Ymtubezznas Residence
No.: 141

The building belonged to Ymtubezznas, a rich Shoan landowner who was the daughter of Hapte Mariam, a judge at Menelik's court. Probably built at the beginning of the twentieth century.

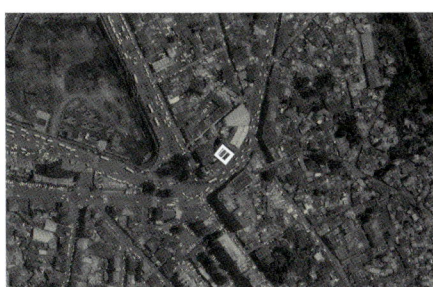
05/2015

02/2021

Badgelling Hotel
No.: 146

Located on Adwa Avenue, one of the city's most representative roads. Indians probably dwelled here. Built in the first two decades of the twentieth century during the reign of Empress Zewditu. Construction of *chikka* and wood. Indian-style architecture. Unfortunately, later steel applications to the façade disturb the appearance.

Heritage at Risk

Menelik Jail
Early 1900s

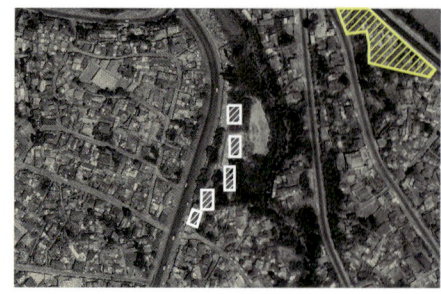
11/2002

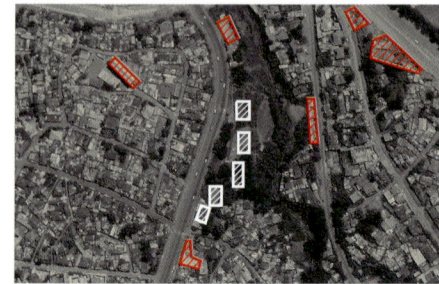
06/2009

***Ras* Kebede Mengasha**
Early 1900s

11/2002

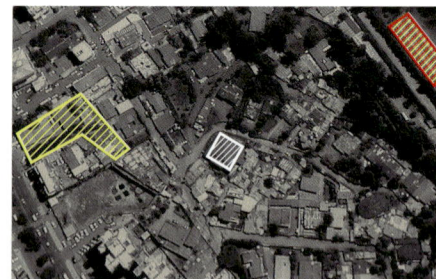
06/2009

Kafay Wale Residence
Early 1900s

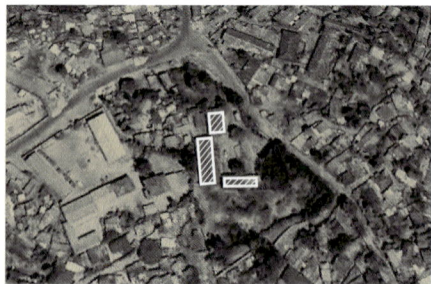
11/2002

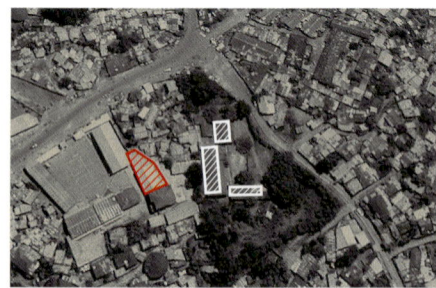
06/2009

***Fitawrari* Agunafer Sebberu Residence**
Early 1900s

11/2002

06/2009

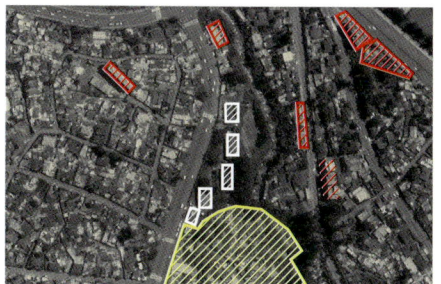

05/2015

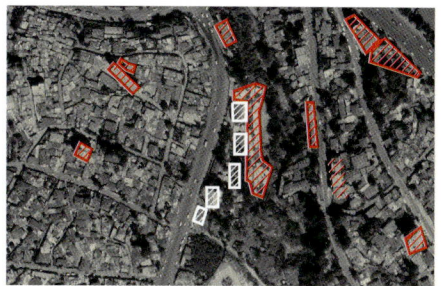

02/2021

Menelik Jail
No.: 16

The big compound featuring five large one-storey buildings served as a jail from the time of Menelik II in the early 1900s until 1961. After that it was converted into a secondary school. It is now the Ethiopia Tikdem No. 2 Elementary School. The old iron grating on the windows is still visible on the administration building.

05/2015

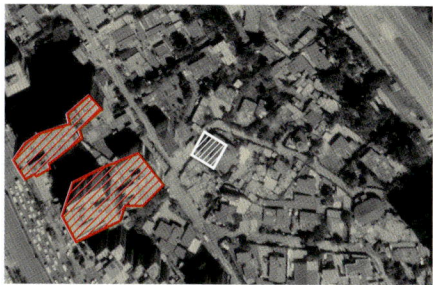

02/2021

Ras Kebede Mengasha
No.: 70

Former residence of *Ras* Kebede Mengasha, who played a key role in the imperial administration under Menelik and was later Governor of Wollo Province. Built in the first decades of the twentieth century. Indian-influenced architecture.

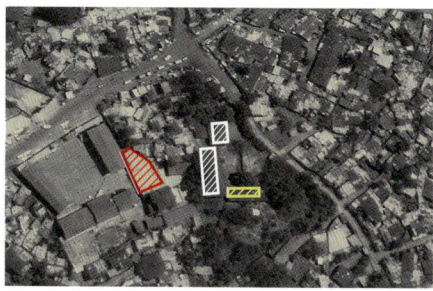

05/2015

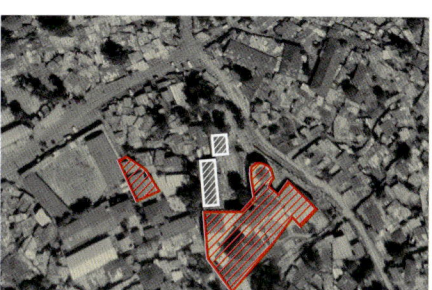

02/2021

Kafay Wale Residence
No.: 183

Former residence of Woizero Kafay Wale, one of Empress Taitu's nieces. Probably built at the beginning of the twentieth century.

05/2015

02/2021

Fitawrari Agunafer Sebberu Residence
No.: 133

Family residence of Agunafer Sebberu, son of *Fitawrari* Sebberu, the commander of the riflemen under Menelik. Built at the beginning of the twentieth century. Early example of the transition from the circular to quadrangular in plan.

Heritage at Risk   231

Hampo Bogasian Residence
Early 1900s

11/2002

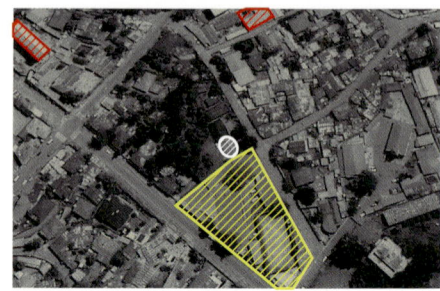

06/2009

Askale Balcha Residence
Early 1900s

11/2002

06/2009

Casa del Fascio / *Ras* Adefrisew
Early 1900s

11/2002

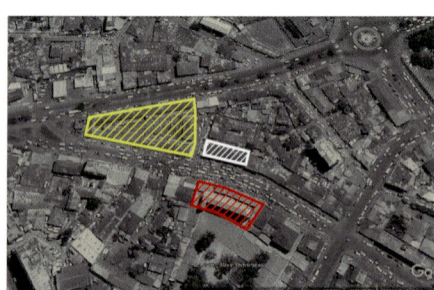

06/2009

***Grazmatch* Sahle Mariam Residence**
Early 1900s

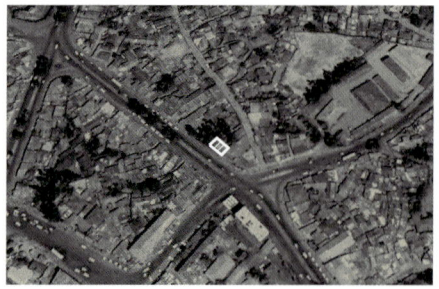

11/2002

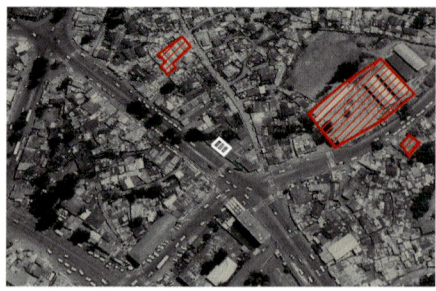

06/2009

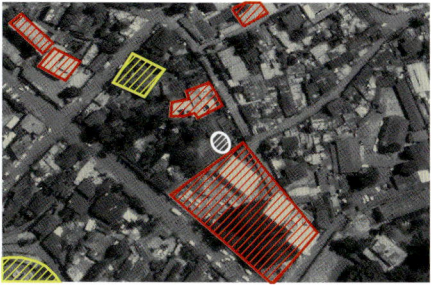
05/2015

02/2021

Hampo Bogasian Residence
No.: 188

Residence (two buildings) of the Bogasian family. Built by Krikorios Bogasian, an honoured supplier of various merchandise by Menelik. Built in the first two decades of the twentieth century. Decorated by Menelik II with the Star of Solomon. Oval plan, wall with adobe plastering. Among the very interesting residences in Arada.

05/2015

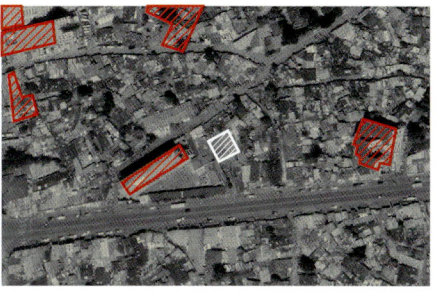
02/2021

Askale Balcha Residence
No.: 155

Former residence of Woizero Askale Balcha, daughter of *Dejazmatch* Balcha, a hero of the Battle of Adwa. Built at the beginning of the twentieth century. Currently used as school. Gingerbread wooden decoration runs around the roof. The owner was the daughter of Askale Balcha, a strong opponent of *Ras* Tafari Makonnen, the later emperor Haile Selassie.

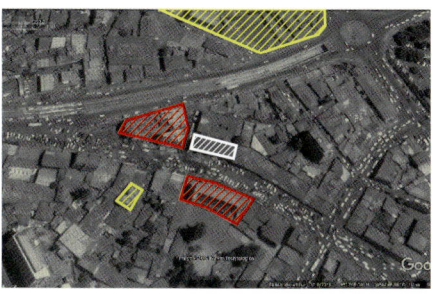
05/2015

02/2021

Casa del Fascio / *Ras* Adefrisew
No.: 28

The building was the first 'Casa del Fascio' used by the Italians after the invasion. Probably built in the first two decades of the twentieth century. Originally the residence of *Ras* Adefrisew, it was selected as the headquarters of the fascist party.

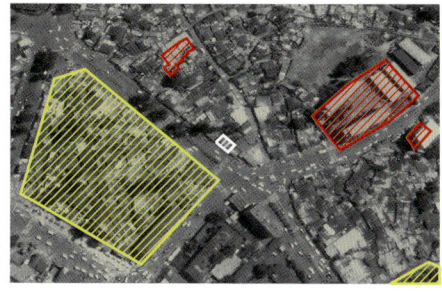
05/2015

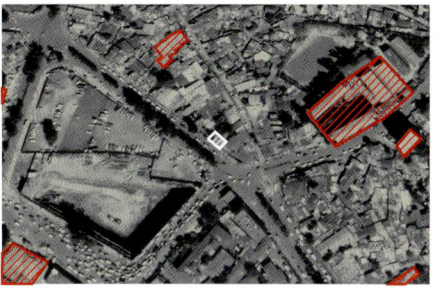
02/2021

Grazmatch Sahle Mariam Residence
No.: 182

Former residence of *Grazmatch* Sahle Mariam, who worked for the Italians as a translator in the 1930s. Built in the early twentieth century.

Heritage at Risk   233

Sheik Ojele House
Early 1900s

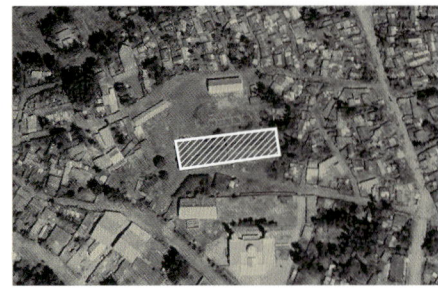
11/2002

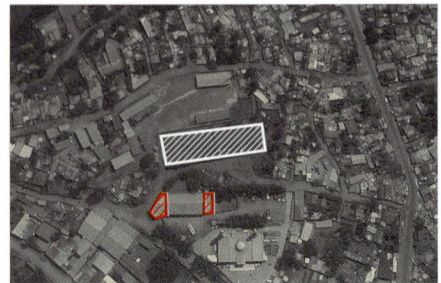
06/2009

Azalech Gobena
Early 1900s

11/2002

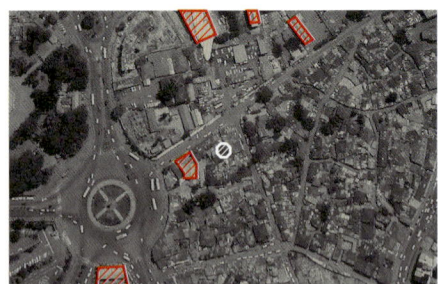
06/2009

Artin Avakian Residence
Early 1900s

11/2002

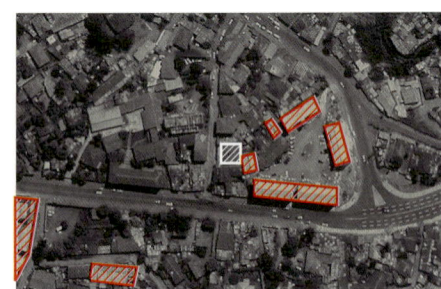
06/2009

Ras Abate Bwayalew Residence
Early 1900s

11/2002

06/2009

234

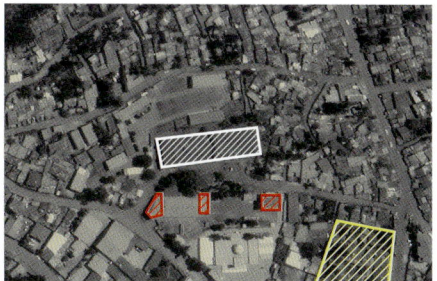
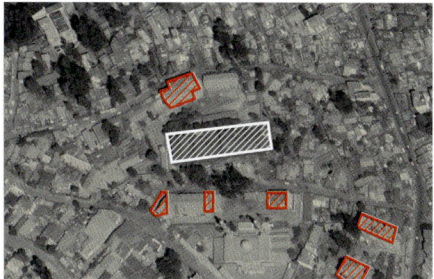

Sheik Ojele House
No.: 8

Former Residence of *Sheik* Ojele Al-Hasan, who was ruler of Asosa and helped *Ras* Makonnen to conquer the Beni Shangul in 1897–1898. Built at the beginning of the twentieth century. Indo-Islamic-influenced architecture.

05/2015 02/2021

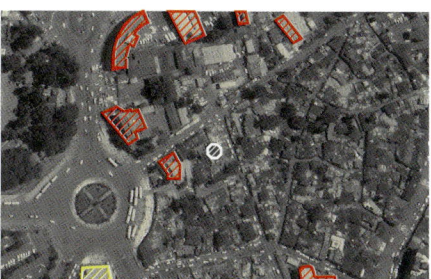

Azalech Gobena
No.: 24

Former residence of the first Ethiopian female minister. It is said that the house was built at the beginning of the twentieth century by a Polish or Russian lawyer.

05/2015 02/2021

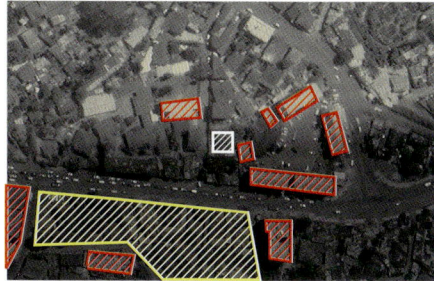

Artin Avakian Residence
No.: 48

Owned by an Armenian constructor in 1924. Built of stone and *chikka*. Characterised by an interesting veranda around the ground floor and large multiglazed windows on the second. floor. (OTNF)

05/2015 02/2021

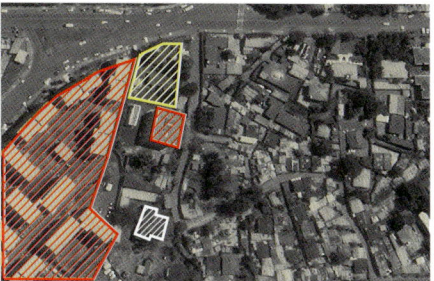

Ras Abate Bwayalew Residence
No.: 80

Former residence of *Ras* Abate Bwayalew, one of the most important military leaders of Menelik's court. The architect was probably *Ras* Abate himself. Built at the beginning of the twentieth century.

05/2015 02/2021

Heritage at Risk

Ghiorgis Armanis Residence
Early 1900s

11/2002

06/2009

Kachini Residence
First two decades of the twentieth century

11/2002

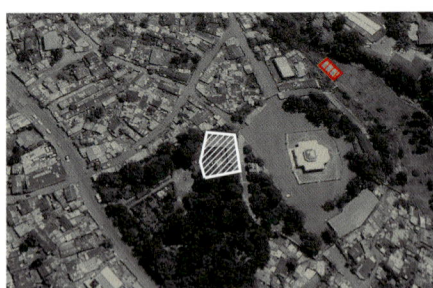
06/2009

Bizunesh H / Michael Res. / *Kegnazmatch*
Early 1900s

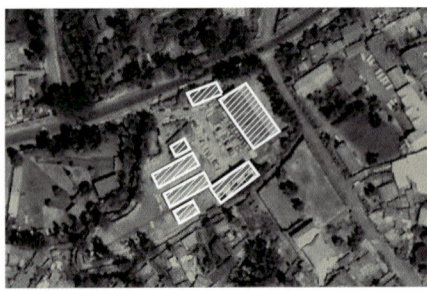
11/2002

06/2009

***Dej.* Mekuria BantYirgu**
1903

11/2002

06/2009

05/2015

02/2021

Ghiorgis Armanis Residence
No.:185

Former residence of the Greek merchant Ghiorgis Armanis. The building dates back to the first decades of the twentieth century. It is unusual due to the contrast between the hexagonal plan of the ground floor and the circular plan of the upper floor.

05/2015

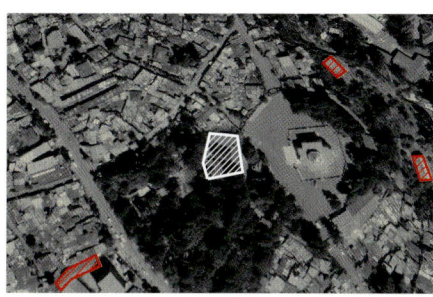

02/2021

Kachini Residence
No.: 138

Former residence of the Armenian Kachini. Built in the first two decades of the twentieth century.

05/2015

02/2021

Bizunesh H / Michael Res. / *Kegnazmatch*
No.: 75

Former residence of *Kegnazmatch* Mulugeta. Built in the first two decades of the twentieth century. A large compound with several buildings. The main building has two floors.

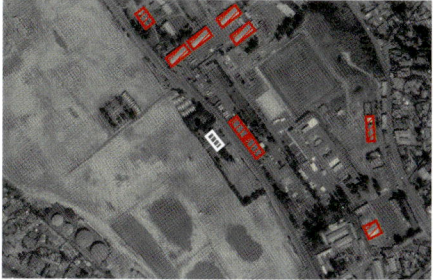

05/2015

02/2021

Dej. Mekuria BantYirgu
No.: 103

This huge field was granted by Menelik to the Imperial Club. Initially used as a polo, tennis, football ground etc. and for state ceremonies and social gatherings. Created in 1903.

Heritage at Risk 237

Muse Fasika Residence
Early twentieth century

11/2002

06/2009

Ahmed Salah / Shashib-Haiset
Early twentieth century

11/2002

06/2009

Andreas Kavadias Residence
Early twentieth century

11/2002

06/2009

Agafari Kelele Residence
Early twentieth century

11/2002

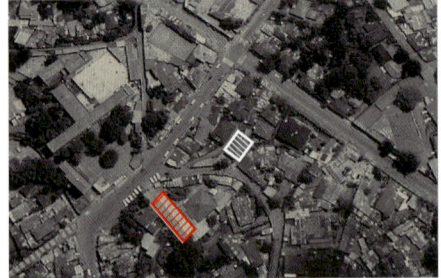

06/2009

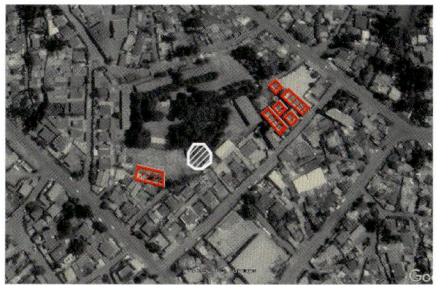
05/2015

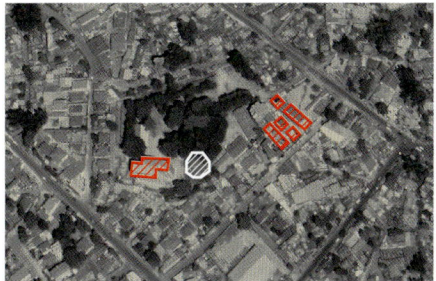
02/2021

Muse Fasika Residence
No.: 6

Former residence of Muse Fasika Wolde Mikael, a nobleman at Menelik's court. Built in the early twentieth century. It shows a blend of Abyssinian and European architecture.

05/2015

02/2021

Ahmed Salah / Shashib-Haiset
No.: 38

Former residence of the Indian Shashib-Haiset family. Built at the beginning of the twentieth century. The building reproduces a typical nobleman's residence of the Indian region of Gujarat.

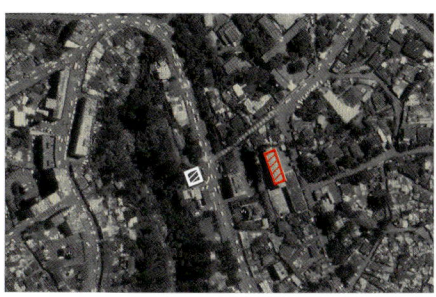
05/2015

02/2021

Andreas Kavadias Residence
No.: 168

Former residence of the Greek Andreas Kavadias, the founder of *Amro*, the first printed newspaper in Addis Ababa. Located near Arat Kilo Sq., it was built during Menelik's time at the beginning of the twentieth century.

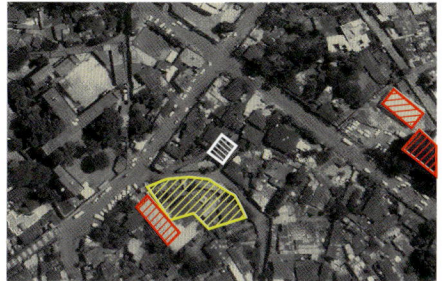
05/2015

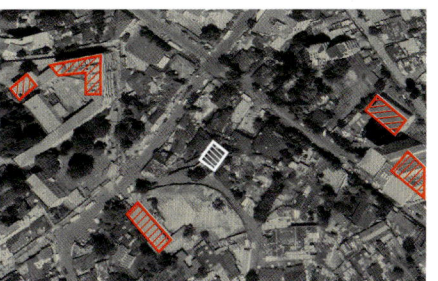
02/2021

Agafari Kelele Residence
No.: 167

Former residence of Agafari Kelele. Built at the beginning of the twentieth century. Indian-style architecture.

Heritage at Risk   239

Old Municipality / *Negadras* H / Giorgis Agid
1906

11/2002

06/2009

Bank of Abyssinia
1907

11/2002

06/2009

Etegue Taitu Hotel
1907

11/2002

06/2009

Cinema Ethiopia
1908

11/2002

06/2009

240

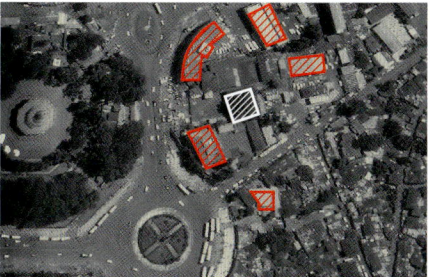

05/2015

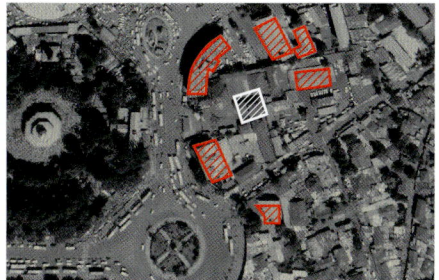

02/2021

Old Municipality / *Negadras* H / Giorgis Agid
No.: 23

Former residence of Haile Giorgis Agidew, appointed 'Head of Merchants' by Menelik. He later chaired the cabinet. Functioned as Municipality from 1916–1964. Built 1906. Used as AA Supreme Court until mid-2008. The house is empty and the adjacent demolition and construction works are a threat to the building, which is already rapidly decaying.

05/2015

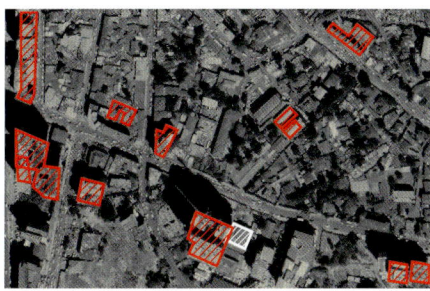

02/2021

Bank of Abyssinia
No.: 47

The Bank of Abyssinia was founded in 1907 as an Anglo-Egyptian company and was the first bank of Ethiopia. Designed by Sebastiano Castagna. Built by the Italian constructor Vaudetto. Completed in 1907. Neo-classical style.

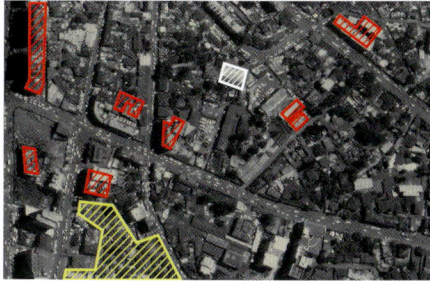

05/2015

02/2021

Etegue Taitu Hotel
No.: 44

This building was the first hotel in Addis Ababa and accommodated mostly Ethiopian dignitaries, diplomats, and foreigners. Constructed on the order of Empress Taitu. Designed by Minas Kerbekian. Built in 1907.

05/2015

02/2021

Cinema Ethiopia
No.: 40

First post office opened in Addis Ababa on 20 July 1908. It functioned until the Italian occupation in 1935. The elegant two-storey building with surrounding verandas was damaged during a fire in 1936. After renovation, it functioned as the Cinema Italia until 1941. It now hosts the Cinema Ethiopia.

Heritage at Risk

Dej. **Ayalew Birru Residence**
Around 1910

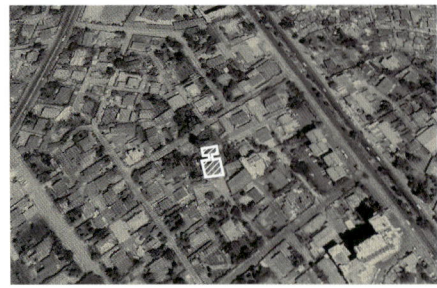

11/2002

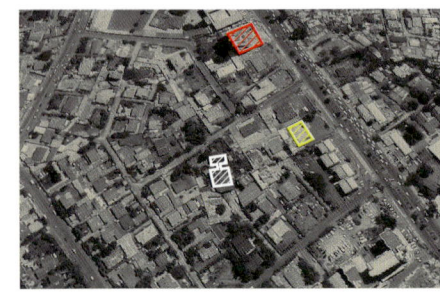

06/2009

Dej. **Asfaw Kebede Residence**
Around 1910

11/2002

06/2009

Afrika Andinet School / Nigist Zewditu's Gu
1913

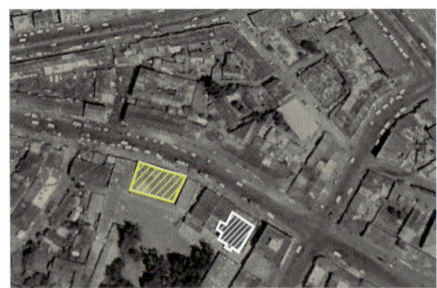

11/2002

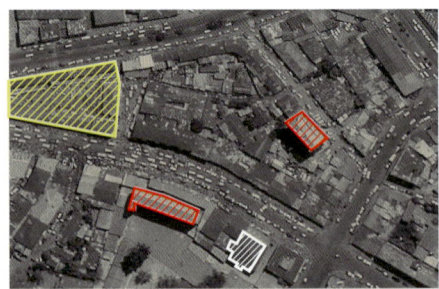

06/2009

Alfred Ilg Residence / Arenti Ashakian
1912–1913 (probably incorrect in database)

11/2002

06/2009

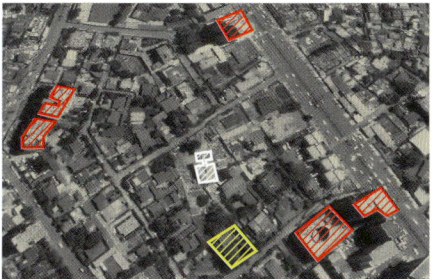
05/2015

02/2021

Dej. Ayalew Birru Residence
No.: 69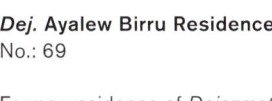

Former residence of *Dejazmatch* Ayalew Birru, son of *Ras* Birru Wolde Gabriel and Governor of the Simien Province. Supported the Italians during their occupation. The residence consists of twin buildings bridged by a covered passage.

05/2015

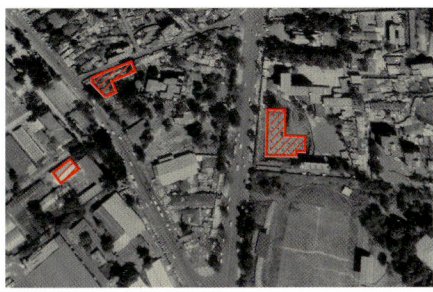
02/2021

Dej. Asfaw Kebede Residence
No.: 101

Former residence of *Dejazmatch* Asfaw Kebede, the administrator of Haile Sellassie's palace. The residence consists of two buildings. Built in the 1910s. Indian-influenced architecture. Though government owned, the very bad state of the building may lead to utter destruction if no measures are taken.

05/2015

02/2021

Afrika Andinet School / Nigist Zewditu's Gu
No.: 29

Previously a hotel, it was built around 1913 and presents Oriental-type details. A construction has been added.

05/2015

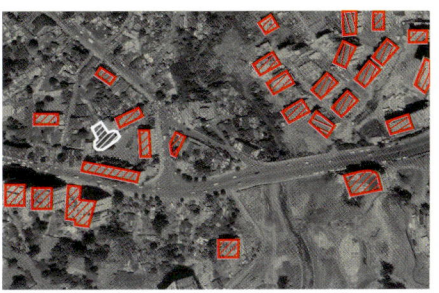
02/2021

Alfred Ilg Residence / Arenti Ashakian
No.: 49

The Swiss Alfred Ilg was an important technical advisor of Emp. Menelik II. The former oval thatched roof was later covered with corrugated steel and thus converted to polygonal. Later owned by Dr. Lorenzo Tiezaz, a diplomat under Haile Selassie and later Minister of Foreign Affairs. It also served as one of the first schools of Menelik's time.

Heritage at Risk 243

Tiezas (Azaje) Terrefe W/Gabriel
1913

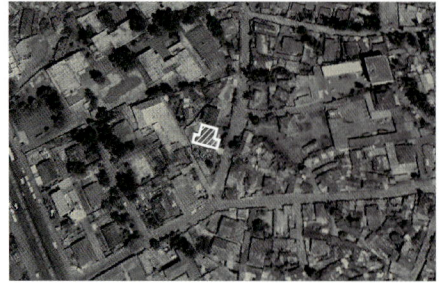

11/2002

06/2009

Ras Kassa Hailu Estate
1910s

11/2002

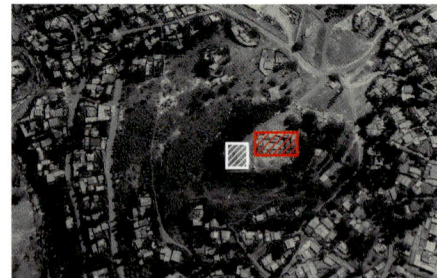

06/2009

Muse Nazareth & Bagdra Iyana
1910s

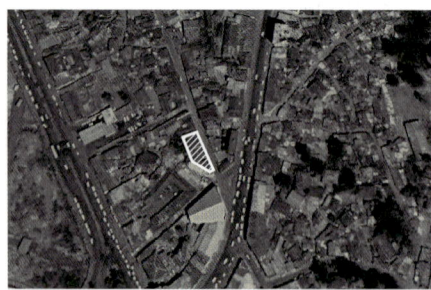

11/2002

06/2009

Matig Kevorkoff Residence / Elias Hotel
1910s

11/2002

06/2009

244

05/2015

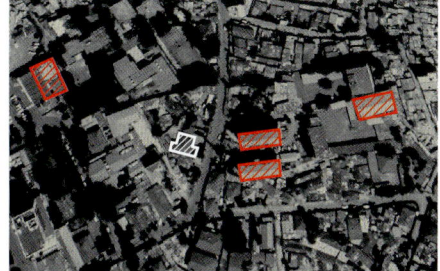

02/2021

Tiezas (Azaye) Terrefe W / Gabriel
No.: 14

The first owner of this building is still unknown. Haile Selassie gave it to Azaye Terrafe as a reward for his services in the palace administration. Built between 1913–1917 (reign of Lij Iyasu). The villa is richly decorated, the construction being made of stone masonry and wood. The roof decoration shows Indian influences.

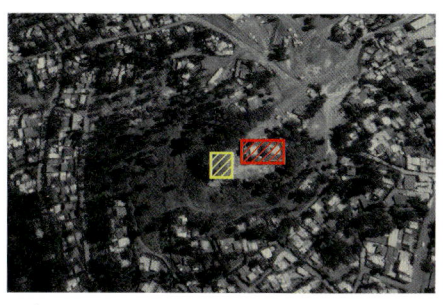

05/2015

02/2021

Ras Kassa Hailu Estate
No.: 121

Former residence of *Ras* Kassa, who brought the *tabot* of Mariam Church, which was in the neighbourhood, to his residence and transformed it into a church.

05/2015

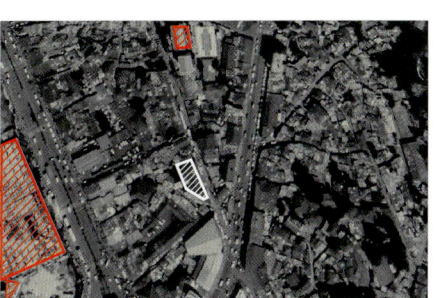

02/2021

Muse Nazareth & Bagdra Iyana
No.: 41

The old merchants house in the central Piassa area is boldly located on the sharply pointed corner of Dej. Afewerk St. The sharp building's corner is a landmark in the area. The construction consisting of plastered masonry, wood, and corrugated steel is in very bad shape.

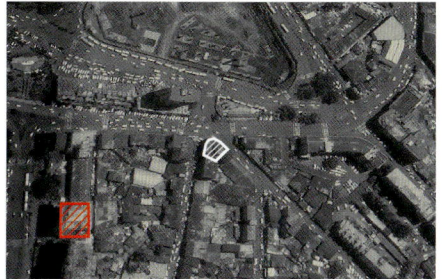

05/2015

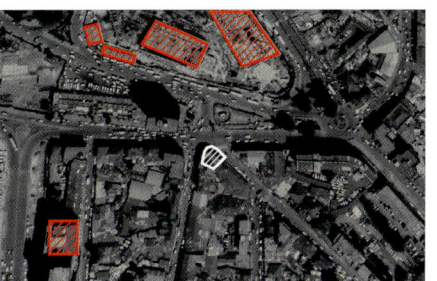

02/2021

Matig Kevorkoff Residence / Elias Hotel
No.: 144

Built on the order of the Armenia trader Matig Kevorkoff to be used as a shop, a store, and as the headquarters of the tobacco monopoly. Built in the 1910s. Armenian architecture.

Heritage at Risk   245

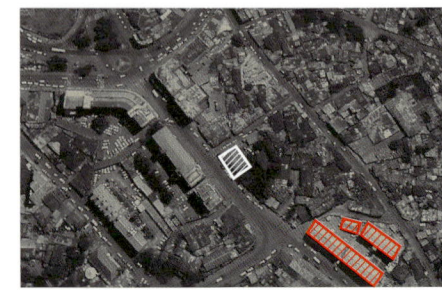

Besmelian (Elias) Residence / Avekian
1915

11/2002

06/2009

Balambaras Shaka Buluhu Residence
1915

11/2002

06/2009

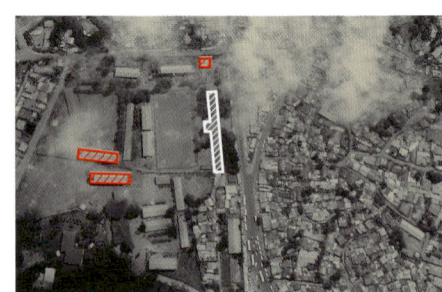

Dil Betgil School / Keg. Beyene Yimer Res.
Around 1915

11/2002

06/2009

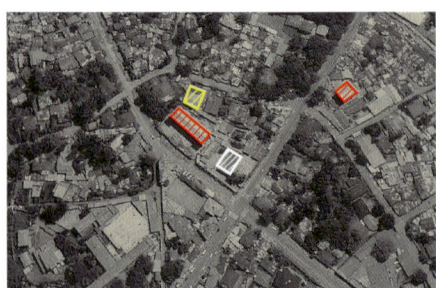

Muse Yakob / Agop Bagdasarian's 1st Res.
1910s

11/2002

06/2009

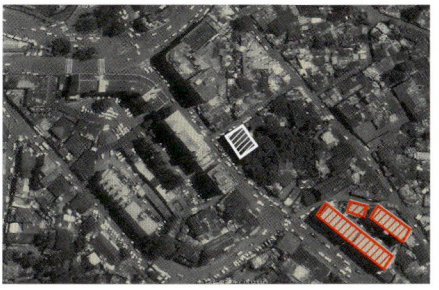

05/2015

02/2021

Besmelian (Elias) Residence / Avekian
No.: 142

Former residence of the Armenian Elias Besmelian, brother of Samuel, who became the first secretary of the US Embassy in Addis Ababa. One of the notable heritage examples in the Piassa area. Construction in natural stone, with rich wooden attachments: pillars, verandas, windows with exterior shutters.

05/2015

02/2021

Balambaras Shaka Buluhu Residence
No.: 100

Former residence of *Balambaras* Shaka, a high-ranking official of Emperor Selassie's court. Built in the early 1920s. The building was destroyed due to overuse and lack of conservation efforts in January 2007. The empty space now serves as an extension of the already formerly existing schoolyard.

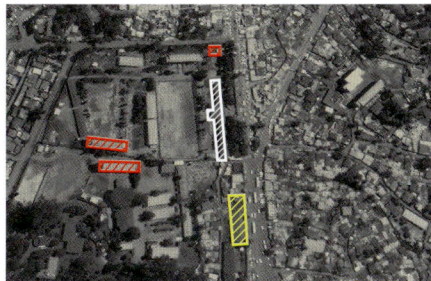

05/2015

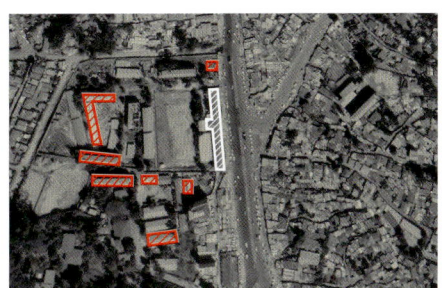

02/2021

Dil Betgil School / Keg. Beyene Yimer Res.
No.: 122

Former residence of Beyene Yimer, Director of Post and Telegraph under Menelik and Minister of Foreign Affairs between 1912–1916. The building was the Menera School for Girls from 1962–1972. Built at the beginning of the twentieth century.

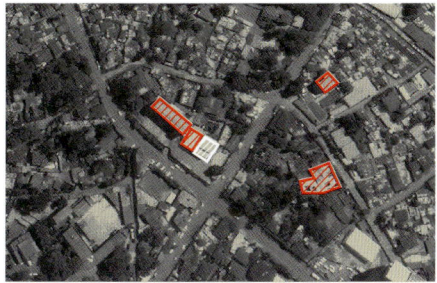

05/2015

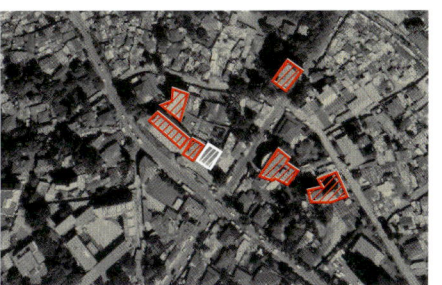

02/2021

Muse Yakob / Agop Bagdasarian's 1st Res.
No.: 164

First residence of the Armenian Agop Bagdasarian, former residence of Muse Yakob, one of the first goldsmiths at Menelik' court. After he left, it became the new residence of the Armenian Agop Bagdasarian. Built in the 1910s. Renovated in the 1990s.

Heritage at Risk   247

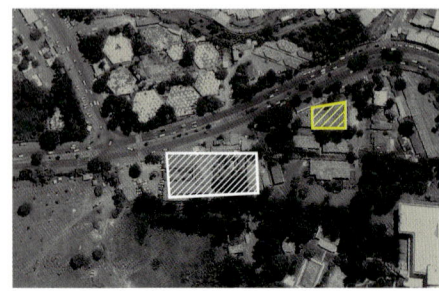

Finefine Hotel / Hotel d'Europe
1915

11/2002

06/2009

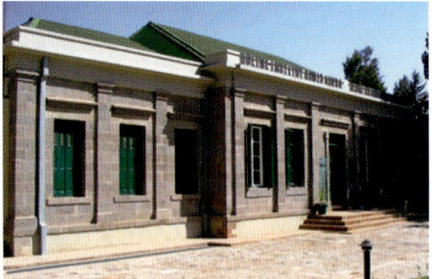

Crownprince Asfa-Wossen Res. / Goethe
1910s

11/2002

06/2009

***Balambaras* Wolde Semait**
1915

11/2002

06/2009

Dimitri Petros Residence
Around 1915

11/2002

06/2009

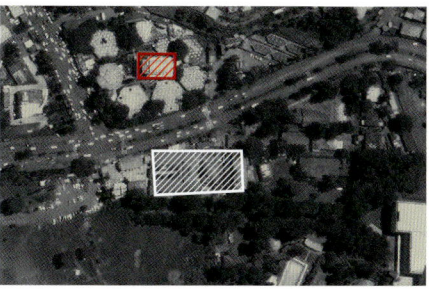 

05/2015   02/2021

Finefine Hotel / Hotel d'Europe
No.: 60

Hotel d'Europe (initial name), located in the hot springs area, was reopened on the request of Haile Selassie to improve the spa facilities in the early 1930s. It still has its own bathing huts. Designed by the Armenian Minas Kerbekian in 1915.

 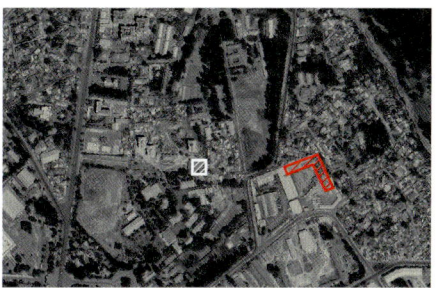

05/2015   02/2021

Crownprince Asfa-Wossen Res. / Goethe
No.: 158

Former residence of Lij Iyasu, the Emperor of Ethiopia from 1913–1916. The residence building was destroyed during the *Derg* period. The building still existing functioned as an *aderash* ('reception hall'). Probably built in the 1910s.

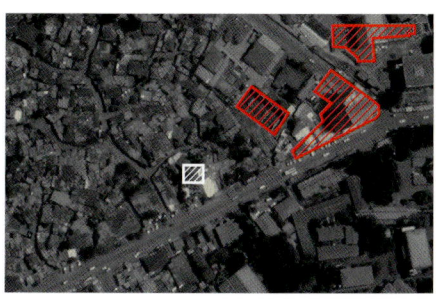 

05/2015   02/2021

Balambaras Wolde Semait
No.: 173

Former residence of *Balambaras* Wolde Semait. The construction is *chikka*, with a variety of wooden elements: elaborate glazing windows including wooden shutters, gingerbread decoration following the roof eaves.

05/2015   02/2021

Dimitri Petros Residence
No.: 172

Former residence of the Greek Dimitri Petros. Before the Italian occupation, the building hosted the Olympia, a renowned restaurant and nightclub.

Heritage at Risk   249

Medehane Alem School
Around 1915

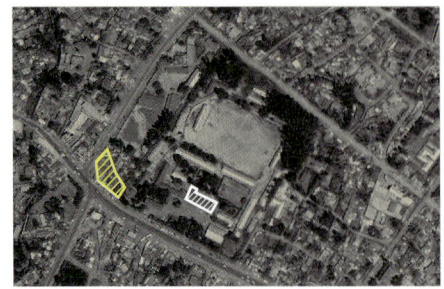

11/2002

06/2009

Ras Nadew Aba Wolo Gatehouse
1910s

11/2002

06/2009

Muse Minas Kerbekian Residence
Around 1915

11/2002

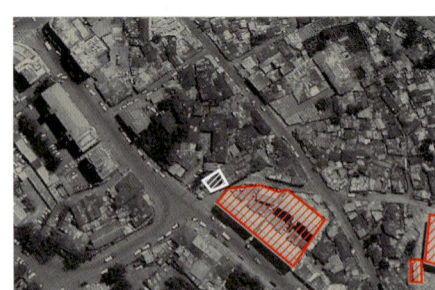

06/2009

Gebre Mariam Gari Residence
Around 1915

11/2002

06/2009

250

05/2015

02/2021

Medehane Alem School
No.: 4

Interesting one-storey building used as a school. The surrounding veranda facing the large courtyard has wooden pillars supporting the protruding roof, adding charm to the ensemble.

05/2015

02/2021

Ras Nadew Aba Wolo Gatehouse
No.: 57

Gatehouse to the compound of *Ras* Nadew Residence, originally on the same compound and now approx. 100 m further south on a separate parcel. At present it is used as a '*kebele* house'. It obviously has some attached shacks for informal housing.

05/2015

02/2021

Muse Minas Kerbekian Residence
No.: 43

Former residence of the Armenian Minas Kerbekian, a key figure in the local building and road construction sector during the first three decades of the twentieth century. Designed by Kerbekian himself. Built in the early twentieth century. Minas Kerbekian was also the architect of the Mohamed Ali House and surroundings.

05/2015

02/2021

Gebre Mariam Gari Residence
No.: 162

House belonged to Gebre Mariam Gari, chief of the palace's guards under Menelik II and founder of the French school. He protected the Emperor from Lij Yaasu's attempts to dispossess him of his title. Later he was one of the notables involved in the resistance against the Italian occupation.

Heritage at Risk   251

Grazmatch Terfe Residence
Around 1915

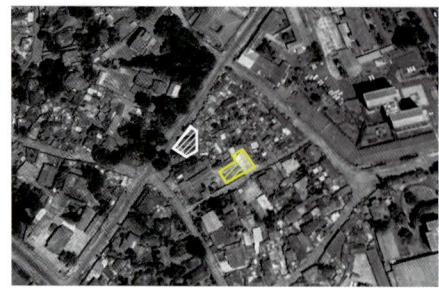
11/2002

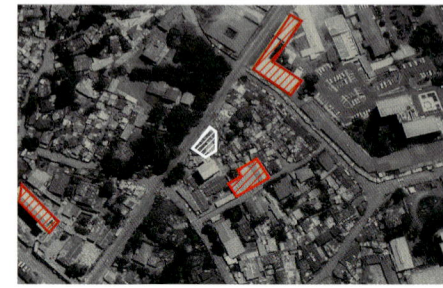
06/2009

Dej. G / Sellassie Bariyagabir Residence
Around 1915

11/2002

06/2009

Dej. W / Gebriel Residence (Arada)
Around 1915

11/2002

06/2009

Arbeynoch Residence
1915

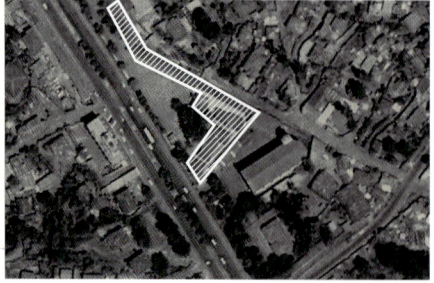
11/2002

06/2009

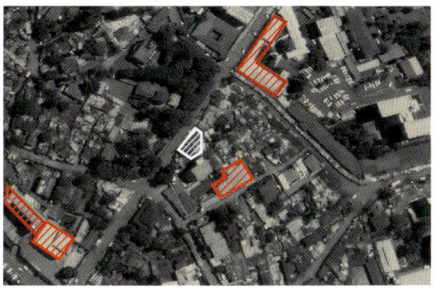

05/2015   02/2021

Grazmatch Terfe Residence
No.: 163

Former residence of *Grazmatch* Terfe, who received the land from Menelik.

05/2015   02/2021

Dej. G / Sellassie Bariyagabir Residence
No.: 58

Former residence of *Dejazmatch* Gebre Sellassie Bariyagabir, a well-known member of the Ethiopian aristocracy. Built in the 1920s. One of the biggest historic houses in Addis Ababa. Indian-influenced architecture.

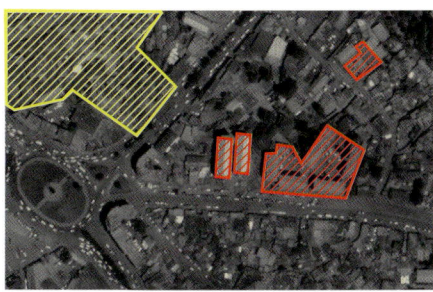
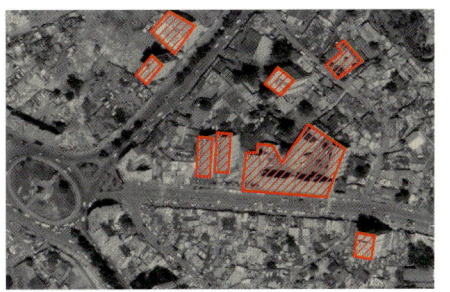

05/2015   02/2021

Dej. W / Gebriel Residence (Arada)
No.: 35

Same owner as master plan no. 2. One of the few existing noblemen's *Ghebbis* and Aderashes in AA. The circular Aderash is linked by a staircase. The material is *chikka* and stone, covered with corrugated iron sheets.

05/2015   02/2021

Arbeynoch Residence
No.: 11

The Arbeynoch 'patriots' residence served as such for the veterans of the war against Italian forces in 1886. Built during the Menelik II reign, it became a school in 1935. In 2005 / 2006, large modern school buildings were added in order to avoid classes being held in shifts. The new construction dwarfs the original, which has hardly undergone any changes.

Heritage at Risk   253

Customs Office La Gare
Around 1924 – demolition decided

11/2002

06/2009

Yekatit Hospital 'Vittorio Emmanuele' / Bet
1924

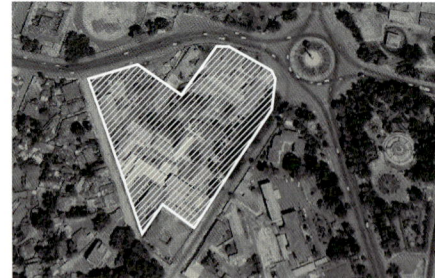

11/2002

06/2009

***Ras* Birru W / Gabriel Res. AA Museum**
1920s

11/2002

06/2009

Tsehafi Tiezaz Haile Wolderufe Residence
1920s

11/2002

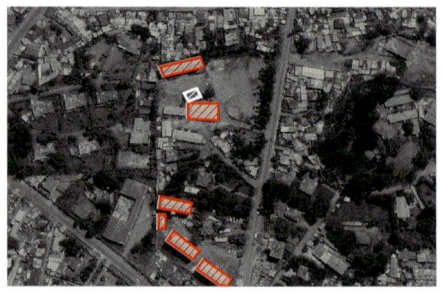

06/2009

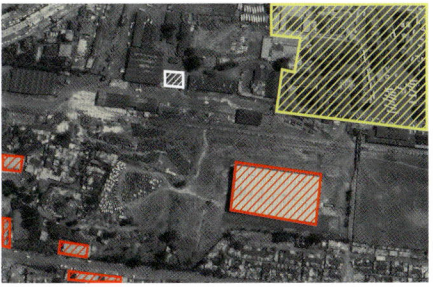
05/2015

02/2021

Customs Office La Gare
No.: 62

The former Customs Office attached to the Djibouti Railroad is located in a vast area near La Gare. A rectangular, solid stone building with exterior plastering alternating with natural stone masonry around windows and on the building's corners, it features two elegant exterior stairs and hosts a large interior, two-storey hall.

05/2015

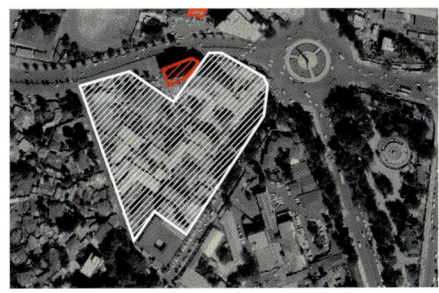
02/2021

Yekatit Hospital 'Vittorio Emanuele' / Bet
No.: 156

The hospital complex includes several buildings. It was constructed in 1924 and named Beth Saida. During the Italian occupation, it was enlarged and called Vittorio Emanuele after the King of Italy. It was designed by Balanos.

05/2015

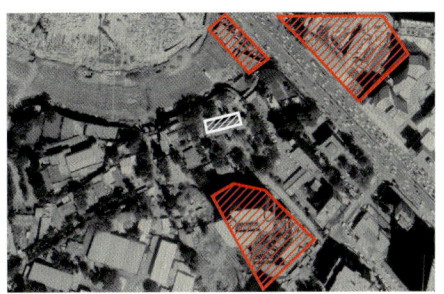
02/2021

Ras Birru W / Gabriel Res. AA Museum
No.: 67

Former residence of *Ras* Birru, an honoured *Dejazmatch* at Menelik's court. He was a notable advisor to Menelik II in the early twentieth century. Built in the 1920s. Outstanding due to the dimension of the complex and its decorations.

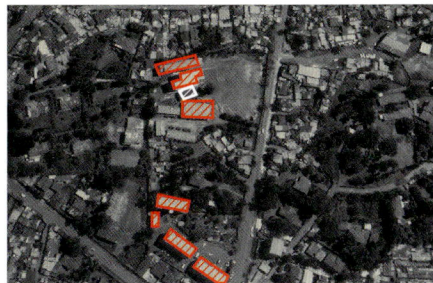
05/2015

02/2021

Tsehafi Tiezaz Haile Wolderufe Residence
No.: 114

The building is part of a larger complex. It has a beautiful veranda and some old decorations.

Heritage at Risk   255

Tafari Makonnen School
1920s

11/2002

06/2009

 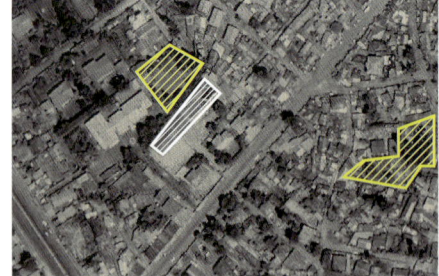 

Dej. **Enqu Sellassie Residence**
Around 1920s

11/2002

06/2009

Mintiwab Desta Residence
1920s

11/2002

06/2009

Dej. **W/Gebriel Residence (Kolfe Keranio)**
Between the 1910s and 1920s

11/2002

06/2009

05/2015 02/2021

Tafari Makonnen School
No.: 112

The former Tafari Makonnen School was funded by the private treasury of *Ras* Tafari to improve the school situation in Addis Ababa. It was completed in 1925.

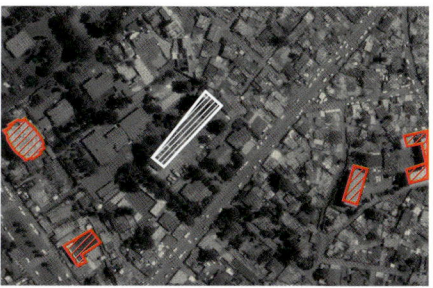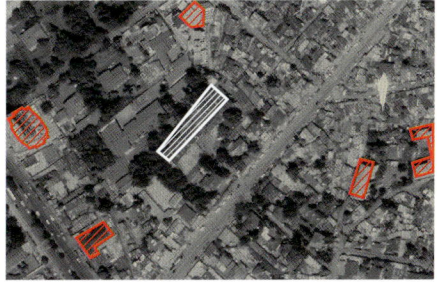

05/2015 02/2021

Dej. Engu Sellassie Residence
No.: 10

The old building has apparently been modified over the course of time, but the remaining features are still important enough to be considered. The construction shows a mix of unplastered brick masonry combined with wooden supports, analogue to European frame houses. It may be the only house with this construction in AA.

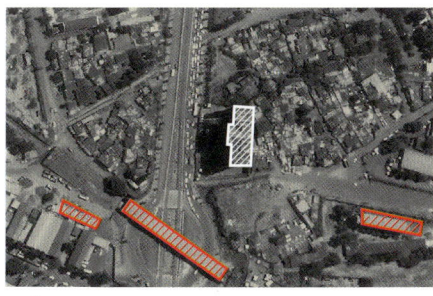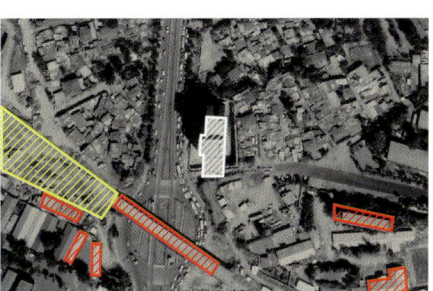

05/2015 02/2021

Mintiwab Desta Residence
No.: 187

Former Residence of Woizero Mintiwab Desta, who actively participated in the establishment of the Ghandi Memorial Hospital. Built in the 1920s.

05/2015 02/2021

Dej. W / Gebriel Residence (Kolfe Keranio)
No.: 2

Belonged to *Dejazmatch* Wolde Gebriel, who was the administrator of this quarter and used to hold the periodic meeting of his religious association here. Built between the 1910s and 1920s.

Heritage at Risk 257

Dej. Letyibelu Gebre Residence
1920s

11/2002

06/2009

Balambaras Guebre Medhin Residence
1910–1920s

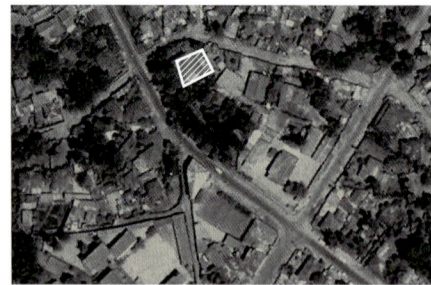
11/2002

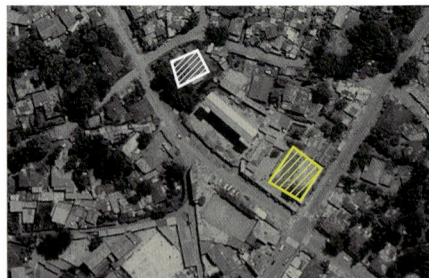
06/2009

Ras Tesema Nadaw Residence
1920s

11/2002

06/2009

Afanegus Nasibu Meskele Residence
1920s (incorrect in database)

11/2002

06/2009

05/2015

02/2021

Dej. Letyibelu Gebre Residence
No.: 94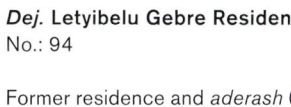

Former residence and *aderash* ('reception hall') of *Dejazmatch* Letyibelu Gebre, the first minister of Haile Selassie's *Ghebbi*. Constructed by Indian and Pakistani builders. Built in the 1920s.

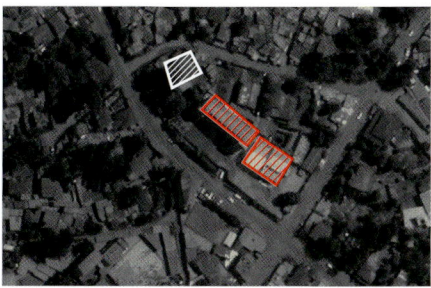
05/2015

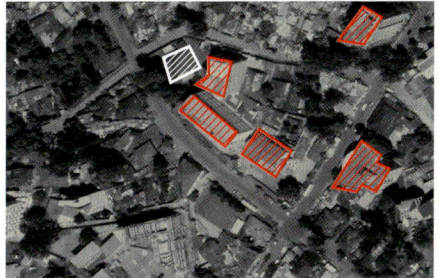
02/2021

Balambaras Guebre Medhin Residence
No.: 166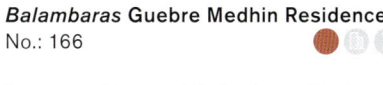

Former residence of *Balambaras* Guebre Medhin Gofa, Minister of Agriculture. Built in 1910–1920s.

05/2015

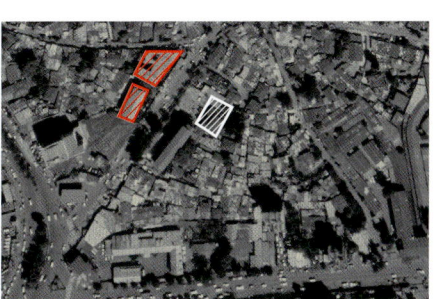
02/2021

Ras Tesema Nadaw Residence
No.: 88

This building stands in the former *Ras* Tesema's *Ghebbi*, a powerful 'ras bitwaddad' under Menelik. His former residence does not exist anymore. The present building was designed by the Armenian architect Minas Kerbekian and built in the early 1920s.

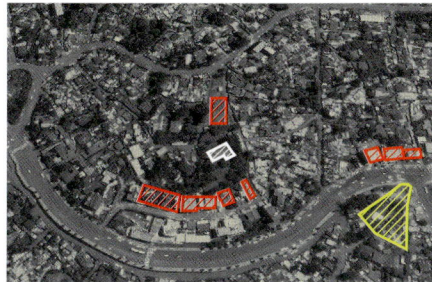
05/2015

02/2021

Afenigus Nasibu Meskele Residence
No.: 106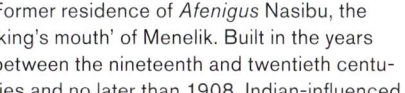

Former residence of *Afenigus* Nasibu, the 'king's mouth' of Menelik. Built in the years between the nineteenth and twentieth centuries and no later than 1908. Indian-influenced architecture.

Heritage at Risk 259

Dej. H / Silassie Gugsa Residence
1928

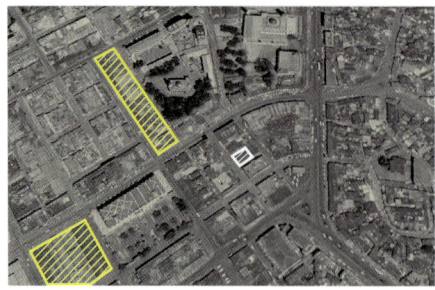
11/2002

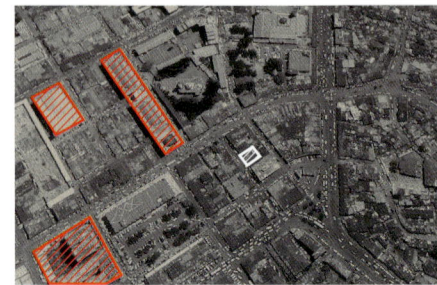
06/2009

National Museum
1920s

11/2002

06/2009

Agop Bagdasarian's 2nd Residence
1920s

11/2002

06/2009

Muse Christo Magliaris / Negadiras Residence
1920s

11/2002

06/2009

260

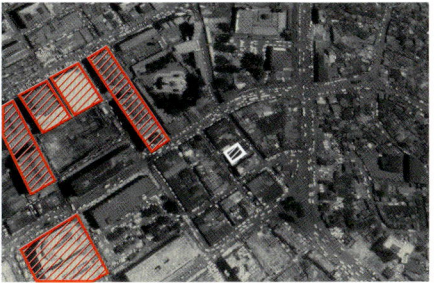

05/2015

02/2021

Dej. H / Silassie Gugsa Residence
No.: 32

Located in the Merkato area. The building is a landmark in the area. Built before 1928, it was modified into a shop during the Italian occupation when the present Merkato got what was then its 'new' urban shape.

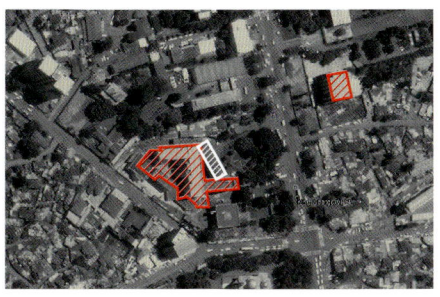

05/2015

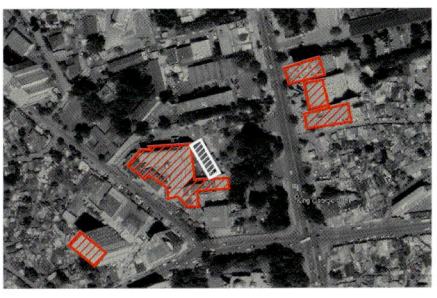

02/2021

National Museum
No.: 90

Served multiple purposes before its current function as the National Museum. The actual building was probably built by the Italians. It was the residence of the mayor of AA during the occupation. It also served as the residence of the Duke of Harar, *Ras* Makonnen, and as the Ministry of Foreign Affairs under Emp. Haile Selassie.

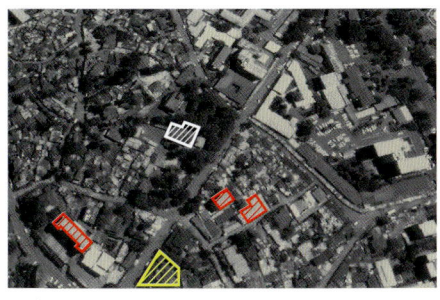

05/2015

02/2021

Agop Bagdasarian's 2nd Residence
No.: 164

Bagdasarian's second residence, around the corner from the first in Welete Yohanis St. It is currently the Ethiopian Association of the Blind. There is an interesting interior ceiling painting, probably by a Russian artist, with motifs of European landscapes.

05/2015

02/2021

Muse Christo Magliaris / Negadiras Res.
No.: 13

Former residence of the Greek lime factory owner Christo Magliaris. During the Italian occupation, it was the residence of an Italian general. Built between 1910 and 1913. Indian-influenced architecture. Other sources say it was built in the 1890s.

Heritage at Risk 261

Tsehafi Tiezas G / Silasie *Negadras* Tsemru
1920s

11/2002

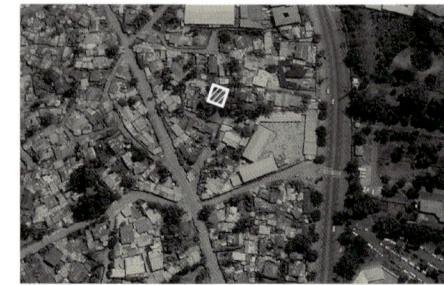
06/2009

Fitawrari Atnaf Seged Residence
1920s

11/2002

06/2009

Teshome Berhe Residence
1930s

11/2002

06/2009

Kuraz Printing Press / Mega Enterprise
1930s

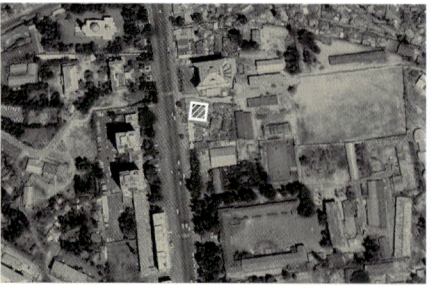
11/2002

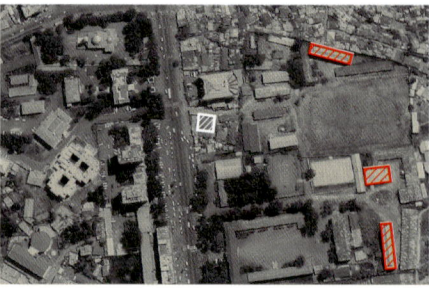
06/2009

05/2015

02/2021

Tsehafi Tiezas G / Silasie *Negadras* Tsemru
No.: 116

Former residence of *Negadras* Tsemru, son of Guebre Selassie, Menelik's famous chronicler. Traditional-style house.

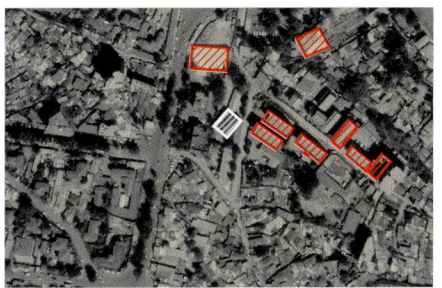

05/2015

02/2021

Fitawrari Atnaf Seged Residence
No.: 74

Former residence of *Fitawrari* Atnaf Seged. He received the land during the reign of Zewditu. Probably designed by the Indian architect Woli Mohammed. Built in the 1920s. Indian-influenced architecture.

05/2015

02/2021

Teshome Berhe Residence
No.: 170

Former residence of Teshome Berhe. In 1939 the Englishman Mr. Buck established a school here. Built in the 1930s. The peculiar feature of the building is a small tower with a fancy roof and small pane windows.

05/2015

02/2021

Kuraz Printing Press / Mega Enterprise
No.: 87

The house functioned as an office during the reign of Haile Selassie. Built in the 1930s. It was later used by Kuraz Printing Press. Indian-style architecture. The carved wood finials and curved roofs clad with corrugated steel are interesting.

Heritage at Risk 263

Night-time coffee at the *Afenigus* Nasibu Meskele Residence

Parts of the building, home to 18 families, could collapse at any time.

The Mohammed Ali House partly collapsed in May 2023.

Epilogue

I didn't choose this topic.
It feels like the topic chose me.

The infrastructure and societal conditions that I benefit from by living in Germany and having a contract at the Technical University Berlin allowed me to put a great deal of time and coordinated knowledge into this book. Additionally, being a white *ferenji* sometimes opens doors for you in Ethiopia, while others have to struggle a lot more.
Indeed, as a researcher, I was blessed with a context where people have a culture of sharing – sharing knowledge and data, without which this project would never have been possible.
I was also blessed with the incredible hospitality of the poor residents of some of the old houses. Although there may have been personal interest involved or the hope of personal benefit, I cannot tell you how grateful I am to have been able to have a cup of coffee and *tenadam* together with friendly families in Ethiopia. Their hope is that officials in their country will start to care for the old houses, their homes, and preserve them to facilitate a safe and dignified living environment for them. I dearly hope that this book can contribute to making their wish come true!

Endnotes

- Batistoni, Milena and Chiari, Gian Paolo, *Old Tracks in the New Flower – A Historical Guide to Addis Ababa* (Arada Books, 2004).
- BBC News, 'Letter from Africa: Ethiopia's Lost Armenian Community', 2020. <https://www.bbc.com/news/world-africa-51672965> accessed 21 March 2023.
- Feyissa, Getnet, Zeleke, Gete, Gebremariam, Ephrem and Bewket, Woldeamlak, 'GIS Based Quantification and Mapping of Climate Change Vulnerability Hotspots in Addis Ababa', 2018. <https://doi.org/10.1186/s40677-018-0106-4> accessed 24 March 2023.
- Giorghis, Fasil, and Gerard, Denis, *The City & Its Architectural Heritage – Addis Ababa 1886-1941 – La Ville & Son Patrimoine Architectural* (Addis Ababa: Shama Books, 2007).
- Giorghis, Fasil, and Gérard, Denis, *The City & Its Architectural Heritage: Addis Ababa* (Shama Books, 2019).
- gtz (now giz) – Urban Governance and Decentralisation Programme, 2009. 'Addis Ababa Urban Heritage Database' (collaboration with the NGO Addis Woubet).
- Harre, Dominique, 'Trading Ports' Influences in Addis Ababa Early Domestic Architecture', 2015.
- Harre, Dominique, 'The Indian Firm G. M. Mohamedally & Co in Ethiopia (1886–1937)' / 'La Firme Indienne G. M. Mohamedally & Co En Éthiopie (1886–1937)', 2015.
- Harre, Dominique, and Gashaw, Wondimagegn, *Addis Ababa – Old Piazza: 3 Self-Guided Tours* (2018).
- INTBAU, 'INTBAU Ethiopia Talk Series Session 3 with Brook Tefera Belay', 2021. <https://www.youtube.com/watch?v=vajvZoBV2VA> accessed 14 March 2023.
- Khan Academy, 'READ: The Berlin Conference', n. d. <https://www.khanacademy.org/humanities/whp-origins/era-6-the-long-nineteenth-century-1750-ce-to-1914-ce/x23c41635548726c4:other-materials-origins-era-6/a/the-berlin-conference> accessed 21 March 2023.
- Link Ethiopia, The Tafari Makonnen School, n. d. <https://www.linkethiopia.org/article/the-tafari-makonnen-school/> accessed 28 March 2023.
- Pankhurst, Richard, 'Menilek and the Utilisation of Foreign Skills in Ethiopia', *Journal of Ethiopian Studies* 5 (1): 29–86, 1967.
- Pankhurst, Richard, 'The Indian Door of Tāfāri Mākonnen's House at Harar (Ethiopia)', *Journal of the Royal Asiatic Society*, vol 1 (3): 389–91, 1991.
- Pankhurst, Richard, 'The Role of Indian Craftsmen in Late Nineteenth and Early Twentieth-Century Ethiopian Palace, Church and Other Building', *Journal of the Royal Asiatic Society*, vol. 5 (1): 11–20, 1995.
- Sacchi, Livio, *Architectural Heritage in Ethiopia. Two Imperial Compounds in Mekele and Addis Ababa* (Skira Editore S.p.A., 2012).
- Societa geografica italiana, 'Regione di Gullelie-Addis Abeba (Finfinni) schizzo topografico / Bollettino della Societa Geografica Italiana', 1909. <https://collections.lib.uwm.edu/digital/collection/agdm/id/320/> accessed 8 March 2023.
- Wikipedia, 'Armenians in Ethiopia', 2022. <https://en.wikipedia.org/w/index.php?title=Armenians_in_Ethiopia&oldid=1124470639> accessed 20 March 2023.
- Wikipedia, 'Climate of Ethiopia', 2023. <https://en.wikipedia.org/w/index.php?title=Climate_of_Ethiopia&oldid=1144505355> accessed 23 March 2023.
- Woodwell Center, 'Climate Risk Assessment: Addis Ababa, Ethiopia', 2023. <https://www.woodwellclimate.org/climate-risk-assessment-addis-ababa-ethiopia/> accessed 23 March 2023.
- Zewdu, Eleni, 'A conservation – restoration study on the of historic premises Teferi Mekonnen School, Addis Ababa', 2018.

Glossary

Addis Ababa	= Amharic for 'new flower'
Afenigus / Afe Negus	= aristocratic title (lit. 'Mouth of the King')
Amharic	= official language in Addis Ababa (from the Ahmara region)
Arada	= historical district of Addis Ababa (= Piassa after 1936)
Balambaras	= aristocratic title
Battle of Adwa	= defeat of the Italian colonialists in 1896
Beni Shangul	= region in the west of Ethiopia
Bitwoded	= aristocratic title (lit. 'loved')
Chikka	= local composite material, a mixture of mud and straw
Chikka wall	= a wall constructed with *chikka*, similar to wattle and daub
clear story	= double-height room
Dejach / Dejazmatch / Dej.	= aristocratic title
Derg	= socialist party that ruled Ethiopia from 1974–1991
ETB	= Ethiopian Birr (currency of Ethiopia)
fascia	= a vertical frieze or band under a roof edge
finial	= an element marking the roof-top, often decorative
Finfinni	= the Oromo name for Addis Ababa (the city lies in the Oromia region)
Ferenji	= Western foreigner
Elfiñ	= Amharic for 'Imperial Residence'
Enqual Bet	= Amharic, literally 'Egg House'
G/…	= prefix for name (read 'Gebre')
Ghebbi	= Amharic for 'Imperial Compound'
Gibir	= Amharic for '(big) festival'
H/…	= prefix for name (read 'Haile')
Haile Selassie I	= Emperor of Ethiopia from 1930–1974 (before *Ras* Tafari)
Hintsa	= Amharic for 'building'
Mashrabiya	= a type of projecting oriel window enclosed with carved latticework
Jharokha	= a window projecting from the wall on an upper story
Kebele	= smallest administrative unit (now *woreda*)
Kegnazmatch	= aristocratic title
Massawa	= port city on the Red Sea, now in Eritrea
Negadras	= aristocratic title: 'head of traders'
Northern Shewa	= historical region of Ethiopia, formerly an autonomous kingdom
Ras	= title for a prince (lit. 'head')
Sefer	= indigenous settlement form in Ethiopia
Sheik	= aristocratic title
Tenadam	= plant served with traditional Ethiopian coffee
Tej-bet	= place to drink honey wine (Tej)
Tukul	= vernacular round or oval house
W/…	= prefix for name (read 'Wolde')
Woreda	= administrative districts in Ethiopia
Zuquala	= Mt. Zuquala is a volcano in the south of Addis Ababa

Historical dates 1886–1936

1865	Menelik proclaims himself King of Shewa.
1881	Menelik moves the capital from Ankober to Entoto.
1886	Menelik and Taitu have a temporary house built by the hot springs of Filoha.
1889	Establishment of the *Ghebbi*. The area is named Addis Ababa.
1892	Introduction of eucalyptus.
1896	Defeat of the Italian colonialists in Adwa.
Since 1897	Establishment of many European legations.
1898	Process of unification of the Ethiopian Empire is completed.
1913	Death of Menelik – Lij Iyasu (Menelik's grandson) becomes Emperor.
1917	Lij Iyasu is deposed by Empress Zewditu (Menelik's daughter).
1917	The Franco-Ethiopian railway reaches Addis Ababa.
1930	Death of Zewditu. *Ras* Tafari Makonnen is crowned Emperor Haile Selassie I.
1931	Abolition of slavery.
1936	Italian troops enter Addis Ababa.
1941	End of the Italian occupation.

PICTURE CREDITS

DISCLAIMER:
Despite our research, the copyright of certain images cannot be identified.

If there are several graphics on one page, they are credited from top left (#1) to top right to bottom left to bottom right.

1 INTRODUCTION

AAH_team
- 10-11

Dreshaj, Arita
- 36 (handdrawn after original: Societa geografica italiana (1909): Regione di Gullelie-Addis Abeba (Finfinni) schizzo topografico / Bollettino della Societa Geografica Italiana)

Fikiremariam, Eden
- 72, #1

Giorghis, Fasil
- 22, #1
- 23

Girmay Gebreegziabher, Tadesse
- 69-71

Nani, Flagote (Architecture by EES)
- 18

Nieder, Piet
- 4
- 6
- 8
- 12
- 22, #2
- 38, #1
- 44-66
- 72, #2

Okazaki, Rumi
- 38, #2
- 39-43

Public domain
- 14 (unknown photographer, link: https://snl.no/Menelik_2)
- 15, #1 (unknown photographer, link: https://commons.wikimedia.org/wiki/File:Zewditu_and_favored_priest.png)
- 15, #2 (unknown photographer, link: https://commons.wikimedia.org/wiki/File:Emperor_Haile_Selassie_I.jpg)
- 20-21 (ETH-Bibliothek, Walter Mittelholzer, link: https://picryl.com/media/eth-bib-strassenszene-in-addis-abeba-abessinienflug-1934-lbs-mh02-22-0985-98334e)

Sacchi, Livio
- 26-35

Tafesse, Hilena
- 73

2 PHENOTYPE: THE CASE STUDIES

AAH_team
- 74-75
- 80
- 92-92
- 93, #2
- 97, #1
- 102
- 108-109
- 111, #4
- 112
- 117-118
- 127, #3
- 128
- 134
- 135, #2
- 139, #1
- 141-142
- 146
- 151, #4
- 152-153
- 157-159
- 163, #3
- 164

AAH_team - based on originals by Yoseph Beredet, ABBAArchitects
- 143

AAH_team - based on originals by Abnet Gezahegn Berhe
- 97, #2-5

AAH_team - based on originals by Addisu Yisma
- 165

AAH_team - based on originals by Eden Fikrmariam
- 113

AAH_team - based on originals by Livio Sacchi
- 81
- 87
- 119
- 113
- 122-123

AAH_team - based on originals by Tadesse Girmay
- 129

AAH_team - based on originals by Tadesse Girmay, Fkereselase Sifir
- 103

Amorim Vasques, Ruben
- 93, #1

Ashagre, Henock
- 124, #2
- 125, #3
- 149, #2
- 150, #1-2
- 161, #2 and 5
- 161, #1 and 3

Ben Kiran, Maroua
- 147

Benti, Dawit
- 136, #1
- 138, #1-2

Castracane, Federico Guglielmo
- 156

Dahmen, Charlotte and Kahlenberg, Rasmus
- 107, #2-3

Dalakouras, Christos
- 91
- 111, #1-3
- 163, #1 and 2

Dreshaj, Arita
- 140, #2 and 3

Duarte Rodríguez, Lía
- 151, #1-3

EiABC (Tadesse Girmay)
- 110, #1
- 136, #2-3
- 138, #3-4

Feistl, Christine
- 96, #1 and 5

Foltyn, Maciej
- 99

Gérard, Denis
- 110, #3
- 140, #1

Girmay Gebreegziabher, Tadesse
- 88
- 89, #2-3
- 94
- 95, #1
- 125, #1
- 148
- 149, #1 and 3
- 150, #3-4
- 154-155

Google-Earth
- 145, #2-3

gtz 2009 (Philipp Schauer, Dr. Omnia Aboukorah-Voigt, and others)
- 144, #1

Hatem, Nagham
- 127, #1 and 2

Jemaneh, Sophia
- 85, #1 and #4
- 96, #2-4
- 116
- 144, #2-3
- 145, #1 and 4

Leoni, Sara
- 133
- 135, #1
- 137
- 139, #2

Lustina, Martina
- 79
- 84

Maharjan, Kamal
- 107, #1

Nieder, Piet
- 89, #1
- 90
- 93, #2
- 95, #2-5
- 98
- 100-101
- 104-106
- 124, #1
- 125, #2
- 126
- 130-132
- 160
- 161, #1 and 3-4
- 161, #2 and 4

Okazaki, Rumi
- 76-78
- 82-83
- 86
- 114-115
- 120-121

Sifir, Fkereselase
- 110, #2

Sönmez, Selen
- 85, #2-3

3 GENOTYPE: INFLUENCE ANALYSIS

AAH_team
- 166-167
- 174-175
- 177, #1 and 3
- 177, #3
- 179-181
- 183, #3-4
- 184-185
- 194-195
- 198-199
- 203

Archive PSN
- 191, #1, #2c and #4
- 192, #2

Ashagre, Henock
- 189, #2

Dreshaj, Arita
- 171, #5-6
- 172
- 173, #2-3
- 201, #2

EiABC (Tadesse Girmay)
- 187, #4

Girmay Gebreegziabher, Tadesse
- 193, #3

Gérard, Denis
- 177, #2d

gtz 2009 (Philipp Schauer, Dr. Omnia Aboukorah-Voigt, and others)
- 169
- 177, #2e, 2f
- 178, #1b, 1c, 1d, 1f, 1g, 1h and 1j
- 186, #3
- 188, #3-4
- 189, #1 and #3-4
- 191, #2e, 2f and 2h
- 192, #1b, 1c, 1d, 1e, 1f, 1g, 1h, 1i
- 197, #2
- 201, #4b, 4c, 4d
- 202, #1c, 1d

Khanghahi, Saba
- 168
- 183, #1-2

Nieder, Piet
- 177, #2g
- 186, #1-2 and 4
- 187, #1-3
- 188, #1
- 191, #2g
- 192, #1a
- 193, #2
- 197, #1
- 197, #4b
- 202, #1b
- 202, #3

Okazaki, Rumi
- 177, #2c
- 191, #2b
- 192, #3
- 201, #1, #3 and #5

Public domain
- 171, #1-2 (Bernard Gagnon, unchanged, license: https://creativecommons.org/share-your-work/licensing-considerations/compatible-licenses)
- 171,#3 (Francisco Anzola, unchanged, license: https://creativecommons.org/licenses/by/3.0/deed.en)
- 171,#4 (Sharanbhurke, unchanged, license: https://creativecommons.org/licenses/by-sa/4.0/deed.en)
- 173,#1 (Ninaras, unchanged, license: https://creativecommons.org/licenses/by-sa/4.0/deed.en)
- 177, #2a "Entoto Palace" (David Stanley, unchanged, license: https://creativecommons.org/licenses/by/2.0/)
- 177, #2b "First palace of Menelik II 1" (Felitsata, unchanged, license: https://creativecommons.org/licenses/by/2.0/)
- 178, #1a "Katedrála sv. Jiří v Addis Abebě (Etiopie)." (Ondřej Žváček, straight lines, license: https://creativecommons.org/licenses/by-sa/3.0/deed.en)
- 178, #1e "Zewditu" (unknown photographer, link: https://commons.wikimedia.org/wiki/File:Zewditu_and_favored_priest.png)
- 178, #1i "Haile Selassie" (unknown photographer, link: (unknown photographer, link: https://commons.wikimedia.org/wiki/File:Emperor_Haile_Selassie_I.jpg)
- 188, #2 "Katedrála sv. Jiří v Addis Abebě (Etiopie)." (Ondřej Žváček, straight lines, license: https://creativecommons.org/licenses/by-sa/3.0/deed.en)
- 191, #2a "Entoto Kidist Ragel" (myeralan, unchanged, license: https://creativecommons.org/licenses/by/2.0/deed.en)
- 191, #2d "Rennell Rodd Mission 1897" (Unknown, unchanged)
- 191, #3 "Dawoodi Bohra at Siddhpur" (Snehrashmi, lines straightened, license: https://creativecommons.org/licenses/by-sa/3.0/deed.en)
- 193, #1 "Red Fort Delhi" (Biswarup Ganguly, unchanged, license: https://creativecommons.org/licenses/by/3.0/deed.en)
- 197, #3 "Armenian Church" (DonCamillo, unchanged, license: https://creativecommons.org/licenses/by/3.0/deed.en)
- 197, #4a "Finfine Adarash restaurant" (Sailko, zoom-in, license: https://creativecommons.org/licenses/by/3.0/deed.en)
- 197, #4c "Mari & Vakhinak Bekaryan in 1918, Addis Ababa, with Armenian school pupils" (Unknown)
- 201, #4a "First palace of Menelik II on the Mount Entoto in Addis Ababa" (Felitsata, unchanged, license: https://creativecommons.org/licenses/by-sa/4.0/deed.en)
- 202, #1a "St George Cathedral in Addis Ababa (Ethiopia)" (Ondřej Žváček, straighten lines, license; https://creativecommons.org/licenses/by/2.5/deed.en)
- 202, #2 "St George Cathedral in Addis Ababa (Ethiopia)" (Ondřej Žváček, straighten lines, license; https://creativecommons.org/licenses/by/2.5/deed.en)

4 GENES: ARCHITECTURAL ALPHABET

AAH_team
- 204-217

5 URBAN TRANSFORMATION: HERITAGE AT RISK

All thumbnail photos 222-263 are by gtz 2009 (Philipp Schauer, Dr. Omnia Aboukorah-Voigt, and others)
All mappings on satellite images 222-263 are by AAH_team

AAH_team
- 218-219

Dreshaj, Arita
- 222, #1-4

Moges, Elizabeth
- 264, #4

Nieder, Piet
- 264, #1-3

Stahlschmidt, Robert
- 220-221

The Making of

Expert talks during the pandemic with gte students in the summer term of 2021

Architectural photography in February 2022: Henock Ashagre, Tadesse Girmay, Piet Nieder

Working session at DOM publishers with gte students in the winter term of 2022/2023

About this Book

The present work has been realised at the Chair of Building Technology and Design (gte) at Technical University Berlin. The chair funded a series of expert talks in the summer term of 2021. In the winter term of 2021, the chair facilitated a teaching collaboration with Fasil Giorghis that allowed a vivd academic exchange on urban heritage with a focus on design appliactions. In the winter term 2022, the chair hosted a seminar on the comprehensive representation of the collected material and research outputs. Throughout the years of study, the chair provided its infrastructure and expertise to put this work into a concise and accessible form. In the picture credits, the work realised during these two semesters is indicated as 'AAH_team', short for 'Addis Ababa House_team'.

Summer term 2021: research kick-off, drafting texts, graphics and CAD drawings, supervised by Piet Nieder

#2 Case Studies

Case Study 1	Martina Lustina
Case Study 2	Selen Sönmez
Case Study 3	Ruben Amorim Vasques
Case Study 4	Feed Furaiji
Case Study 5	Kamal Maharjan
Case Study 6	Klajd Cullhaj
Case Study 7	Onur Degirmenci
Case Study 8	Adèle Lebaudy
Case Study 9	Nagham Hatem
Case Study 10	Rami Anis
Case Study 11	Maroua Ben Kiran
Case Study 12	Christine Feistl
Case Study 13	Lía Duarte Rodríguez
Case Study 14	Federico Guglielmo Castracane
Case Study 15	Sara Leoni
Case Study 16	Sara Leoni
Case Study 17	Bachir Benkirane

#3 Influence Analysis

Climate	Adèle Lebaudy, Federico Guglielmo Castracane, Onur Degirmenci, Selen Sönmez
Material	Bachir Benkirane, Kamal Maharjan, Lía Duarte Rodríguez, Rami Anis
Local	Klajd Cullhaj, Ruben Amorim Vasques
Indian	Feed Furaiji, Nagham Hatem
Armenian	Christine Feistl, Maroua Ben Kiran
European	Martina Lustina, Sara Leoni

#4 Arch. Alphabeth Work of the entire group

#5 Heritage at Risk Work of the entire group

Winter term 2022/23: editing of graphics and content excluding texts, supervised by Piet Nieder

#2 Case Studies	Christos Dalakouras, Sophia Jemaneh
#2 CAD site plans	Arita Dreshaj
#2 CAD axonometries	Ebrar Sayan
#2 CAD drawings	Fabian Gutheil
#3 Influence Analysis	Arita Dreshaj
#3 Matrixes	Christos Dalakouras, Fabian Gutheil, Robert Stahlschmidt, Sophia Jemaneh
#4 Arch. Alphabeth	Ebrar Sayan, Robert Stahlschmidt
#5 Heritage at Risk	Robert Stahlschmidt (supported by Arita Dreshaj, Ebrar Sayan)

Unless noted otherwise, all texts by Piet Nieder
With the following exeptions:

Case Study #1: text by Martina Lustina
Case Study #2: text by Selen Sönmez
Material Influences: text by Bachir Benkirane, Kamal Maharjan, Lía Duarte Rodríguez, Rami Anis

Acknowledgements

The editor would like to thank:

Fasil Giorghis (EiABC), for his untiring scientific exchange throughout the past two years.

Tadesse Girmay (EiABC), without whose support this research would not have been able to be initiated.

My talented gte students (in alphabetical order): Rami Anis, Bachir Benkirane, Federico Guglielmo Castracane, Klajd Cullhaj, Christos Dalakouras, Onur Degirmenci, Arita Dreshaj, Christine Feistl, Feed Furaiji, Fabian Gutheil, Nagham Hatem, Sophia Jemaneh, Maroua Ben Kiran, Adèle Lebaudy, Sara Leoni, Martina Lustina, Kamal Maharjan, Lía Duarte Rodríguez, Ebrar Sayan, Selen Sönmez, Robert Stahlschmidt, and Ruben Amorim Vasques.

Thank you to the whole gte team, especially Prof. Claus Steffan and Tanja Stanke. Thanks to our tutors: Antonello Prezioso, Cathy Burmester, Anna Mönke, and Verdiana Greco.

Special thanks to EiABC students: Tesfaye Abebe, Ayana Kebede, Habtewold Tadesse, Beemnet Mulugeta, Yeabsira Tesfaye, Biruk Zelalem, Tewodros Sntayehu, and Yohannes Deribe.

For providing graphical material: Addisu Yisma, Eden Fikrmariam, Bilisaf Teferri, Yoseph Beredet.

Continuous scientific exchange on Addis Ababa's heritage: Rumi Okazaki (Shibaura Institute of Technology, Tokyo), Livio Sacchi (Ud'A, Pescara), Nicole Baron (BUW), and Monika Wiebusch (GTZ).

Scientific exchange: Philipp Misselwitz (TU Berlin), Maheder Gebremedhin (The Urban Center), Genet Alem (TU Dortmund), Fabienne Hoelzel (ABK Stuttgart), Mari Paz Agúndez Lería, Nadine Appelhans (TU Berlin), Dawit Benti (EiABC), Prinz Asfa-Wossen Asserate.

Thank you to everyone who supported me during my field research: Besa Wendmagegn, Ammanuel Feleke, Yamman Hebbo (GIZ), Hennok Ashagre, Dr. Petra Raymond (Goethe-Institute Addis Ababa), Helawi Sewnet.

Thank you Princess Maryam Senna Asfaw Wossen (Addis Woubet) for your kindness and trust.

Others: Anteneh Tesfaye (TU Delft), Jonathan Le Péchon, Martin Buchholz, Nahu Senay Girma (Addis Woubet), Michael Maiwald (GTZ, rip), Silye Maiwald, Omnia Aboukorah-Voigt, Adey Tadesse, Nicola Borgmann (Architecture-Gallery Munich), and my wonderful family Jana, Rena, and Thomas. Thank you, my dear Saba, for your invaluable support.

Thank you!

TOP-supporters: Saba Khanghahi, Fabian Hesse, Monika Wiebusch, Rena and Thomas Nieder and the institutions: Chair of Building Technology and Design (gte, Prof. Claus Steffan), DÄV (German-Ethiopian Association), and TU Delft.

Further supporters: Dick van Gameren, Marc Angélil, Hans Witschurke, Hannes Rutenfranz, Jana Nieder, Christoph Rauhut, Julia Mauser, Ralf Keller, and Ellen Gottwald.

… and many more.

Biography of Piet Nieder

Piet Nieder is a practicing architect and researcher at Technical University Berlin. His doctoral thesis looks at the potential of traditional building techniques for architectural solutions in transforming urban territories in Ethiopia. He holds a Master of Science in Architecture from ETH Zurich. Between 2012–2013, he taught architectural design at the Ethiopian Institute for Architecture, Building Construction and City Development (EiABC) of Addis Ababa University.

The Deutsche Bibliothek lists this publication in the *Deutsche Nationalbibliografie;* detailed bibliographic data is available on the internet at *http://dnb.d-nb.de.*

ISBN 978-3-86922-867-9

© 2024 by DOM publishers, Berlin
www.dom-publishers.com

This work is subject to copyright. All rights are reserved, whether the whole or part of the material is concerned, specifically the rights of translation, reprinting, recitation, broadcasting, reproduction on microfilms or in other ways, and storage or processing in data bases. Sources and owners of rights are given to the best of our knowledge; please inform us of any we may have omitted.

Proofreading
Sandie Kestell

Design
Piet Nieder

Printing
Tiger Printing (Hong Kong) Co., Ltd.
www.tigerprinting.hk